T0144418

The Old Home Place

Moods And Modes - Vagrant Writings

by George W. May

Turner Publishing Company

Turner Publishing Company

Turner Publishing Company Staff:
Heather Warren, Designer

Publishing Rights:
Turner Publishing Company

ISBN: 978-1-68162-293-4

Library of Congress Control #:
2001089986

Table of Contents

Books By the Same Author

History of Massac County, Illinois, 1955

Massac Pilgrimage, 1964

Students' History of Peoria County, Illinois, 1968

Charles E. Duryea - Automaker, 1973

Down Illinois Rivers, 1981

Massac County 1955-1982, 1983
(20 page update booklet)

History Papers on Massac County, Illinois, 1990

Walter West's Probation
(a novel of the Regulator-Flathead War), 1993

Massac Biographies, 1998

For information address the author at
Metropolis, Illinois 62960

Preface

In this incongruous collection of my writings comprising various literary forms, one may trace the development or non-development of my literary power from age 12 to age 90. Playwriting is not represented for the drama is not for me.

How may such a hodge-podge be justified? I have been reluctant to publish this book because of its disparity of material and its evidence of amateurish writing skills. I feel I am far short of even modest talent.

In extenuation, what follows is part apologia and part explanatory, but not abjectly and lacking in some spirit and independence. Some other related thoughts creep in.

Originally, my purpose was to collect these fugitive writings and to leave them in some form to be read by my kin, my children, grandchildren and select friends and acquaintances with no thought of publication. The project gradually gave birth to the thought of publishing the manuscripts. Any book, by anyone, must have something to offer else why had the author gone to the trouble of writing it. Early on, I had no thought of wide distribution (many to be given away) and certainly not of monetary profit.

Some may say this book is my "swan song," that I have scraped the bottom of my literary trunk, that I am finished. That may prove true. I think of an instance: Jerome Cardano, an Italian scientist, compiled a last volume of his *Opera Omni*, made up of "things left out" of his other books, a sort of cleaning up of all the chips left in his workshop. So I have rather done. Perhaps at my age I should cease writing. What, then, is left? Some say honor; some, charity - both the refuge of the elderly. I only hope the reader will be indulgent and make allowance for my "showing off." It is about as Lord Byron said: "Years steal fire from the mind as vigor from the limb." Thoreau once said that every author writes in the faith that his book will last through the ages. Most writers are deluded but I am under no such illusion.

There is a Russian word *kitsch* that means vulgar or show off, as applied to bad art; something useless but often found in the bric-a-brac trade. *Kitsch* might well be applicable to some books (offbeat, uninteresting, ornate, wordy) but often with a lofty message, but badly crafted. To read such books could indicate a depraved taste but could also be a true extension of experience. One might simply be amused reading the feeble, fumbling, over-ambitious books.

Some may accuse me as a dilettante, a dabbler in literary forms. I plead guilty. Really, I place myself at the bottom of the literary totem pole. Lacking high skill, I must blame it on my heredity, my training or upon every facet of my environment or circumstance. Truly, we are what we are, with divine limitations.

Pursuing the points made above, consider any book, third rate or whatever, is worthy in some respects. It is the man's record, his experience, in novelized form or in autobiography. There must be a few kernels worth saving. The writer's efforts should not be curbed. We have a free press in America. Anyone may publish if the contents are within the bounds of decency and laws of defamation. The old Roman Pliny thought that even a bad book had some merit. And Dorothea Brande says: "Even a bad book is tolerable when you are engaged in probing it for the reasons for its stiff, unnatural effects." For the writer himself, Wash Young says: "It is a pleasure merely to do one's best, even if nothing happens."

Thomas Merton and many another writer have said that if a writer is too cautious to write anything because of a fear of criticism he will delay publication forever.

Not to belabor my points to excess, which I have perhaps done, I repeat that I have no illusions about *Moods and Modes - Vagrant Writings* and how it will be received. Likely, it will be a Russian *nyet*. That will be all right. Stendahl said: "Do not try to falsify and praise a book beyond its merits, merely to avoid hurting the author's feelings." I am prepared. My primary purpose is to leave you, my children and grandchildren, this book as part of my legacy and I am doing this simply because I want to.

Kind reader, if there are to be any outside my kin and friends, excuse all these words which approach a diatribe and an over-blown apology. This heterogeneous bag of writings goes out upon a long-suffering reading public which, perforce, is made to diet largely upon contemporary styles of writing.

G.W.M.

November 1, 2000

Stories

Simpatico

Ras Wehmer knew Mexico. He ought to-he had traveled extensively through 18 states in that republic. But he was hardly prepared to meet the raw crowd that jeered and insulted him in the plaza of Santa Catarina that hot day.

He was taking his *siesta* on a *plaza* bench like the other people of that lazy *pueblo*. When the *siesta* began every shop had shut up and within five minutes not a soul could be seen. Three loose *burros* wandered slowly here and there in and out of private gates. The *policia* pulled up his chair, carried it within the carcel and folded up until two o'clock.

Two o'clock finally tolled in the church across the *calle*. Ras sat up suddenly, rubbed his eyes and looked around. The heat was still sweltering. Now at the stroke of the second hour the little *pueblo* awakened. Almost at once, it seemed, the little town took on life. Men came in from every street and moved toward the *plaza*. What was strange was that almost every man and boy carried a banner or a placard. What was this, thought Ras? A *fiesta* or fair day? He had no knowledge that it was a special day.

He read the banners closely as they approached: "Down with the foreigners," "Down with exploiters," and numerous others couched in no uncertain terms. What did it mean? His interest was suddenly aroused. Ras had seen nothing like it lately; since the little trouble in Morelia two years ago, to be exact.

The paraders were now gathering in the plaza. Ras addressed one of their number who did not seem to be as excited. "What does it mean, senor?"

The rough man looked at him curiously. His eyes fell to his guarchis. They returned to gaze at Ras. Funny fellows, these peones, thought Ras; so bashful-like yet possible to be so fierce.

"*Con permiso, señor*," he said, "We do not wish the foreigners here. They take our land, our oil; they take everything. We show why we do not like it." He swept his hand over the crowd.

Several had gathered around Ras while they were talking. They saw he was American and he saw they knew it. More gathered around. Some jeered and insinuated. Ras saw that many were drinking.

"*Americano! Americano!*" shouted one of the mangy fellows. "Why is he here? Does he not see our banner?"

The powder-keg was upset and Ras knew it. The cry was repeated around the circle. Certainly he had been caught in the rougher element, if there were any responsible ones around. Ras doubted if there were any.

Their looks became lowering and threatening. The rough circle was inflamed my *mescal* or sodden with *pulque*. Ras knew the character of these men in such small *pueblos*. They felt no restraint; they had none. Once before he had felt the barest tip of a long knife and he had no wish to feel one again. Obviously, his situation was dangerous.

Why hadn't the little girl in the *cantina* across the street warned him of probable trouble? She was a sweet little *señorita*, about 17, he guessed, hard to tell about their ages sometimes. He had stopped there for a drink after tramping the hot dusty road from Monterrey. Yes, he was out on another lark, a hike to Saltillo this time over that stiff up-grade road which wound in and out those sharp pinnacles of bare stone.

He had jabbered to her in Spanish. She had such a come-on look he couldn't help telling her about himself. He had let out confidences that if it had not been for his egotistical nature, he would never have given.'Did she work here all the time?' 'Where did she live?' 'Was there anyone playing the bear now?' Dangerous talk for a stranger in a little town like this, even if it were only in jest.

She had asked about him. Yes, he was out to enjoy the country first-hand. His headquarters were in Monterrey, Hotel Fronterrizco, Calle Hidalgo at corner of Puebla. Did he like Mexico?'

'Ah, yes, mucho.' He had been so amiable, so tolerant, so polite that she had lisped at him 'Very *simpático*.' He had thrilled to that apellation from so sweet a mouth. He knew it meant that she considered him a person who appreciated Mexico and the Mexicans at their true worth. Well, by george, he appreciated her.

These reflections were not helping him at the situation which now faced him. Around him rumbled an angry, intoxicated mob of *peones*. Squalor and poverty lay back in those huts in the hills. For this day that was left behind in the excitement of an affair which afforded a chance to get drunk. Here was sport aplenty: an American, a foreigner alone in their midst. Their crazy visions conjured up a hated enemy.

As yet no one had been so bold as to lay a hand on him. It would come, thought Ras. He tried to look across to where the policia had been sitting. He ought to be there now, if he tended his job, thought Ras. Should he attempt to push his way out toward, the *carcel*?

Ras stretched his neck to look over the slightly-less taller *peones*. Far too many wide sombreros were in the way to see much. Jumping up, he did see a number of horses tied to the lone hitching post on the far side of the *plaza*. The men followed his gaze. Impossible to make a dash for a horse. Ras saw no weapons in sight but he was certain there were knives about. It would not do to show hostility. "*Gente sin razon,* "People without reason." Yes, that was the kind of people they were. In desperation he ventured to push gently out of the circle. For the first time he felt the touch of hands upon his arm. It was from behind.

He whirled. Two villainous pair of eyes looked at him. An almost uncontrollable anger beat in his breast. He made a perceptible move toward them; then stopped.

They gazed at each other intently, like cats about to spring, but waiting. Silence fell.

There was a slight motion behind Ras. Then he heard that sweet, sibilant voice say: "What ees the matter, senor traveler?"

All turned to face her. She was beautiful, compelling. Damn she was!

Ras explained.

"Ah, señores, she cried gleefully. "You do not understand. He is all right. He is one of us he is *muy simpático*. Come, I buy you all drinks."

They all melted away like a snow in June and Ras was left alone, stunned in his isolation.

—1930's

That Mexican Gal

Hugo looked up as new passengers sifted in from the Guaymas station. He looked them over casually: a bald businessman with his loquacious wife but strangely-contrasting quiet baby; two school boys in leather sandals and loose blouse; a number of country youths from the hinterlands with guitars slung over their backs; a tired, brown house-wife, two mesh sacks dangling low from her hands. Hugo's eyes turned from this sameness. Almost to the border and no excitement yet.

Carambra! Who was that?

Shuffling her way along came a substantial figure down the aisle. She reached a seat near Hugo, paused, looked up and down and around and sank into it.

The train started. Vendors faded back from the car windows to prepare for the next train, 12 hours later. Hugo saw it, hazily, slug-gishly. His eyes returned to the lady.

Not bad looking - couldn't be over 30 and probably not nearly that. Eyes a little prominent. Fair-skinned for a Mexie. Big enough, yes. But not too substantial to preclude the probability of a once good figure.

She was gazing around again, searching, as if calculating the stature of each male passenger. Her eyes rested on Hugo's temporary traveling companion, a thread salesman working out of the capital. Her scrutiny finished, she blinked her eyes toward Hugo. He seemed to feel it. He looked up. Their eyes met.

For one moment her eyes seemed to bury deep into his consciousness. He fidgeted and turned away, uncomfortable.

The train rattled along. No danger of being overheard. He inclined toward the thread man. "What is she?" he asked timorously.

The man laughed and passed it off. He arose. "We'll see."

Animated conversation between the two.

Now the wild boys, Indians, of course they were. One could tell by their looks-Yaquis, no doubt-they started up. Wilder music, not boisterous, wild-primitive, sweet. Those words-what were they? Unfortunate man! Was he just now experiencing the soul of the true aborigines? Had he wasted a month across the border? So late, too late to linger longer. He leaned forward.

The thread man returned. He touched Hugo lightly. "Be friendly *amigo*, she says for you."

"That music, señor," said Hugo huskily. "Dios! That's wonderful".

"Not bad, *amigo*. But they will get better before we reach Hermosillo."

"Why?"

"The more drink, the more abandon, the better *músicos*. Come, fren."

"Wait. Who is she?"

His companion shrugged. "Who knows? Who cares to know? Some pleasure, some beguilement for us."

"What's she doing on this train? Where's she going?" persisted Hugo.

"Well, señor," he began patiently, "she's alooking for her *marido*, ah, her husband. He left her *a la frances*, as you say." He shrugged again.

"Where is she from?"

"Mexico City."

"Heavens! Relentless woman. Will she find him?"

"Quite immaterial, señor. She says if she finds him not, she will find another, perhaps before she reaches Nogales, *no es verdad*?"

They moved toward her, where she was already making room.

She poured out *tequila* from a bottle which she had in her satchel. She passed it. The thread salesman sipped. Hugo passed. "Too wild," he said.

"Maybe *vino* is more better." She drew forth a large green bottle.

"Don't care if I do." He drank the wine. She gave him two more.

Presently the señor arose and sauntered forward, close to the musicians. Hugo stayed.

He knew he should leave, too. He shouldn't notice her; he shouldn't encourage her. He told himself that. But something in the strange pornographic tempo of the wild boys' music intoxicated him, led him on. Maybe it was partly the wine. He was talking to her recklessly, exhilaratingly, confidently. *Diantre*! Here was the chance!

There was only a brief stop at Hermosillo; then the train ran on over the vast wasteland through the night.

The Yaquis left the train at Llano. Sleepiness overcame Hugo. He dozed. Morning dawned chilly on the desert. Hugo awoke, then Nogales at eight o'clock. Gone were the passions of last evening.

A voice was asking softly. "Ees the *Señor* Hugo's health good this morning?"

"Rotten," he said. "I'll be glad when I cross the line. These second-class seats are deucedly hard after riding 72 hours on them."

Hugo collected his two pieces of baggage, a laundry case of Mexicana and a guitar. He had not played it last night. The boys were too good for him.

The S.P. train stopped and he alighted. He strode toward the custom house. He heard someone following close behind. He turned. It was Teresa, the gal of last night.

"What's up?" he interrogated idly.

"Ah, *señor*. Maybe we can cross together, ah, as man and wife. It will be a great help to me. It will not trouble you much. Just for this little time."

"You're loony," he cried. What could she mean? "No, *señora*, no, no." He passed into the custom house and opened his luggage. Teresa opened hers beside Hugo's.

"Man and wife?" asked the officer, looking over his spectacles.

"Yes," said Teresa before Hugo could reply.

"She's not," exclaimed he furiously.

"Let's see your card, sir," said the man. "Hmm, single at Laredo." He looked up and a grin of enlightenment came over his face. "Got hooked up, eh. OK then. Close your baggage."

Hugo had heard that the officials were very indulgent toward tourists. Well, what should he do? Let her pose as a favor until she got across; then shake her off? He thought quickly, warily. No, it was too risky. Of course, he could prove he wasn't married to this impostor. But it would take some wiring, some time.

"I say again she's not my wife." He flushed hotly. "I never saw the woman until yesterday afternoon

The officer scratched his head. It was plain the Americano already regretted his hasty romance.

"Telegram, *señor*," announced a boy coming up.

The officer looked at it. "Hmm, Laredo. Wonder what?" his countenance assumed seriousness as he read it. "You say you do not claim this *señora* as your lawful wife?"

"Devil, no," yelled Hugo.

"Read," commanded the officer.

Hugo scanned the yellow paper: BE ON LOOKOUT FOR WOMAN STOP ABOUT 25 YEARS OLD STOP HAS TRIED TO GAIN ENTRANCE TO US POSING AS WIFE OF VARIOUS MEN STOP LAST CHECK AT MATZATLAN STOP DETAIN.

That goes for Hugo when in a jovial mood at the club he tells about that good-looking *señorita* he had in Old Mexico.

—1930's

The Hag of Nizhni Tag

Alexeiev Feodor looked out of the car window up to the forest-clad slopes of the low Urals, which began to be dimly outlined in the distance. Then he stretched his long legs as far as the forward seat would permit and yawned. It had been a long trip, but happily he would get a long rest in Ekaterinburg before beginning the long trek back.

But this last prison inspection lessened the anticipation of the pleasures he would enjoy in the big city. He had seen enough horror and human misery the past three months to last him some time. He made a wry grimace of distaste at the thought of visiting Camp No. 18.

The distortion, however, changed rapidly to one of complacency, as he reflected what a rise he had taken the past five years under the present regime. From mediocrity station he had risen rapidly in the favor of the Stalin circles. Promotion had followed promotion. He was now the inspector of camps. His duty was merely to secure statistics and look through the camps in a cursory way.

He had eaten well at Perm. So well, in fact, that he slept as the monotony of the ride lulled him into insensibility. He awoke once or twice to see the low mountains about him. Somewhere, on the other side lay the camp.

It was dark when Nizhni Tag was called out. He alighted, worn and hungry and made his way to the best hotel. He would not visit the camp that night.

He reached the camp late next morning. Two long rows of buildings faced one another at the foot of the mountains which reached westward. Prisoners were already returning with loads of timber. Feodor watched them come in. He saw their pained, emaciated faces. Always, he could hardly look upon those poor convicts. The job had not hardened his sensibilities, rather, they had been made keener. The greater number of the prisoners were there for purely political reasons. Many were ignorants, scarcely knowing for what they had been sent there for.

Feodor turned to the main building and entered. He showed his credentials to the one in charge. Together, they entered the buildings, one by one. In several were found women. They had the looks of those sunken to the lowest depths of despair, ill-nourished, haggard and spiritless.

"Ah, ye devils," exclaimed a voice from a door they were approaching. It came from an old hag. Her voice rose to a shriek as the two drew up and stopped.

"Ye demons of punishment," she yelled. "Infamous castigators."

"Shut up," commanded the manager, threatening to strike her.

She pointed her bony fingers toward the mountains. Her decrepit body shook as she went on heedlessly. "That's what I say. Stop me, if you will. Strike me down. 'Tis no more than has been done in the forest."

Feodor's companion made a move as if to strike her, then, letting his hand fall, said smiling, "Let her yell. She's crazy. We're used to it. Let's move along."

As they walked on down the row she continued to vituperate them. "Oblansky, Kursov, Romanoff," she cried, the names being separated by scathing language.

The two returned and faced the hag again.

Screeching "Oblansky, Kursov, Romanoff," she flew at Feodor, clawing and scratching.

He tried to shake her off.

The manager seized her and tore her off. He flung her violently to the floor. "Lay there, fool," he cried angrily.

She lay still a moment, then slowly got up. She faced Feodor. His head was turned from the miserable wretch. She pointed a bony finger at him and said, "Alexeiev Feodor, you don't seem to remember me."

He whirled to face her, as if he had been pricked by a Czarist sword.

Astonishment and stark amazement showed in his face. In wonder, he asked, "You, you, do you know me?"

"Why not? Haven't I talked with you many times? So long ago, five, 10, these 18 years have gone by. No wonder. Doubtless, I am much changed. But you look very much the same. I wonder I didn't recognize you at first. After you left, a few minutes ago, I collected my shattered memory enough to remember. Ah, it's you, Alexeiev."

"Who is this woman, Kocinski," demanded Feodor, turning to his conductor abruptly.

"Ah, er, I think the registry shows her to have been Orlav Ferma. Sent up from around Moscow back in 1920. Know her?" Kocinski looked at him half-mockingly.

"My God, yes. That is, I did know her, well, too and the whole family. All were ex...," He stopped short. This was a tight-mouthed job. He could easily say too much, even if he did not really mean it.

And this was Orlav Ferma, whom he had known when he was a mere youth. She had been a substantial property owner in those days. Often he had visited the family. He had spent many hours in their home. Oblansky, the youngest son, had been his favorite companion in those brief years. Where were they now? Feodor had left Kozlof and lost all further account of them. So they had been victims of the Soviet idea. And this was Madame, in a convict camp in the far-off Urals. He could scarcely make himself believe it.

Well, what could he do? Jeopardize himself, his job, his very life, in a useless effort to secure the discharge of this once dear friend? Did she expect it? Would she reproach him unless he did make an effort?

Back in the main building, Feodor asked, "Could I beg to recommend that Madame Ferma be released from the sentence?"

"You have been so nice, so companionable, I don't see why not," Kocinsky smiled broadly.

He was one man who kept his word.

Orlav Ferma and Alexeiev Feodor are in America now.

Oh, why did Feodor happen to come to America? He lost his job, but he was out of the country before the case came up before the Spies Tribunal.

—1930's

Spanish for Pretty

George Rhodes looked up from the row of beans which he was picking and gazed across the road to Glen Pasco's truck farm. He was not looking at Pasco's house nor for Pasco himself. His gaze settled upon a little house nestled among Pasco's apple orchard. There lived the Martinez family: Luis, Otilia and the daughter Marie de los Angelos. They were employed by Pasco to work on his truck farm. The Ben Rhodes farm was second only to old Pasco's, which was known all over the Elgin country.

George's look was rewarded by a wave from the Martinez home. A bright handkerchief fluttered from Marie's hand at the side path which led directly to the Pasco house. George signaled in reply. He shouted, "I'll be over again tonight." Another wave of the handkerchief answered for welcome.

"Sweetest little girl I ever knew, even if she is a Mex," mused George following her figure until it was lost among the trees. "Too bad dad is so prejudiced against them. He seldom hires a Mexican unless he knows about them for sure. I know Luis is all right. Dad hasn't been around the family as much as I have. "Too bad," he muttered, as he fell to his knees again.

Night came. The truck was loaded with green beans and corn, ready to start the next morning for Chicago. Supper over, George walked the 300 yards to the Martinez home and knocked.

"It ees our George again," said Luis, welcoming him in. "How ees your back after all the bean-picking, *amigo*?"

"Pretty stiff, Luis," George laughed. "but still able to walk here. Where is Marie?" he asked with ill-concealed eagerness.

In answer, Marie came out of the kitchen. She was dressed coolly and simply but in a most charming mode. Her olive skin shone softly in the light of the living room. George's eyes could scarcely leave her. Luis looked at her in unfeigned admiration, while Otilia restrained hers by taking up some needlework.

"Too tired to walk a little, Marie?" George asked, after an interval of small talk.

"On, no. My work was nothing today. But you, perhaps, you are too stiff?"

"Oh no," replied George. The work of the day was forgotten.

"Then come." Marie seized his arm and they passed out into the road.

"Want a drink, after the hot day?" he asked.

"If you do," she replied, gleefully.

They walked down the road to a station a half-mile away for soda water. Lingering only a short while, they returned to Marie's yard.

"Want to walk through the orchard? I have a nice little bower just a little way behind the house. I made two little seats under a tree just for me and you," said Marie.

"Two little seats for you and me," repeated George. "Are they together?"

"Oh yes, of course," Marie replied. "Why would you ask that?" And her voice trilled in a merry laugh.

"But your feet, your shoes," he remonstrated with an attempt at sincerity, "they will get soiled in the dew."

"Oh no, foolish boy." she laughed again. "There is a path. Come." She snuggled to him closer to keep her feet in the narrow path.

Marie had performed her work well. George saw two rustic seats. They were not together, but he seized Marie's implication and moved them side by side.

"You like the farm, Marie?" he asked when they had been seated.

"Oh much, George. I have lived in town so much where we couldn't have a decent garden. The little plants would come up through the ashy soil so strong, then grow sickly and never do well. It was sad to see them linger so. They never had a chance to grow like they do on Pasco's or your farm. Oh, I like so much the little plants come up, then grow and grow and at last make the fruit or grain."

"You really like growing things, don't you, Marie?"

"Oh so much. I would like to live on the farm always. But dad, he talks of going back to the railroad." She signed heavily, as if to return to that life would grieve her deeply.

George looked upon her bowed head. A wild burst of love beat in his breast for the strange little Mexican girl. No, she was woman with a wonderful love for the soil, that noblest of human sentiment. It was not the first time she had uttered her desires. Everyday, every night, she had let slip, here and there, little intimations that she loved the truck gardeners life.

Did he dare to press that beautiful head to him and tell her that she could be his, that she could have this life if she would say so?

Then the kind but firm image of his father arose before him. He would never sanction it. He would not hire one of them to say nothing of marriage with one.

He touched her hair gently, caressingly. She looked up. He kissed her undemonstratively. She did not scold him.

"Doesn't Luis like his work on the farm?" he asked.

"Yes, I suppose so. He never complains. But he says he can make more money on the old railroad job."

"That's true," agreed George. "But tell me, Marie, is money always the only consideration?"

"No, no," she whispered.

"For instance?"

"Love, George." She looked into his eyes as if to seek agreement.

Their arms clasped one another and their lips met. George knew there was no other girl for him. He looked into her dark eyes and upon her sweet face. "Tell me," he asked, "what is the Spanish word for pretty?"

"*Bonita*," Maria responded.

"Then I will call you my little Bonita," and he kissed her again.

"Just a moment, boy," she said, laughing and breaking away. "I will call you '*Jorge*,' Spanish for George. How do you like having your name changed?"

"Fine," he cried and chased her to the house.

A week passed in which George made the market every morning. He was up and on the road long before daylight. Occasionally he made day trips to Elgin but for the most part smaller truckers supplied that market. Saturday night he took Maria to a show, stopped for eats at a place near the edge of Elgin and reached the Martinez home about midnight.

A light was still burning in the front room. The couple was surprised for it was long past the parent's bedtime. "Someone must be sick," said Maria.

"I'll just step in with you," said George.

Neither was sick, but Luis jumped up upon their entrance and seemed a little excited.

"What's the matter, dad?" asked Maria.

"Oh, nothing. I just have a decision to make and I am having trouble making it. I couldn't sleep. I thought I would wait till you two came in. Then if you weren't too sleepy, maybe you could help me."

"What is it, Luis?" questioned George.

"I have been in Elgin today, down at the shops and they tell me I can get on the railroad again if I want to. The job is over at Rockford and a good one, too."

"You are trying to decide whether to take it or to stay here?" finished George.

"That's it," returned Luis.

Maria's form seemed to sink and her eyes dropped toward the floor. George was silent.

Luis looked at them, puzzled. "Well, what would you do, *amigo*?"

"Take the job, I suppose," replied George, reluctantly.

"You don't seem very keen about it," remarked Luis, seeing Maria's dejected mood.

"I don't dad," she replied, lowly, "I don't want to leave here. I like it here best."

"That's it, Luis," spoke up George. "I don't want you to leave, either. I'd miss you a lot and especially Maria, I'll be frank in saying."

"Struck?" said Luis, soberly.

In answer, George passed one arm around Maria and took one of her hands in his. "Yes."

The following week the Martinezs moved to Rockford. It was a sad day for the lovers. George vowed he would visit her every chance he got. True to his promise, he was in Rockford the following Saturday where he stayed until Sunday.

This continued for a month until Ben Rhodes remarked to his son, "Going it pretty hard, aren't you? Can't you forget the Mex?"

"No, I can't and please don't call her a Mex."

Rhodes smiled broadly. "You called them Mexies yourself when they moved in."

"It's different now," said George, ill-humoredly.

The next trip Luis told him, "I can get you on the welding job if you want it. Of course, you weren't on the job long down on the I.C., but I think you will do well enough for the work here. You and Maria could be together every day. What do you say?"

George considered a few moments. "All right, Luis, I'll take the job if they will have me. I hate to leave the farm, though. Dad will be as sore as boils."

Sunday morning a month later, George and Maria visited the two truck farms. Pasco's little tenant house was still unoccupied. The couple walked through the orchard to the rustic bower and lived over again the happy hours of their earlier nocturnal meetings. They looked about the fertile acres. Their looks met and they signed.

"So close, yet so far from us," said Maria.

"Maybe it will not be always so, Maria. This is a good job Luis put me on to. Maybe I can save enough money to get a place someday."

"Some day, Jorge," signed Maria. "That is far too long."

Silence. Then Maria said quietly, "You remember that Pasco wants to sell out and retire."

"Why, yes. We saw the sign along the road some minutes ago. It's been there a year. Why do you mention it?"

"Just a thought, George, a vain hope, a daydream. Maybe he would make some arrangements for us to take over the place."

"I doubt it, Maria. Of course, he likes us all. It would take real money to buy his farm. It's hopeless to think of buying it. But why let us wait. Let's go over and tell dad we are going to marry today, before we start back to Rockford."

"Your dad, he wouldn't help you out?"

"No use," said George, brusquely. "Come, let's go over and see the folks a few minutes, get married and start for Rockford."

"*Bueno*," said Maria, lightly.

The father and mother greeted them warmly. Ben had missed his son. He knew without asking that George's heart was right here.

"How much do you suppose old Pasco wants for his place," George asked of his father.

"Plenty," replied Ben. He looked at the couple quizzically. "Why?"

"Oh, nothing, just idle curiosity." George looked away across to the field of corn which would be ready for the pulling within a few days.

"Of course," continued Ben eyeing them closely "he might come down a little considering that he seemed rather eager to retire. I have an idea I could drive a very good bargain with him."

This assurance did not inspirit the couple any. They stood silent, dejected. Ben Rhodes hadn't volunteered help nor encouraged either one in their love, nor in their desire for a farm life.

George looked up. Throwing off the mood with a feint at lightness and gaiety, he announced, "Well, good-bye, mother and dad. We will marry in Elgin this afternoon and then be on our way to Rockford."

"Hey, hold on, wait a minute," cried Rhodes.

They stopped.

"Wait one more week," pleaded Rhodes.

"For what?" asked George.

"To marry. You said you were going to get married this afternoon."

"What's the idea, dad?"

"Oh, er, just wait one more week, please," begged Rhodes with sincerity. "I, rather, I wish you would wait until this time next week. Then come over and see us again, son."

"Well, I don't see the implication, Dad. But we will do as you request," George promised.

Sunday they ate dinner with George's parents. Mrs. Rhodes made much of Maria. The father was indulgent toward the lovers' frequent glances at one another. He smiled, a sort of grim but secretly, happy kind. Dinner finished, they all went into the front room. Rhodes looked at George and Maria grimly. The mother backed him up but a faint smile flickered around her lips in the tense moment that the elder Rhodes faced the lovers.

"I have seen your affection for each other. I have also seen that I cannot stop it even if I wanted to. George, you are your own boss and can make a living for yourself. But I know where your heart is, it is on the farm. I don't believe you are satisfied in Rockford, son. I don't believe you will ever like it anywhere except on a farm. Love of the soil is powerful, son. It has drawn great men to it as by a magnet.

"Therefore, my son and daughter," he said, taking a long envelope from the library table, "I present to you the deed to the Pasco place. Yes, you can pay me as you will and can."

A hush of astonishment claimed the couple. Then they flew to big Ben Rhodes, who was smiling broadly, all show of grimness gone. Mrs. Rhodes joined the happy trio.

"I had been talking to Pasco before you came home last Sunday, but our negotiations had not been completed. I wished to present the deed to you on your marriage day and I have done so." The father met their questioning looks.

"Oh, yes. Pasco will move out soon. Until then you may stay with us."

George pulled out the marriage license and held it up beside the deed. Then he replaced both in the same pocket. "Come, Bonita, sweet, Let's rush to Elgin." And they ran to the car.

"Know what I'll do with these documents?" asked Maria, as she kissed the deed and the license. It was long past midnight and they were speeding toward Rockford.

"Put them under lock and key, I suppose." George laughed and reached over to pinch her.

Not on your life, Jorge. I'll frame them and hang them side by side on the wall."

And she did.

–1930's

The Show That Didn't Show

The Little Chancy Side Shows were booked to appear on Wednesday night only in Brockton.

"Having been placed behind schedule by the recent series of high winds, rain and storms," the bills read, "We regret to inform that we will be able to appear in BROCKTON only on WEDNES-

DAY night. Come one, come all, only one chance to see this spectacular array of artists." Few of the citizens of the little town of Brockton took the thought to reflect that the bills were printed in form, irregular space being allowed for the hand-typed insertion of the place and time.

One citizen in particular did. Cy Wilson, member of the village board, scanned the bill contemptuously, threw it down and spit on it. He had been the lone one who opposed the coming of the show. "Another gambling troupe, a graft, a disgrace to the intelligence and good name of Brockton," he said in presenting his arguments against permitting it to enter.

"Wal, the younguns must have their fun," contended Abe Lukens, a favoring member. "Have no ideer I'll go out myself."

"You will be the first one there," predicted Wilson.

It was Wednesday morning of the show day. The show was even now setting up its canvases at the foot of the steep, rocky hill just outside the town. It was in a level field near an old barn which was partly filled with last year's hay and afforded scant protection to the harvest within. But the boys had a grand time playing hide-and-go-seek in it.

Cy Wilson was the center of the small group of idlers about the townhall, as he concluded his unfavorable encomium of the Little Chancy Side Shows.

Slim Maynard, the town's most professional ne'er-do-well, spat furiously and spoke up, "That just it, Cy. You don't want us to have a bit of variety. Same old amusements with the same old crowd."

"You don't seem to be weakening under the strain," laughed Luna Wisco. "You don't look a day older than you did 10 years ago when I first hit this hollow."

A general guffaw followed.

"Anyway," said Wilson doggedly, "I would have given a lot to keep this outfit away."

"A feared for the morals of his Sunday School son, I guess," remarked Jonas Dyer to Wisco, as they moved away towards the show out of earshot.

All the others moved slowly after them except Wilson and Maynard. The latter followed the crowd with his eye until they turned the corner. Then he looked at Wilson.

"You say you would have given a lot to keep this outfit from showing?" he asked.

"Yes," returned Wilson irritably.

"Maybe it won't show after all. Something might happen to prevent it," said Maynard, looking at him significantly. "Another storm, a wind, fire, might burst it up," he added.

"No such luck," returned Wilson grimly.

Ten minutes later Wilson went home for dinner. He splashed the water savagely. The bar of soap bounced out of the bowl onto the floor. He pitched it back in. He toweled his face and hands angrily.

"The show's all set up, dad," said Adolphus timidly.

"What of it?" growled Wilson.

"Oh, nothing," returned Adolphus foolishly. He had intended making a request, but seeing his father's irate mood, thought it wise to defer it until after dinner.

The meal put Wilson in better humor.

Adolphus was quick to take advantage. "I would like to have a little money, dad," he said.

"What for?" He turned on his son.

"For the show tonight."

"As I expected," said Wilson angrily. "All right, here's 25 cents."

"But, dad, that's hardly enough."

"That's as much as I always give you and you've always managed to get along with that."

"Yes, but I am older. An 18-year old boy needs more money than a 10 year old boy. All the fellows will have money. I don't want to be the only one without any."

"Well, that's all I'm going to give you," he said abruptly, as he left the room.

Adolphus' face flushed with indignation. Slowly, he left the house and walked down the street, away from the show grounds. His head was bowed and he looked neither to the right nor left.

"Hi, Adolphus," someone greeted.

He looked up to see Slim Maynard lounging on a wooden bench across the street. He was in no mood to parley with Slim and in his righteous anger, was mind not to return the greeting.

Slim followed up with "Hey, come over."

Adolphus suddenly felt the desire to unload his anger and walked over.

"Why you look as glum as a squeezed lemon. What's wrong?"

"What would you think of your old man if he gave you only a quarter for a circus day, or a show like tonight?" demanded Adolphus, his light blue eyes flashing fire from underneath a frizz of yellow brows.

"I'd think he was the dirtiest man in town," said Maynard unhesitatingly. "Come," he added, "have a cold pop on me."

Over the drinks, Slim continued to expound upon the necessity of boys of Adolphus' age having money to spend.

"How much would you say a fellow like you ought to have for a night like this one?" asked Slim.

"I should say at least $2.00," calculated Adolphus.

"Shucks, that's about half enough. Make it $5.00 at least," returned Slim. He looked at his companion searchingly. He leaned over his bottle and whispered confidentially, "How would you like to earn that much, real easy tonight, huh?" He whispered still lower.

"Bring us two more bottles," ordered Slim loudly, as the whispered conversation ceased.

Night saw the Brockton populace milling around the tents set out in the open field. The minstrels were doing their stuff with a catty band on the ticket stage. Loki, the crazy alligator boy, was heard croaking inside his tent. Somo, the fat woman, was demonstrating one of her featherweight tricks. Zaga, sees all, knows all, pleaded for a chance to tell one the secrets of one's future life. The popcorn man, the soda pop vendor, the whirl-a-wheel man dolefully announced that the supply would run low, "Get yours while you can." Small boys ran hither and thither among the crowd, knocking bottles of pop out of people's hands and stepping on women's corns, fearful that they would miss something and trying to be everywhere at once. Then that terrible moment arrived when the Master of Ceremonies announced that the seats were insufficient to accommodate all that would want to enter and that one had better rush for their tickets before all seats were taken, "only one show, first and last chance."

In that moment, a yellow flame darted out from the old barn. Then another. Scarcely had the ticket sellers detached their first ticket, when the lurid flames from the old barn illuminated the place and made the weak show lights look pale in comparison. All eyes turned toward the fire; the boys and what men who happened to be unencumbered with babies, hastened the hundred yards to it. Loki, Somo, Zaga and all forgotten for the moment.

Hearing the yelling and commotion, the manager darted out from a tent and shouted "What's the matter?'

"Fire, a little fire," said a minstrel.

"Curse it," fumed the manager. "That little fire will cut out half our crowd."

And so it proved. A stiff wind was blowing already and sparks were lighting on the canvas. Alarmed, the showmen threw down their instruments, left their posts and prepared to fight the fire. They had hardly decided on this action before the larger tent caught fire and burned a two foot hole before it could be gotten to and put out. Then another spark lit. Now the other canvases flared up, until it required all their attention to keep down the threatened conflagration.

With Loki darting about and yelling in his efforts to beat out the sparks, with Somo milling about in common with the townspeople and with dark minstrels cutting up more than they would have on the stage, there was little use in continuing the show. The whirl-a-wheel prizes were knocked over in hopeless confusion and a long pole, used to beat out the sparks, had crashed into Zaga's crystal and shattered it into a thousand pieces.

"Pull stakes!" shouted the manager when all danger from sparks had ceased. It was now 11 p.m. and the more sober minded had already gone home. Only a remnant of boys and hangers-on remained. A tame show could not hope now to attract attention after the excitement which had transpired.

Abe Lukens drew alongside Cy as the latter started to leave. Cautiously and in a low tone, he said, "Did 'cha know the barn was set?"

"Set?" exclaimed Wilson. Then a slow look of recognition came over his face. He stopped short.

"Slim Maynard," he half whispered, as if to himself.

"Hardly think so," returned Lukens. "I saw him a dozen times right around the open stage. He was right there when the fire first started. I was the first fellow to see the fire and start towards it. Want to know who I saw coming towards me, just as I started out?"

"Yes," returned Wilson.

"Are you sure?" asked Lukens doubtfully.

"Yes! Speak it out."

"Adolphus, your son," said Lukens. He widened the distance between them several inches, as if fearful how Wilson would respond.

"Stop, what are you insinuating?" demanded Wilson. He could see no connection, no reason in this rash accusation.

"Don't get sore, Cy," said Lukens deprecatingly. "I may be wrong. I just wanted to put you wise in case some inquiries were made."

"Well, I don't believe it," said Wilson.

"Look at the boy's right hand when you get home," said Lukens. "I think you'll find he has an ugly burn and he had it before the canvasses started catching fire."

"Well, the old barn was hardly fit for kindling anyway," said Wilson. "And the hay," he added, "wasn't fit for seed, mostly weeds, half rotten and molded by now."

"You look at Adolphus' hand," said Lukens again as they came to Wilson's gate.

"I will," he returned as he turned in.

Next morning, as he faced his father at the table, Adolphus' hand was bandaged. His father said nothing until the meal was over. Then he spoke.

"Where'd you get that burned hand?" asked Wilson.

Adolphus looked surprised at his father's knowledge. He replied, "Down at the show last night."

"How?"

"Putting out a flame on one of the tents."

"That's funny, Adolphus. Abe Lukens says he saw your burned hand before the sparks ever started catching."

Adolphus paled and did not reply.

Wilson noted the change and shot at him. "Did you set the old barn afire?"

The son hesitated, at a loss as to what to say to excuse himself, or to frame an alibi.

"I did, dad." He trembled.

"What for?"

"For money," said Adolphus meekly.

"Money! How could that make you any?" thundered Wilson.

"Slim Maynard was to give me $5.00," returned Adolphus, now resolved to tell the truth. Maybe it would awaken his dad to the danger of being miserly towards him. "Slim gave me half of it yesterday afternoon. He was to give me the other half if the fire stopped the show. I am to collect this morning."

Into Wilson's mind came the inkling of what had happened. Still it was not all clear. His son's next declaration dissolved the situation.

"Slim said that you declared you wanted the show run out of town. He said we could burn the old barn, the wind was just right, the old barn wasn't worth anything. He said you would pay him to break up the outfit. Isn't that right, dad?"

He looked at Wilson, whose head was now bowed in thought or shame; he couldn't figure which it was.

Wilson looked up and took a deep breath. "That's partly true, son. He kept at me wanting to know what it would be worth to me to run the troupe out. Finally, I said $25.00 to have my way would be worth that much. The other fellows on the board were so strong against me.

I had no idea my statement would suggest to him any such wild scheme. In fact, I said it rather idly. But now I see how strong mere suggestion is to a weak fellow like Slim. So he didn't have the nerve to do the job himself? No wonder, that's arson, son." He looked at Adolphus seriously.

"But, dad, the shack wasn't worth much. It wasn't insured."

"That makes no difference," replied Wilson, his tone and manner becoming kinder every moment. "If a man burns property worth nothing, wouldn't he burn property worth something? It's the principle, son. Just what was the job Slim shoved on you?"

"To slip in the barn, fire the old hay and skip as fast as I could without being seen. Unluckily, I was looking to see if anyone was coming up on me and scorched my hand pretty badly."

"Both guilty, in a way," mused Wilson. He shoved his hand in his pocket and pulled out a pocketbook. "Here's your $2.50. I'll talk to Slim right away this morning." He rose and put on his hat to leave, then turned to ask, "Son, I thought you wanted to see the show. If you burned it out, how did you figure you could see the acts?"

"Slim said we could see a much better one over at Shellville two weeks from now," answered Adolphus.

"Another show? Shut up!" roared Wilson, drawing back the palm of his hand as if to strike him. Then he slammed the door.

—1930's

Jimmy's Graduation

"All ready for the graduation exercises Saturday?" asked Walton from across the street.

Jimmy Ryan, a lad of 13, looked up and stopped hoeing in the garden. "No," he called back regretfully, "Guess I'll not get to go."

"What!" exclaimed the Ayers boy. He stopped and looked across at Jimmy incredulously. Then he came over. "Why not?" demanded Walton.

"Well, er, you see, I don't have clothes fit to wear to the exercises, that's the reason."

This year, contrary to the usual custom, almost everyone wanted mass graduation exercises. It was all very fine and all had favored it. But then Jimmy had not thought, at the time, what it involved. Only within the few days had he realized that everyone would be dressed in his best, new suits, ties, shirts and everything.

Jimmy had no new suit nor scarcely an old one. Mr. Ryan hadn't had work lately and well, it looked as if Jimmy would have to call for his diploma privately after the exercises.

"Aw, don't let that keep you out," said Walton. "Brush up your old one and come on."

"No," returned Jimmy regretfully but determinedly. "I will not go unless I can be dressed properly."

"Well, then," pursued Walton, "couldn't you borrow a suit?"

"I wouldn't do that." Jimmy drew up a little proudly. "All the kids would know it. Put yourself in my place, you wouldn't want to do it."

Walton had to admit that himself, but he left Jimmy, saying cheerfully, "After all, there's a whole week yet and something may turn up."

Jimmy *was* disappointed. He had done so well in school, his teacher had praised his work so, that he hated not to be able to take part in the final triumph of receiving the well-earned diploma from the hands of the superintendent. But seemingly, there was nothing he could do about it.

Concluding thus, he fell to work furiously and soon his thoughts were far away. After all, he had the entire care of the garden this season and he had made some plans of his own in which he was very much interested in carrying out.

Suppertime, he repeated the conversation he and Walton had had.

"It will be too bad," sighed Mrs. Ryan, "but I don't know what we can do about it. Of course, I could try mending your old suit, I'll just do that tomorrow."

"Don't do it, mother, please," interrupted Jimmy. "It'll be all right if I am not present. I'll get my diploma anyway."

"Yes, I know, but you had counted on it so much." Mrs. Ryan signed again, then her face lighted up.

"Perhaps we could buy you a suit at Elleston's Shop and make arrangements to pay later. Surely, we could do it within a few months."

"Let's don't," returned Jimmy. "We need the money for other things."

"You're mighty serious, son. Most boys would yell until they got a suit."

"Maybe being given the sole management of the garden has made me so," Jimmy said and laughed.

Friday morning, Walton stopped along the garden fence and greeted the young gardener. "Any developments?" asked he of Jimmy.

"Any what?" said Jimmy. Then quickly, "Oh, you mean the garden, well, you see the beans are up, the lettuce is about ready to eat, but the cutworms ..."

"Naw, I didn't mean that," responded Walton brusquely, "I meant about the exercises tomorrow."

"Oh," laughed Jimmy, "I had almost forgotten about it. I have been so busy here."

"You mean you haven't looked around to find out if you can get the clothes, or, or haven't decided to wear the best you have already?"

"That's it," replied Jimmy.

"Well, you're some boy, I must say," remarked Walton good humoredly. "Say, Jimmy, had you thought about earning money for the clothes, or would you do that? Of course, I know you're busy now, but later?"

"By the time I earned enough, it would be too late, maybe I could earn enough to buy one by the time high school opened up in the fall."

"Well, I must get down town on this errand," said Walton, leaving.

Jimmy returned to his work. Work as fast as he could without endangering the plants with his hoe, he could not entirely brush away his disappointment. Tomorrow, everyone would be in the big hall; he would be there in the garden, alone of all the boys and girls. Resting a few moments, he was forced to brush some tears away.

It was well that they were only a few, for Walton was returning from his errand and would stop. It would hurt his pride to let Walton know that he felt the disappointment so keenly. He must keep up the bravado.

"Say, listen Jimmy," Walton exclaimed, quickening pace and almost running himself into the fence. "I got you a job, you can get your new suit."

Jimmy flung down the hoe excitedly and ran to the fence. The trampled beans went unheeded, as Walton explained.

"I wanted to help you, I felt as if I ought to, gosh, you do want to be in the exercises, don't you? So at Elleston's I stopped and asked him if there was a chance for a boy to buy a suit and work it out some way, you know. I told him who it was and that you would be left out unless someone gave you a break. Mr. Elleston thought a few moments, then asked what you were doing. 'Gardening,' I told him, 'has all the management of it this year and it's a pretty big one, too.'

'Tell Jimmy to come down today and we will make some arrangements. I can use him in the mornings cleaning up and probably if he has any extra garden produce, I can use some of it. Send him right down.'

"You ready?" demanded Walton.

For answer, Jimmy gave a leap and bounded over the fence. Then he stopped abruptly, "have to tell Mom," he said. He darted indoors and came out again in a run. "It's all right."

After supper, Jimmy dressed himself in the new suit. He looked at himself a little bashfully in the glass. Mr. and Mrs. Ryan surveyed him praisingly.

At that moment, Walton came in.

"I was so excited this afternoon that I forgot to thank you for getting me that job," said Jimmy. "Thanks a lot."

"I'm afraid that if it had not been for Walton, Jimmy would be out of the fun tomorrow." Mrs. Ryan smiled, then quoted: "Pride goes before a fall and Jimmy almost fell."

—1930's

Murder In The Oil Country

A huge black shadow played across the face of the mile-distant limestone cliff overlooking a little valley near Merwick City. Its form was human but its extremities trailed off into the texture of the cliff. It darted here and there, now in natural form, now assuming the most grotesque attitude.

The height of the oil boom was on in Southern Illinois and almost anything could happen fabulous. Many a poor one had been made rich overnight. Business had leaped up; building had taken an unprecedented boom. Speculation, serious talk and idle rumor filled the air. Whole townships had been leased. Giant oil ruled all. But so far nothing so fantastical as a human giant had appeared.

To a party of four youths who were encamped at the foot of a hill lying opposite the limestone cliff, the great bulky shadow was but a concomitant to the exciting times. They had located themselves for the night in an old abandoned shack which stood in a sassafras thicket mixed with persimmon not a mile off the main highway.

"I say, fellows, we are not getting anywhere standing here," remarked a fiery-haired, freckled youth of 16.

"Well, what do you want us to do, damsel?" asked Ben, the son of the town's only banker.

"Let's get some supper. I'm hungry."

Induced by James and Ben, the two others, Joe Allston (the grocer's son) and Bonnard Dowell, dug into the duffel bag and brought out utensils. They darted frequent glances at the agile shadow. The sun had scarcely sunk behind that cliff when the strange shadow suddenly disappeared.

"What do you suppose it is?" asked Bonnard, somewhat awed.

"Don't know," replied James. "Let's get some supper first and talk about it later."

Released from nine month's work in the little high school, the four boys had felt the urge for adventure. Even though they expected only a night or two out, they had begun the trip with eagerness. Warm spring days had come. Their pent-up energies had to have expression.

A hundred different subjects were brought up for discussion around the campfire after supper. But the mysterious shadow was most talked of.

"I say, fellows," said Ben, the largest and strongest of the four, who was now 19, "I say we have adventure right here at hand the first night out."

"Suppose we cross the valley to the bluff first thing in the morning," suggested James. His red hair matched his impetuous nature.

"OK with us," the others chorused.

The next morning they walked a quarter mile down the road and crossed Clifty Creek. Here they were forced to take off their shoes to ford the creek which had risen during the heavy rains the previous morning. It was that rain which had delayed their start the day before. They were now only five miles from Merwick City.

"Heah, look here!" ejaculated Joe, who was the first to set foot on the other side.

"What is it?" asked Bonnard.

"Footprints, giant footprints," cried Joe excitedly.

All hurried across.

Sure enough! The giant imprint of a shoe showed plainly on the moist roadway. Each one measured about 12 inches in width and 38 in length.

Bonnard looked frightened. Although not the youngest, he was recognized as the least daring. "What can they be?" he half-whispered.

"Footprints, of course, dummy," said Joe.

"But whose?" persisted Bonnard.

"It must be the giant's," said Ben seriously. "Looks as if we might run into something. These tracks were undoubtedly made last night."

"But where did they come from?" questioned James. "Look here. They start from the side of the road; there are none on the other side of the creek."

"Probably the giant came from up the creek," remarked Ben. Of course he could not really believe that there was a real giant abroad. He had read that there had been comparative giant men in modern times, even now was there one in own state; yes, it was a possibility, but he brushed the idea aside.

His thoughts were broken into by Joe's exclaiming "Let's follow them! We have to go by old Steve Morton's place anyway. Maybe he's seen them, too, and the shadows."

Two hundred yards off the road, at the end of a private lane, squatted the old man's ramshackle house. The boys turned into the driveway. The giant tracks had also turned. Thirty yards from the front gate and just past the barn lot, the tracks disappeared as completely as they had appeared down at the creek.

A little barking terrier announced their arrival. Old Morton came out on the porch. The boys hesitated, the dog might bite. "Wait, I'll be there. I can't hear you." He leaned over the fence and cupped an ear.

"We would like permission to explore the bluff back of your house," explained Ben. "We are boys from Merwick City and want to scout around."

"Did you see the big shadow last evening and the giant footprints down by your horse lot?" James blurted out, pointing in that direction.

Ben gave him a withering look.

"Yes, I did, yelled Morton, suddenly showing anger. "I saw it last night and this morning, and have seen it for a week. I don't like this tomfoolery. No," he cried, his fury mounting. "no, I won't let you roam around my place. There's been an army around here lately, surveying, breaking down fences and wanting leases on my 200 acres. I've ordered the whole push to stay off."

"But" began Ben, ever polite.

"No, can't have you boys or anyone else around and that settles it. Move on." and Steve spit furiously and strode into the house.

The same day Steve Morton stamped angrily over the dirt road to the main highway which led to Merwick City, five miles southeast. He walked in the exact steps of the giant, kicking and stamping at each one until they ceased at Clifty Creek. "Some fool trying to scare me," he muttered to himself. "Look at those tracks. Too close together not to be a man's.

Sheriff Ramp looked up from his desk to see a pair of beady eyes peering at him through the fretted grill. "Hello, Mr. Morton," he exclaimed. "Don't see you here very often. What can I do for you?"

"Huh. You may get to see more of me if you don't arrest some of those fellows trespassing on my place. Why, just this morning..." and he told about the latest culprits.

"Well, now," said Sheriff Ramp slowly. He had come in office on a landslide over his opponents. Voters had wanted a new man, a fair and square man, one who would show no favorites in executing the law. In Ramp the people had found their man. He had already gained the reputation of "taking his man."

"Is your land posted?" asked Ramp. He was careful and calculating.

"No, it is not," returned Morton.

"Then you do that the first thing. How are you in town?"

"Afoot."

"Then I'll take you home and together we can locate the best places to post your premises.

"Sheriff," said Morton huskily "there's something else, too."

"Why, what's the matter, Mr. Morton?" noting the half-frightened look which had come over the old man.

"I don't know, sheriff," he said in a low voice. "I don't know. Something mysterious. I have tried to forget it and believe it some joke. The boys have seen it. I admit, sheriff, that I am a little shaky."

"Hm, well, let's go if you are ready," said Ramp, putting on his hat.

They stepped out of the courthouse and came face to face with the amiable tavern owner Leon Firsch. He was accounted the wealthiest in and around Merwick City. His pleasant disposition had enabled him to gain success. He owned several farms, had stock in this and that, and was even now deeply interested in the oil boom. During prohibition years he had almost completely disappeared for a time; then had reappeared, more pleasant and wealthier than before.

He greeted Sheriff Ramp and Morton collectively and asked of the latter "Have you decided to give me a lease yet?"

"No," growled Morton.

"Say, Mr. Morton," asked Ramp, as they passed on. "Didn't you have a son who was sent to the penitentiary years ago, for a short time, because of some convicting evidence of Firsch?"

"Yes, I have a son who got just that, in Chicago now, and I have not liked Firsch since. He could have cleared my son if he had wished. But I think he was shielding someone else."

They jumped into Ramp's car and sped rapidly to the Morton place.

"They tell me that Firsch has leased thousands of acres around here," remarked Ramp.

"That's what he told me about a month ago," said Morton. "He wanted an oil lease on my place, said he would even buy it. I refused him.

"Why, man," he said to me, 'where's your reason. You can't hold out on me like this after offering you four times what it's worth,' he said, pulling out a checkbook. 'I will write you a check for $25,000.' Oh, he has the money. 'It's enough to make you comfortable for the rest of your days.' I said if it was worth that much to him, it might be worth as much to me to keep it and have all the profit in my pocket. Ha, ha,' cackled old Steve. 'We all, young and old, have the oil fever."

Sheriff made no reply. The fording of rough little Clifty Creek required all his attention. But he was thoughtful as he turned into the lane.

It was late in the afternoon when Ramp drove away. Twice as the afternoon advanced they had seen light shadows cast up against the limestone cliff, which arose a little more than 200 yards back of the farmhouse and a little to the north. Each time they had approached the foot of the cliff the shadows had disappeared.

The sheriff stopped at the end of the lane which led to the old shack. He got out. The thicket hid the cliff. He walked to the shack, at whose elevation he hoped to be able to see over the thicket. He stopped short, surprised. A bright fire burned in front of the shack around which were gathered crouching figures. "Oh, the boys, of course. I forgot," he laughed.

The four boys leaped up, alarmed at seeing the sudden approach, for they had not heard the car behind the dense growth of saplings.

"It's all right boys," the sheriff laughed. "Guess you saw the strange shadows over on the bluff?"

"Yes, sheriff, we have." The boys were going to explain further but he stopped them with "Yes, I already know. The old man told me. There he goes again!" he exclaimed. Everyone looked. The shadows were getting into more curious shapes than they had even the night before.

"What do you make of it, sheriff?" asked Ben.

"I don't know yet, but I have ever so small a hunch. If you boys want some real adventures, I suggest that tonight you hide down by the creek. You may see something."

"Gee! Great!" ejaculated the three less sober-mannered youths.

"But stay out of Morton's way. He may be crazy. Talks like it."

The following morning a heated discussion took place around the breakfast table. Frequent laughing and bantering intermixed. "I told you James," said Joe, "to get a good position and stay, if you heard the giant coming."

"I did but I became tired and got a crick in my leg and had to move."

"A good scout you'd make," growled Koe.

"Say, weren't you fellows a little scared when you heard that clomp, clomp down the road," ventured Bonnard. "I more than half-expected to see a 10-foot giant come striding down the creek."

"You would be scared," ridiculed James. "You should have guarded the camp. Here we are without any meat for breakfast because that 'possum carried it off."

"How do you know it was an opossum?" asked Bonnard.

"I saw its tracks," informed Ben, who had taken little part in the discussion. "It is unfortunate that James kicked some gravel into the creek. The man might have hidden his wooden shoes close by and we could have gained possession of them. Anyway, we know for certain that the shoes are a fraud. Even in the dim starlight we saw him take them off."

"What's the next move?" asked James.

"Tell the sheriff what we've learned," said Ben.

******

"Well, things do look a little bad for you, Mr. Morton," the sheriff said, looking at the old man listlessly fingering his frugal supper in the county jail.

"But why should they?" repeated Morton for the tenth time that day.

"We've gone over all that," said the sheriff kindly. "I regret caging you up here but circumstances forced me to arrest you this morning."

"But my word, my character. Isn't that worth anything to you. Have I ever been accused of the least misdemeanor, let alone murder."

"Well, perhaps not cold-blooded murder but had you thought that, possessing the strong character you have, a plea of self-defense might go a long way with a jury? I'm impartially suggesting, understand," said Ramp.

"No, never," shouted Morton. "I will never say that I killed Bob Sayer. I never injured a man bodily in my life, so help me."

"Too bad you lighted your pipe with that note you found on your door." mused Ramp.

"I did not think, never thought," said Morton, weakly.

"You say it said: 'Meet me across the creek by the old hollow sycamore at nine o'clock a.m. and you will learn the truth' Then, as you almost reached the creek bank, you heard a shot and going over you as a voice cried for help, found Bob Sayer shot to death and a pistol lying near him. I could not have been far behind you and I heard the shot. Was the dead man on your land?" asked Ramp.

"Yes, just barely," said Morton.

"Then I came up and saw you bending over Sayer with the pistol in your hand. You explained all to me and we looked around but found no one. Then I arrested you."

"That's right," returned Morton.

"One more question, Mr. Morton. Understand, I am only trying to help you. I believe you are absolutely innocent; after all the evidence is quite circumstantial. The question is, Mr. Morton, what do you know about this Bob Sayer?"

"Practically nothing. He bought that place which lies east about three quarters of a mile opposite mine. He's been on it about a month."

"Who sold it to him?"

"Don't know, there's been so much buying, selling and leasing around here the last several months," returned Morton.

"Hey, Sheriff," he continued anxiously, "what's to become of my stock? I have two horses, six head of hogs, a cow to be milked and a dog to be fed. It's six o'clock now."

"How will the four boys do?" asked Ramp.

"What! Those boys who were out there yesterday? They can't do chores. Besides, how do you know but they are in to some of this trick work?"

"I hardly think so," said Ramp, repressing a smile. "They saw the giant last night about midnight and..."

"The giant! What, who was it?" interrupted Morton excitedly.

"Fine boys, these are, adventurous, too. I'll call them up and take them out to do the chores." he said as he reached for the telephone.

"I hope the cow is not a kicker," laughed Ben as he merrily swung the bucket on the way to the barn. He thought this was the chore requiring the steadiest patience and he happened to have had the most experience with the bovine tribe. The other boys fed the horses and hogs. The chickens had gone to roost. The animals must have thought it was a holiday for they were fed twice as much as old Steve fed them. The terrier was not forgotten. The next morning the old rooster looked up in surprise at the handful after handful of corn that were cast around. It was eight o'clock before all the chores were completed. They had supper afterwards. It was an unusual position for the boys. It had been so sudden and unexpected that the novelty of it had not yet been fully appreciated.

James expressed it when he said as they sat around the kitchen stove: "Who would have thought yesterday that tonight we would be farmers and in full possession of Steve Morton's house."

"It is rather a quick rise," smiled Ben. "Who will be the housekeeper and cook, the errand boy, the chore doers and the farmer himself?"

Laughingly, they assigned positions and discussed various matters until bedtime. "A good farmer gets up early, you know," said Ben, who as the eldest had been chosen to represent Morton. "Let's turn in."

He added: "We may laugh about ourselves, boys, but you have to admit that Morton is in a serious position tonight. Let's hope he gets out of it quick."

The following day the boys thoroughly explored the bluff, top and bottom and all around. There was nothing to be found to help solve the shadow puzzle. They visited the scene of the fatal shooting and looked about the premises carefully. No need. Ramp and Morton had already covered it. They did not roam the flat meadowland as the sun was near setting.

Again, as they neared the house, the great silhouette darted upon the face of the cliff, even more terrifying in appearance since they were now closer than they had been at the old shack. Ben led the way up to the foot of the cliff. They wound in and out among the huge fragments with which the cliff's foot was strewn. Frost, rain and wind had surely but steadily eaten into stony tentacles.

As they neared the smooth solid wall the mimicking profile vanished. "Now where is it?" asked Joe.

"Find it if you can," returned Ben, puzzled.

They watched until the last sunbeam faded from the windows of the house across the valley on the opposite bluff. Ben looked in that direction, long and hard. He moved some steps away from the others and resting his arm upon a huge stone, took out a nail and scratched some odd designs upon it. He came back, muttering to himself. "Could it be possible?"

After supper Ben announced: " I want to arise before daylight in the morning so I must turn in or I'll oversleep."

"What for?" asked Bonnard, a proven sleepyhead.

"I have a long watch I want to make tomorrow," and he detailed his plan.

"How'd you figure it out," demanded James, rather amazed at Ben's budding detective ability.

"It may not turn out the way I've figured; then the laugh will be on me. But first I want some food to take along to last all day. Can you fix that much from what is left over, cook?" he jested. Joe still had on old Morton's apron.

"We'll see, husband," returned Joe.

"I want something to read also," continued Ben. "Wonder what there is here in that line?"

A search uncovered some farm papers, a Bible and some law books of 1900 vintage. Ben wrapped a cord around the papers and a law book and said, "Guess these will do. If I'm working on a case I might as well read-up on the law. Hm. You'd think Morton was a reader, his wife being dead so long."

"That's just the reason he isn't," said Joe. "Doing farm work and house work both, he doesn't have time."

"Remember, boys" said Ben as he prepared to retire, "don't any of you approach the cliff all day. I'll be back a little after sunset tomorrow."

Ben returned the following evening, wearied from inactivity and hunger. But a happy sparkle came into his eyes as he devoured the warm food.

"Well, how did you manage the cow," he laughed between mouthfuls.

"Aw, come on, drop it," his companions chorused. "Out with it, tell us what you found."

"I'm not entirely certain yet, but almost. I want to do some spying tonight to complete the case against the giant man."

"Where? The same house?" asked James.

"Yes, the one over on the opposite bluff," returned Ben.

"But would the sheriff approve?" asked Bonnard, advisedly.

"I don't know but I think it will be all right."

"Oh, yes. We had a visitor," informed James. "The sheriff came out to see how we were coming along."

"Any developments?" asked Ben.

"No. None," replied James.

"Now boys," said Ben, arising from the sadly-depleted table, "let's put up a light against the great wall for a beacon. I got a line on the house today. We can use that line to locate what I want to find tonight. Who goes with me?"

All three volunteered. Bonnard backed out when Ben outlined his plan in detail.

"Shall I toss a coin?" asked Ben of the other two.

"Choose the one you think best for the job," said Joe. "Suits me."

"Then get your cap, Joe" said Ben. "After all you're the slimmest boy and we may need to do some squeezing in and among those rocks tonight."

After a short night's sleep Ben tramped into Merwick City and reported to the sheriff.

"Joe and I left about nine o'clock" he recounted. "It was dark and pretty hard going after we left the old shack. As we went up the side of the bluff we found rocks, thickets and briars. Our shins suffered plenty. Then we took out the compass. Carefully, by the light of the flashlight and the guide light on the opposite bluff, we found the correct line of vision. What gave us trouble was finding the proper altitude. But knowing the proper north-south line we had only to move up and down the steep slope to find what we were looking for."

"And what were you looking for?" interrupted Ramp with interest.

"The heliograph," said Ben.

"The what?" exclaimed the sheriff, unenlightened.

"A heliograph," informed the boy, "is an instrument which catches the light of the sun and flashes it back. Now, putting a solid object in front of it of course will shut off the light that much. That explains the shadows over on the cliff and it explains why it happened only in the afternoon, though with some difficulty it might be made to flash in almost any direction any time of the day."

"How did the operator know when we approached the great wall?"

"Probably with a powerful telescope. They cut the shadows off when we drew too close because we probably would have seen the source. As it was, however, we found it rather hidden among some huge boulders where the out-flashing light could not be so easily discovered."

"The question is," said the sheriff, puzzled, "what is the motive back of it all?"

"They probably wanted to scare Morton off the place," ventured Ben.

He continued: "Suddenly, Joe and I saw a light in a south window of the Sayer house. We thought the house was deserted since Sayer's death and it mystified us. At first we hardly dared to investigate, but curiosity got the better of us and we did. We slipped into the yard and up to the window with lowered shades. We crouched, listening to voices inside.

"'Looks as if we had the old man out of the way,' said one. 'Yes, he's the same as in the pen if not in the chair,' said another. We peeped carefully but we could not see the faces of any of them. A third voice said: 'Maybe out of the way but not off the place. I can't pay you yet. The deal was...' and the rest was lost by the other two exclaiming 'the deuce, why not?' Then the third voice said: 'Tell you what I'll do. I'll compromise. The boys are still on the place. Every day you handle the works, I'll give you $10. Besides, if things get too hot, I'll pay you the whole sum and warn you when to git.' After a short discussion the first voice said, 'OK, we'll take you up.' As one of them prepared to leave, we slipped behind some rose bushes. He pulled out in a big car and sped down the road so fast that we just barely managed to get the first four license numbers. Then we left for Morton's.'"

"How many numbers were there on the plate?" asked the sheriff.

"Six. We got the first four. Here they are, 5456."

"Shouldn't be so hard to run down the other two. Good work, Ben." and he placed his hand on the lad's shoulder.

"Thanks, sheriff. Do you think any of the three men could have had anything to do with Sayer's death?"

"Don't know, Ben. The old man swears he hasn't shot a revolver since he was a young man. He defies us to find anyone in the United States who sold or loaned him either gun or shells. I believe the old man. I say," said Ramp abruptly, "I'll just drive out and see the fellows."

In the Sayer yard a tall, gaunt man of about 35 age looked at the sheriff coolly. "It's a fact, sheriff, Sayer and I were good friends. That's why he had us down for a visit. Then the old man shot him..."

"Hold on, interrupted Ramp. "Nothing has been proven yet."

"Well, anyway, he was killed."

"Why are you staying on after the death of your friend." Ramp eyed him narrowly.

"The truth is we put all our eggs in one basket. We figured on staying with Bob, maybe working for him, until our visit was over and we had gotten a few dollars wages. Ought to be plenty of work around this burg soon if oil is struck."

"May be a long time," remarked Ramp, dryly.

The two men looked discomfited. Noting their shifty, suspicious glances, he shot at them: "where were you about nine o'clock the morning Sayer was shot?"

Their faces brightened and the gaunt man's lips curled into a smile.

"We were down at the pool hall and that's a fact. We can prove it by the proprietor and half a dozen others."

"Well, good morning, men, and excuse me if I have caused you any anxiety." The Sheriff thought it wisest not to mention the heliograph. If they were implicated in any way and to supply the recently-acquired information might frighten them away. He had no legal justification for arresting them. But he would check up on them at the pool hall. The gaunt one was speaking: "Not at all, sheriff; in fact, you are welcome. We have no apprehension whatever. Why should we."

Sheriff Ramp raced back to town. He searched furiously among his books and papers for the new edition of automobile owners' license numbers.

"Late this year, Mr. Ramp," said the office girl, "We have no copy yet."

He raced to the telegraph office and sent a wire asking if there had been a license issued to a Merwick City resident between the numbers 545600 and 545699. He waited for the answer, tensely. There had been.

He turned the corner and sped down Poplar Street. There was the number, 545617. Now he returned to the courthouse and looked over the deeds to the Sayer place.

Ramp then sped five miles out to a house opposite to the side road which led to the Sayer place. Here he held a lengthy conversation with the wife and oldest daughter. Complacently, he started back, driving more slowly. He turned and followed the side road to the Morton place. A chorus of boys' voices greeted him. Together, he and the boys went over the evidence. The case was made out.

Back in Merwick City, Sheriff Ramp knocked on the door of the big house on Poplar Street.

"I arrest you, Leon Firsch, for the murder of Bob Sayler," said Ramp.

"Impossible! This can't be. Are you crazy, man?" yelled Firsch.

"Just hear me and you will come along," returned the sheriff. First, you sold Bob Sayler that place he bought. Then you tried to scare Morton into selling or leasing his farm. You brought the strangers here to help Bob. Moreover, we have two witnesses to your conversation last night in the Sayler house. We have the license number of the car that left there, and it happened to be yours. As further proof, I have two other witnesses who will swear on oath that your car drove into the Sayer Road the morning of the murder. You alone were in it. Your two friends have furnished a satisfactory alibi; they were not on the place, and - will you come?"

"If you demand it, sheriff," said Firsch feebly.

"What was your motive?" queried Ramp, as he turned the key to a cell.

"Why, Bob enraged me. He wanted an exorbitant sum of money for his oil rights. I told him we would meet Morton on the land line and try to induce him into selling or leasing his place, one more time. I had a good chance. My rage still boiled, and I shot him."

As they all stood on the front porch of the Morton house, old Steve said: "You boys can do all the exploring you want, the place is yours." He surveyed the animals peacefully cropping grass and the happy cackling of hens. "You're good chore boys, too." he added.

"I think we've explored about all we want to around that bluff the past several days." Ben laughed.

"Yes, I think Ben had better apply himself to detective work if he wants to be my deputy some day." And Sheriff Ramp grinned.
                    —1930's

No Madding Crowd

It was just 16 years ago, as I come to think of it, that I first met David Trimble. He was then 14 years old, only a boy and I was one year younger. We were neighbors for a year and during that time I spent many happy hours in his company.

I remember now how I admired him, how I envied him and how I wished someday to be like him, of all the boys I ever met, he was my ideal. I saw in my young mind's eye, the combination of all that was good embodied in this companion.

He was studying music at the time he moved away. He learned quickly. He was precocious in his books, or rather, he was a hard worker. True, he was then immature, but sometimes our hero can be just a boy. Often, in our play, we would stop and I would listen speechless and admiringly to his young piping voice explaining most earnestly and often vehemently, points of his school work.

He loved nature. He spoke tenderly of the flowers in his little garden and of the strolls in the woods. But strangely he did not often invite me to take those rambles with him. "Depart into a solitary place," he quoted. Thus I attributed to him all that my ideal desired.

The following year, he moved away. I received two letters from him at intervals of one year and then I lost account of him. I only knew that he was somewhere in the far Southwest, an ethereal land to my youthful mind.

The years passed and I was busily engaged in school work. I graduated from Balloi College with honors, deriving from its training a love for the sciences. I was placed upon the staff of a prominent research organization for the study of unsurveyed lands in our far Southwest.

My field of endeavor was in a region vaguely called "the most desolate country in the world." It lay 150 miles almost due north of Flagstaff, the nearest railroad point and very close to the Grand Canyon. Little was known about the region. Some settlers had been through that section many years before, but gave such descriptions of the desolation that no one had cared to invade it. Besides, it was said to be haunted and there were Indians. Only with the greatest inducements could be found to lead one to it.

I planned to visit the country in a preliminary sort of way first, to determine the needs for a more extended survey and to discover if I would need white companions to conduct my scientific investigations. Thus, it was that I started out with only two Navajo guides, who seemed to have enough grit in them to defy the ghosts that were supposed to inhabit the canyon. All three of us rode horses.

I received my share of friendly warnings at towns on both sides of the canyon. Definitely, the region was without life: no birds, not even vultures, no animals, no sounds, no vegetable life. It was a dead country. Perhaps it was this absence of the smallest sound that was so eerie and worked on the imagination of the simple people like the Indians and sometimes even the white men. That there were no half-wild outcasts of society it was not so sure, though how anyone could exist there was a mystery. I immediately eliminated men from the list of dangers. Heat and shortage of food and water were my worst fears. I provided well for the latter.

We left Moencopie and rode to Kai Peto, a Navajo Indian trading post, situated among the pines and cedars and at the very mouth of Kai Peto canyon. Fifteen miles farther the region of desolation began and we soon found ourselves in a maze of canyons, but with Navajo Mountain always looming up as the dominating thing on the horizon.

The day was sizzling hot. The omnipresent rocks, staring at us like sore thumbs everywhere, struck my eyes with the force of dazzling hot steel. My head throbbed long before noon, but the guides led on and I followed doggedly. In that vast network of canyons and jumbled rocks, I could not but admire the knowledge of the guides. I felt that, abandoned, I would never find the way back to Kai Peto. In fact, I had given unusual care as to the selection of these two Navajos and trusted that they would not fail me.

In the blackness of that first night, I dreamed of huge boulders weighing upon me and awakened each time with cold sweat on my brow and feeling feverish. I only saw my guides' huddled, wrapped figures, doubtless in a like state of torture.

The second day, about noon, we passed the mouth of a canyon, before which the guides seemed to hesitate.

"What is it?" I asked.

"These two canyons meet again in about half a day's ride," they informed. "It is a sort of island. The right canyon has much deep water in it. It may be hard to pass up it. But the left canyon has no water in it until we pass beyond the upper juncture and ride for two hours. We may not be able to get to drinking water for the horses until after dark."

"Let's push ahead a little faster up the left canyon," I suggested. I knew we could go faster along a dry course than to have to swim the horses very far.

"It may be changed, it may not," said one of the guides. "I have been along the right canyon only once, 20 years ago."

"We go up the left," grunted the other guide.

In about an hour the horses showed signs of uneasiness. We stopped. It was strange with not a breath stirring, not a living thing but us and the horses and where the stillness of the day was like night. The dusky guides were not as calm as at first. The heat waves throbbed against my temples and I felt unnerved. In my lonesomeness, I was glad to have the more elemental horses and Navajos with me. I took a deep drink from my canteen and shook the feeling off, attributing the disquietude to the crushing silence and its unusualness. But neither the horses, guides nor myself could entirely shake it off. The country soon became even more rugged and wild. The precipitous walls towered over the dim forgotten trail of ancient races, as if to hide that land of the dead from prying eyes.

The canyon was a long one. Night began to fall before we reached the juncture of the two canyons. It was dark when we found water and selected a suitable place to make camp.

The older guide looked up the canyon uncertainly. He spoke with the younger in Navajo.

"What's the trouble?" I asked, seeing them look dubiously around.

"Nothing," returned the older, but it did not sound convincing.

With canned heat I furnished, the guides prepared a few bites of hot supper and some coffee. The darkness was so dense it could almost be felt. And the brooding silence! The awfulness of it was not broken, even by the howling of slinking coyotes and which could be appreciated here at least.

We lay down and sought forgetfulness in sleep, but even that was restless.

I know not how long I slept, but suddenly I was awakened by shouts from the guides. I sprang up hastily, half awake, half asleep and was able to hear a low, roaring sound, as of waves on a distant seashore.

We listened, curious, half-terrified. The roar increased until definitely I could tell it was a roar of onrushing water.

Terrified, the Indians shouted, "Water! We are trapped!"

No less excited, I yelled at the top of my voice, "What shall we do? The horses!"

"Take care of yourself," they howled.

Almost simultaneously, there appeared around the canyon curve, a solid wall of water, head high.

There was no escape. The walls were unscalable. I saw the black form of the horses dart past. Thank God, the Navajos had not so far lost their head as to leave the animals fettered.

The Indians prepared for the struggle. I gave a poor gasp of self-assurance and trusting to fate, met the torrent which was now upon me.

I was forced down the first thing and was almost knocked senseless. The next moment I was lifted up bodily and rose to the top of the torrent. Of the Indians, I lost all knowledge. I was quickly rushed down the dark canyon, expecting every moment to have my brains crushed against the rocky, protruding knobs.

I know not how far I floated, but it must have been some distance. Of time - I had no consciousness. Even yet, I do not cease to wonder how I kept from being drowned or mortally injured. All at once, I was conscious of being in still water. Letting my feet sink, I touched bottom at about five feet. It was still dark and I knew not which way to proceed to find shallower water. Edging gingerly along, I managed to find in which direction the bottom of the pool sloped upward and followed upward.

On dry sand at last, I sank exhausted and rested. I got up only to shake off my extreme chilliness, then lay down again. I did this several times, until day began to dawn.

The scene which met my eyes after my last fit of slumber, defies telling. Transported as by magic from the desolation of yesterday, it struck me as incongruous, impossible. I had misapprehensions as to my sanity. For there, before me, not a quarter of a mile off, was a habitation, trees, a garden and a curling column of smoke. The whole beautiful picture lay in a kind of semi-lunar enclosure of rock walls, with a yawning canyon at the far side, behind the tent-like house.

I contemplated the prospect Crusoe-like for some moments. Then I tested my body to see if all was sound. I was sore and bruised, it was true; I knew that last night when I found dry earth. But I wanted to do something to understand this transmigration. I ended by walking towards the oasis.

"I am Cecil Bellamy," I said simply to the little girl who came out of the tent. "I was washed upon the bank by the flood last night. Two Navajo guides and I were making our way to Rainbow Bridge."

She looked at me long, curiously, searchingly. She was about 8 years old, I guessed. I returned the gaze, fascinated by the fine brown hair, brown skin and blue eyes. There appeared in her survey of me a touch of wilderness, yet in her next speech, I detected a subtle note of refinement.

"Daddy has gone to the spring for water. He will be back within a few minutes." she said. "Then we will eat." Perfect grammar, in a child of 8. I could hardly restrain myself from asking the way to the spring. I wanted to see this man. I thought the region was without life, habitation.

"Here he comes now," the child piped up shrilly.

I saw a man of about my own age approaching with a bucket in each hand. Seeing me, he quickened step.

" I am Cecil Bell ..."

The man dropped both buckets and the contents trickled along, unheeded. I stared at him incredulously, he returned my look with fixed eyes.

"Cecil Bellamy," he said slowly and emphatically. His countenance relaxed and he said "And I am David Trimble. Pleased to meet my old school-boy friend again."

The muteness of sudden emotion broken, we returned to the spring, arm in arm, explaining, questioning as we went.

"I had brilliant success here in the west," my friend began, after we had eaten breakfast. "My interest was chiefly philosophy. I got up a series of lectures on my chosen subject and putting into them much practicality, succinct advice and subtle humor, I took the lecture-goers by storm. I also wrote a great deal."

"I was married when I was 22 and the baby, Mina, came to us soon afterwards, not much of a baby now, if you could see her clamber over these rocks and canyons." David glanced at her and laughed. "Unhappily, my wife was drowned while on a vacation jaunt at the seashore and left me with 5-year-old Mina."

"I continued to lecture, but the strain of the crowd became too great for my nature and I desired to seek solitude for more study and reflection. That and seeking surcease from sorrow from my wife's tragic death, impelled me to find some out of the way corner of the west and dwell in it for a time.

"You know, my friend" he continued, "as a youth I desired solitude."

"Yes, I remember," I nodded.

"I wished to spend more time on my writings as well," David went on. "I believe in isolation as the best atmosphere in which to produce. You may grow among society, but you will not produce seed forever, nurtured in it alone.

"My father listened to my plan coldly and especially so when I proposed taking Mina with me. He finally consented to my isolation and to keep it quiet from the world on one condition. That was, to produce one thoughtful, worthwhile book per year.

"I took him up and leaving the promotion of my publications and their sale to a trusted agent, I looked about for a suitable locality. Hearing about the most 'desolate region in the world', I made an exploration of this region. After several weeks, in which I regained some of my physical ruggedness, I discovered this enclosed valley.

"I transported all needful supplies here with the help of Indians from Kai Peto. Then I dismissed all of them except one. After a few months, I had my Indian give out word that I had abandoned the project. This was to throw anyone off the trail who might be tempted hither and especially since such visitors would come by way of Kai Peto. Then my Indian began to get supplies at Goodridge. But with my garden, many food supplies were eliminated. Pah-Nah should be in tomorrow from Goodridge. My father and my agent are my only correspondents and I have not left this place since I came here three years."

"But your daughter, you instruct her I suppose, won't she be handicapped, how long will you stay here?" I asked, amazed at my friend's fanatical desire for isolation.

"Perhaps I should say," David began again, "that I have more than fulfilled the promise to my father. I have produced five philosophical works, besides other miscellanies. One of them is an unpublished manuscript on this region. I have written stories for Mina as good or better than she would read at large. Than I have a few choice books for her. Yes, I have instructed her. As to my success as a teacher, you may be your own judge."

I turned to Mina and catechized her. I found her superior and said as much as I turned to David and smiled.

Towards evening my younger Navajo straggled up. He informed that the other was lying down the right canyon, some ways, with a broken arm and a badly cut head. The younger had caught on to a rock and clung until the flood subsided. I felt some remorse from so far having forgotten them. We went down immediately and brought him up.

"Your flood last night came most likely from a cloud burst on Navajo Mountain," informed David. "It is not generally known that storms occur on Navajo. They are infrequent and it is quite possible for a guide not to know about it, unless he had sojourned here sometime."

"Isn't your place in danger?" I asked.

"No. Our canyon is not fed by Navajo. It is a dry one. You see, our water comes from below, the spring and not above."

We remained several days with David. Then, feeling that our continued presence would not be welcomed, I suggested that we had better move on.

But I had not understood David; I never had when we were boys.

"You are on a scientific expedition, are you not?" he asked.

"I am." I hardly knew how to answer.

"Any helpers to return with you?"

"I think it unnecessary, except possibly the Navajos," I answered.

"Go back, bring in your supplies, tell your guides not to mention this place and return to make this your headquarters," David outlined.

"Too many people around banish solitude," I suggested.

David laughed. "Well, if you are fearful of breaking in on my meditations, you can move some yards away. No, my friend," he said quietly and with sincerity. "Your presence is never disturbing. You understand me, you appreciate my attitude. You do not constitute the world crowd. And the Navajos," he ended "they are a part of the name land."

I spent four years with David. Long before the end of that time, I had explored the region thoroughly, read David's unpublished manuscript and returned to civilization to give my report. Then I came back.

David and Mina accompanied me on several of the shorter trips. I saw the strangely-isolated child in many aspects. Beauty, charm and wildness were blended in her makeup. Several times, Mina and I explored together. She scrambled over the rocks and canyons like an untamed one. It was she who first showed me the 'pumkin patch," stone balls looking like mud and some actually having stems. We saw the crouching camel, the painted sands and other freaks.

It was during my fourth year with David that Mina and I visited Rainbow Natural Bridge for about the 20th time and I dared to draw the girl out about her thoughts on this country, her father's isolation and the great, busy, outside world. It was the first time we had ever gone there alone. Night had fallen and we were sitting around our camp-fire in the eerie silence and in the moonlight shadow of the great arch. She was sitting on the scant pile of wood which I had foraged from the few trees in Bridge Canyon. Her trim, girlish ankles were broadside to me and she was looking up at that great crescent.

"What a bridge," she almost whispered. "I know I shouldn't say that in this land of the unusual, but I can't think of anything else now to equal that simple exclamation."

"The bridge of the ancient dead. No moon, no sun sees them now. They are the dead of the dead," I said, quoting from David's manuscript. "You, you, like this?" I half queried.

"Yes," she returned, "Much."

"You never think of the other world, the great outside world of men, women, boys and girls, other girls like you, yet so unlike you?"

I had had hints from David that his hermitical life was to end sometime, sometime, yes. But when?

"Yes, I think about it sometimes," she said dreamily. "But just now, I like to think about this. Do you like it?" she asked turning her face to me at last.

"Why, yes, with a pretty little girl like you around," I said, hazarding to tease her.

She reddened and arose. "I'm sleepy," she said.

******

It was just 16 years ago that I first met David Trimble and now I have met him again. His charm is as ever. Here will I stay until another philosopher bids my heart to go.

And I have no doubt that it will not be many more years, for Mina has entwined her charms about me in an inescapable tie.

Can a man fall in love with a child?

I did.

—1930's

The Staircase Masons

Don Ignatius was spending the day with his son Albert in a public square. They stopped before a house which was being built and which now reached the second story.

Albert noticed that there were many stonemasons, located one above the other on the stairway steps, raising and lowering their arms successfully. This spectacle excited his curiosity. "Papa, what are these men playing at? Let us draw closer to the foot of the stairs."

Thus they placed themselves at a certain point where they would not be in any danger. They came to a man who was carrying an andiron and taking it to another place on the first floor, which latter, raising his hands above his head, put it in the hands of another who was higher than he and in this manner the object reached, from hand to hand, the top of the second story, where the masons found it and soon used it.

"How seems to you what they are doing." said Don Ignatius to his little son. "Why are there so many persons occupied in building this house? Would it not be better that only one worked at it alone and that each one of the others constructed a house by himself?"

"Certainly so," responded Albert, "and then more houses would be had than there are."

"But have you reflected well upon what you say?" responded Don Ignatius. "Do you know how many trades and skills go into the construction of a house such as this? For that, it would be necessary for each man to learn all about the construction of a building, to perfect himself completely in all these professions and being thus, to employ his entire life in acquiring these different knowledges before he would find himself in a state to commence a building.

"And let us suppose that one could instruct himself in a little while in all that he must be able to know. We see him alone and without any help to dig the earth to pour the concrete and afterwards to go alone to look for the stone, to work it and cut it, to mix the gypsum and the lime and to prepare all which must enter into the manufacture and at last, he must sketch his measurements, form his proportions and build the scaffolds. How much time, does it seem to you, would it require for the fine tiled house to be built?"

"Ah! Papa! It is true. I do not think that one would ever finish it."

"You are right, my child. Then look. In this house is represented all the work of human society. When a man conceals himself and works for himself alone, when timid about lending his assistance to the others; refuses to value the time given to it, then it destroys his efforts in the enterprise and quickly he sees for himself that he must abandon it. On the other hand, if men lend themselves mutually to do and aid, in a little while the most difficult and painful things are performed, even those which have been necessarily the work of an entire lifetime.

"The same thing happens also with the pleasures of life. He who wishes to enjoy them exclusively, cut short a number of consequent joys. More is enjoyed if all unite to contribute something for the enjoyment of others, in which each will find his part.

"You will also some day, my son, enter into the world. Be careful never to lose the memory of these workers. Now you see how their work is shortened and made easier by the little aid which each lends. Now we will return here again within a few days and you will see the finished house. Procure, then, in this world, help from others in your undertakings, if you wish them to help you work in your favor."

—Translated by George W. May from the Spanish of *Biblioteca De Mi Abuelo* (Mexico 1864)

The Aristocratic Stone

The heat was suffocating. The month of August had come to a close and night came over the flat tableland. Gathered in one of the shepherd's huts in the vicinity of Guerande, one of those windowless huts of lower Britany, were several persons speaking within it. In the same room some children played on the threshold of the door.

These persons to the number of four were: Fetiot, the owner of the hut; his wife, Monica, a small and corpulent Briton; the old Jane, mother of Monica; and the collector or treasurer of Guerande and a doctor of medicine at the same time.

Upon a table in the middle of the room smoked a great stewing pan of soup; on the side of that same table was a boiling mass composed of black wheat and sour milk, a kind of black paste which is peculiarly to the liking of the Briton countryman; a jar of water stood near the food, which was surrounded by some clay plates and as many other tin spoons.

"Are you waiting for someone to eat, mother Monica?" asked the collector casting toward the table one of those sidewise looks which indicated a desire to satisfy a violent appetite.

"No, Mr. Mogniot. We will eat when our man (indicating her husband who was cleaning his firelock) has finished."

"The deuce!" exclaimed the husband. "What a time like this, one ought to wait a moment more to be called; but here is my firelock ready, loaded. We will eat when you wish, wife."

This said, mother Monica called the little ones who came, four in number (three boys and one girl).

As each one ate with the appetite of people accustomed to the open air and a laboring life, the grandmother exclaimed, directing herself to the oldest of the children, a lad of 11 years:

"Are you sick, Paul?"

"No, Grandmother," the boy responded.

"Then why are you not eating?"

"I am not hungry," answered the youth, his eyes falling.

"They say you are bashful," replied the little girl.

"Why do you call your brother bashful and timid, Mary," asked her father.

"Because he says he is not hungry at the table and it is only to go to eat at the Aristocratic Stone. Oh! I saw him the other night when the moon was shining." said Mary.

Paul, ordinarily pale, flushed red as fire.

"You have seen me?" he repeated.

"Yes, I have seen you," affirmed the little maiden. "It was Sunday; it has been one, two, three, four, five, six, seven, eight, nine days," she added counting on her fingers. "You said as you did tonight 'I am not hungry', and then when mamma turned to the back part of the hut, you took your plate and began to run so that I could not see more! I wanted to follow you but when I saw that you ran to the side of the Aristocratic stone, where they say ghosts come during the night, the deuce, I was afraid, no more, no less. I waited for you halfway and I saw you return with the empty plate, are you not certain?"

Little Paul, who little by little, had raised his head to the level of his speaking sister, suddenly seemed to take his part and responded resolutely: "Well! Even though I did not eat the soup on the Aristocratic Stone, what is wrong about that?"

"What thing is the Aristocratic Stone," asked the collector. "I have been in the village a month and this is the first time I have heard it spoken of."

Monica responded, laughingly: "It is a very large stone which is there under the end of the little road which leads to Guerande. As it does not move itself, as it does not draw aside for any many, clergyman or villain, it has been called the Aristocrat."

"And the little girl says there are ghosts in this place?" asked the collector.

To this question all lowered their eyes making the sign of the cross, and only the grandmother had the courage to reply.

"Ah! My good Mr. Mogniot, it is too true. Spirits come, ghosts, monks and I know not what. Little Paul, if you wish, you can give us information about it; but the dear child, doubtlessly, has sworn to keep silent about it; that is why he is so pale. He will not live, I am sure."

"Don not foretell that, mother," said the father disturbed.

And looking at her grandson, whose paleness was certainly powerful evidence, she said: "The devil! When have the people of the other world joined themselves to do this work?"

"Explain to us, mother," said Monica, looking alternately at her mother and her son. "About Paul and why have it said? And I have attributed his paleness to failure of appetite!"

"I assure you, mother, that I have seen ghosts in my life," said Paul, repressing a singular smile.

"You would not have seen it, as such, because you would have closed your eyes; but has it spoken to you, child?" the old Jane made to observe.

"Never spoken," said the boy.

"Paul, do not lie," said Mary, "because one night near the end of winter there was a fog so thick that one could not see the end of one's nose, as grandmother said during one of her days of good humor. Mamma told me to look down the highway to Guerande, where you had gone to do an errand. Upon nearing the Aristocratic Stone, I heard your voice and another which seemed to have a cold; then a great, black shadow passed near me and frightened me. You came and asked me what the matter was that I cried out; I told you and added 'who is it? Do you know him to whom you were beginning to speak?' You hesitated a moment, I remember very well, and replied to me, raising your voice: Be still little girl; it is the ghost!' Ah! but that is very true. Bah!"

"Well, was it to mock me that you said 'bah?' replied Paul, imitating his sister's accent.

The prolonged barking of the watchdog put the inhabitants of the hut on the alert. The father was arising to go find out what it was about, when several blue uniforms appeared at the entrance of the only opening of the shepherd's hut.

"No one is to move!" said the chief, placing a sentinel outside the door. Then he added: "We have reason to think that the old proprietor of the castle is hidden around here. We have examined all except this hut. If you will permit, then, good people..."

"Do your duty," responded the Briton shepherds.

Taking advantage of the confusion occasioned by the troop of soldiers in the hut, Paul arose, took his plate still full of soup, and gained the door.

"Where are you going, little man?" asked the guard, seeing him pass by.

"Do you not see?" responded Paul. "I am going to eat in the cool."

"It may be, child, but you cannot go," replied the sentinel, hindering the boy's step. The latter returned, sad and pensive, into the hut.

Scarcely had the following morning dawned when Paul, arising before all the rest, went to take his soup, which he had not touched, and looking out for the guard who was not now at his post, gained the door, ran across the field which extended to the highroad, and arrived at the Aristocratic Stone. He stopped and cast an anxious look about him. The level land was deserted; no sound indicated the presence of anyone. Then Paul, drawing near to the stone, gave it a clever turn. Upon changing its place, the stone let one see an opening - and steps. Paul went down through this aperture; then having previously touched a spring which made the stone return to its place, he reached a kind of cave. A man leaped up at his entrance, saying: "At last, here you are!"

Paul recounted briefly the events of the evening before and offered his food, excusing for it being cold.

"Dear and generous child," said the unknown one, "tell me how at your age you can know a secret which was not known by anyone except the ancient men of the castle?"

"In a funny way," responded the child. "Two months ago I was playing there upon the stone when I felt it move and I saw coming out form underneath the person or lord whom we all thought dead. Upon seeing me you cried out, 'I am lost!; And then you explained to me that you were hiding because if you were found, they would cut off your head; and then you added: 'But what an idea to think that a child would know how to keep silent and guard the secret.' A little stung, I only replied: 'It is for you to test me, sir.' You remained a month hidden here; that is the reason why I am so lean, very lean."

"On account of the secret?" asked the stranger smiling.

"On account of taking you my supper every night," responded the child candidly.

"Ah, my God! Because of me!" exclaimed the stranger. "And I am also the cause of your being lean! Paul, I do not wish it now."

"But, sir" said Paul, "I who run every day over the fields find something to eat; but you, shut up, if you do not eat my supper and a little of my dinner, will die of hunger."

The aristocrat stranger remained overwhelmed, with his eyes fixed on that charming lad, whose sweet paleness attested to the generosity of a beautiful soul.

"Paul," he said at last with force and himself speaking to that child as he would have spoken to a man, "I am the gentleman of this country, the owner of this castle; let me stay 24 hours longer hidden from all eyes, and tomorrow I will be free. Eight days after having parted from here, then you shall come and shall find enough gold to buy whatever you want. Take yourself to your father and tell him where you have it; but only eight days after my departure, do you understand?"

"I comprehend," responded Paul. "And now, good-bye, sir, because they may be looking for me."

Paul came to the surface again; but scarcely had he placed the stone in its place when a uniformed soldier appeared.

"Ah, little vagabond, I have caught you!" said the officer, coming forward toward Paul. "There is an aristocrat hidden around here; tell us where he is and I will be satisfied with you."

"The deuce, you say! But I do not know where he is," responded Paul.

"Ah, so you say," repeated the official.

The boy replied with an air of shamed frankness. "So they say also that the whole forest is full of hollow trees and that in each one there is an aristocrat."

"Well, now, the hollow trees come to show themselves to us," said the officer.

"Oh, none of that, my good sir. I have fear of the aristocrat; they say that they are very bad," responded Paul.

"Little boy," said the officer shaking his head, "I do not know what tells me that you deceive us. What do you come to do at stone? Speak! Not that we have our eyes on you."

"Do you wish to know what I come here to do? Well, then, look!: And immediately cupping his hands as he cried out, he called out: "Hello, eh! Mary, Leon, Victor, Henry - to the Aristocrat!"

And having brought the children by his voice, Paul, helped by his brothers, took a large branch of a fallen tree, put it across the stone, seated his sister and a brother on one end and two brothers on the other see-saw fashion, and said to the soldier: "Look, look at the Aristocrat; I do not move myself from here, but make the tree branch move."

After having looked well, the soldiers saw themselves obliged to leave for Guerande, and eight days later Paul, carrying a great sack of money to his father, confessed all.

"Because of that you are so lean," his grandmother told him.

"Here is something to fatten me," answered Paul, patting the sack of money.

"Papa," asked Mary sometime later, "why did the gentleman of the castle have to hide himself if he did not wish to have head cut off?"

"Nothing in particular, my daughter, but you must know that France was at that time killing everyone who was born of noble parents, or were of the church. It was an unpardonable crime which was punished with death. Some day you may read the history of this memorable revolution, which at the time produced great benefits to humanity and gave the common people their rights. It stained itself with the blood of many innocents. The nobles and the priests had to hide to save their lives. Many, however, did not find a person so charitable as Paul, who helped the lord of the castle in so noble and generous manner."

—Translated by George W. May from the Spanish of *Biblioteca De Mi Abuelo*, Mexico 1864.

Wanted: A Father

The first remembrance of my father was when he came back from the World War I. I was 6 years old. I remember him walking up the grassy path to our door that fine March morning. All nature seemed to have conspired to give him a beautiful welcome. The trees had already budded out and the bluebird and robin had returned. The sun was sending down its gentle warmth. It meant a lot to me, for I had no remembrance of ever seeing him before. I was only 2 years old when he left. He had volunteered in the 2nd Division very early in the war. Three years he had been in France, fighting and wallowing in the trenches and two times in Chambery, recovering from wounds.

As I had grown older, my mother had told me about him. I had seen his picture many times, medium height, heavy set, with pleasing blue eyes looking out from under light locks of sandy hair. I could almost hear him speak and see him move as I gazed at his colored picture. I waited for the time when he would take me in his arms and I could call him "daddy." Ah! Fond hope to be shattered in so few short years.

"My little Bonnie!" he cried as he picked me up in his arms that wonderful spring homecoming. "I've been thinking of you all this long time." He took out his billfold. "See, I have carried your picture all these many months."

He secured work in a factory nearby and we settled down to make up for those years of separation. Two brothers came, three years apart and completed our happy little circle. Only one thing marred this bliss. Archie Widner, my father, drank, at times rather heavily. But we overlooked that in the joy of having him back with us, whole, if not perfectly sound in body.

I was 10 years old when I first received the intimation that perhaps Archie was not my real father. I had gone to the store for a few items of groceries. Several men were hanging about the outside. I came out with the groceries and seeing an interesting display in the window, stopped to look at it. As I started to leave, I overheard one of the men say, "Whose girl is that?"

"Archie Widner's," another replied.

"How many children does he have now?"

"Two," answered the second man.

"Two? I thought he had three, the two boys and the girl. Isn't the girl his?"

"No," replied the second man.

I stopped short, pretending to look at the display. My heart pounded. My eyes felt filling. A feeling of bewilderment came over me. What did they mean?

I hurried home. As it happened, my Aunt Emma was there. Seeing my chance, I recounted to her what I had heard and asked trepidly, "Is it true, about me?"

Aunt Emma looked at me, compassionately, as I thought later and said with some hesitation and with an attempt at brushing it away, "Those men didn't know what they were talking about."

She knew how I adored Archie and she knew how he loved me as no other man could love his little girl. I was satisfied with Aunt Emma's answer for a time. But the words of those men kept recurring to me and impelled me to learn the truth, if the truth had not been told me.

There came a day when my father fell very ill. He was taken to the nearest hospital where the case was diagnosed as cancer. He was sent to another hospital in that large city of Windmer where we lived. The hospital was 15 miles from our home. It almost broke my heart to see him leave. The grave countenances of the doctors and of my immediate kinsmen put a dread in my heart. I was afraid he would never come back to me.

It so proved. I had just reached my 12th birthday, when the news came that he was dead. Tenderly, we laid him in the Masonic Cemetery of Windmer. I was fatherless. Oh, the emptiness in the little home! Deprived so long of a father's love, I had enjoyed only a few years of it before he was taken away. I cried unrestrainedly.

Time softens sorrow and I remembered happy, ever-cheerful Archie only as a beautiful memory a picture even such as I had known before I ever saw him. Curiosity returned to me concerning my baby years and I wondered even more than before if there was something else that had not been told.

Mother had a small wooden trunk which had always been, as long as I had recollected, under lock and key. She never opened it, at least when anyone was around. "What do you have in that little trunk, Mother?" I often asked. "Nothing but a lot of mine and Archie's early love letters, Bonnie," she said. "May I see them sometime?" I fingered the lock.

"No, Bonnie, they wouldn't interest you or anyone else. I don't know why I am keeping them myself. Just had them so long I don't want to destroy them, I suppose." Tears came into her eyes. "Please, Mother," I begged.

"No." She refused firmly, in spite of her emotion.

One afternoon while my mother was at the factory at work, I found myself all alone. It didn't happen often. But the cold rain which was falling must have kept the usual girl visitors away. I sat around the fire in a quiet which I had seldom had before. The dinner dishes I had washed. There was no ironing, no baking, nothing to do in particular but sew. I did not feel inclined to do that anyway. Nor did I feel in the mood to read.

Suddenly my abstracted gaze fell upon the little wooden trunk over in the corner underneath some quilts. Pandora-like, my idleness begot curiosity anew. I thought I knew where Mother kept the key. I looked. Sure enough, after a brief search, I found a key that fit. I looked out the window. No one was in sight, only the driving rain sheeting upon the puddled street. I looked furtively out and around to make sure. No one. I strode quickly to the trunk, lifted off the quilts and fell on my knees before it and unlocked it.

I became so absorbed in reading those old letters that I did not notice the passing of time. Yes, all was explained. Archie was *not* my father. A deep feeling of disappointment came over me. This changed to uncertainty. Who was my real father?

I read on. The clock struck the hour of four but I did not hear. Then I found the name I was seeking, Raymond Oaker. He was my real father. Where was he? Was he living?

Footsteps sounded suddenly on the porch. I had only time to cram the letters back into the trunk when the door opened. It was Mother. The lock was still open and I held the key in my hand.

Mother looked at me a moment, anger showing in her face. Then the flush on her face died away. Quietly and not unkindly she said, "Well, I suppose you found out what you wanted to know?"

"Yes, I did, Mother," I replied.

She took the key from my hand and locked the trunk. We said no more about it.

As time went on, the desire to meet my real father grew intensely within me. My girl companions all had fathers. How familiarly and fondly, yet unconcernedly, would they mention them: the little plans, the gifts and everyday life in which their fathers would figure largely. I could not do that. I felt the vacuum more keenly than any of my friends dreamed of. I wanted a father too. Even if I met Raymond Oaker, would he recognize me? Would he claim me?

My foster-father's brother had come back with us after the funeral. I should regret to condone this relation. (From that time on, he lived in cohabitation with Mother.) But thinking back upon how good he was to us, I cannot bring myself to condemn either of them. William Widner was all a father would be to his family. Our relations were most congenial. He treated us three children as his own, gave us money, fed and clothed us, saw that we went to school and tried to lead us in the right moral actions.

However, I was old enough to realize the unlawful, if not unpleasant relation. It was not a healthy environment for a girl in her early teens, alert and inquisitive as I was. Mother and William gave me almost free rein when I was 15. I could go anywhere, anytime and with almost anyone. I was out late to dances. Aunt Emma, who was 8 years older than I, had a "steady" whom we expected her to marry anytime. She gave me friendly warning in my wild search for pleasure.

Louis Locher was my favorite companion. He was with whom I was most seen. I loved him in my young, violent way. I awoke one morning to the realization that I was to become a mother. I told Louis about it the same night.

"Well, what shall we do?' he asked. He had me in his arms and was kissing me.

"That's up to you, Louis,"

"You mean," he hesitated, "you mean that we can marry?"

"Yes, sweetheart. You know I love you." I felt there was some reluctance on his part. "Do you love me? Would you want to marry?"

"Why, yes, of course." It sounded half-hearted. A sinking feeling of doubt came over me.

"All right." He set no date and I did not press him.

Louis still came to see me, but he did not volunteer to set a definite date. I made no advances, no suggestions. I felt that if Louis would not see me through of his own accord, it would not be right to give him the least chance to make him feel he was obligated to marry me. I was as much to blame for our indiscretion as he.

Not until the last month was almost up did he say one night, "We will go down to the Justice's in the morning and be married." An indescribable sense of relief came over me. Had he considered the thing settled the first night I told him, so many months back?

I am glad to say that I made him a happy wife. Three boys soon joined our family in close succession and welded us together as we had never been before.

"Mother," I asked one day sometime after my marriage, "Won't you tell me about my father, my real father, Raymond Oaker?" Longing for knowledge of him and his love, if he had any to offer me, had never ceased.

"Bonnie, why not let by-gones be by-gones. It has been so long ago. How can you be so interested in him? You have Louis, your babies and us. Let it drop. Why not forget it?"

"I can't mother," I replied. "You don't know how a girl feels who has never had a father. It is even more agonizing to know that you have one living, but have never seen him, even though, as you say, he is or was, living in this state, not 100 miles from here."

"Just the same, forget it now, dearie. Someday maybe I'll tell you all."

Why was my mother so averse to telling me the story? That was what I couldn't understand. Was there some mutual understanding between them about me? Was Mother under promise to keep the truth from me? More than ever I yearned to meet my father.

Mother had suffered from heart trouble for several years. She was still young, 36. Several severe attacks had frightened us. Other times she seemed to be in good health. Another woman I had known had died suddenly from an attack, without warning and without time to say anything. I was fearful lest one of Mother's attacks would also carry her away from me as suddenly. My only chance of learning the facts about my father and his whereabouts would then perish. That was now the reason why I was so anxious for her to reveal what she was withholding.

I was justified in my fears the following year. On a morning in January, Mother had a sudden heart attack after eating breakfast. The doctor was sent for and friends gathered in quickly. It was the worst attack she had ever had. She must have realized its extreme seriousness for she told all the others to leave the room and called me to her bedside.

"Bonnie," she whispered. I fell on my knees beside the bed. "Bonnie, maybe I have been wrong in not telling you what you have wanted to know for so long. Maybe you should know. But before I tell you, let me say that your father, Raymond Oaker, was as fine a man as I ever knew. That is not why I have kept the truth from you; he was not bad."

"He wanted to marry me but I would not. He came here when you were a little baby and renewed the proposal, but I still refused." Mother's breath came short and labored. Only the fact that she was telling me what I wanted to know so long, kept me from refusing to let her go on in that condition.

"Raymond and I were both working in the state hospital at Fordson when we first met. He lived in Eden, a little town south of here, 300 miles. We had a happy love affair, but which was soon interrupted by an old home sweetheart of his who had followed him to the state hospital and found employment. Naturally, he had to give her some attention. She seemed to be one of those kind who runs a man down, even though it is made plain that they are not particularly wanted."

"Meanwhile, I discovered that I was to become a mother. Raymond was in a dilemma. Home folks had practically settled the marriage of

Raymond and Coranne. He did not love her, of that I was sure. But sometimes home ties bind one with almost inescapable bonds. I realized his position. I refused his offer of marriage and told him to marry Coranne, as it had been so arranged."

"He was loath to give me up. But I still firmly refused and he went back to Eden and married Coranne. I vowed, for the love that I bore him, that I would never reveal anything to mar his happiness or to compromise his character among his home folks. I have kept that vow all these years. I came back to Windmer, where you were born and married Archie shortly after your birth. Then he went to the war. You know the rest."

Mother closed her eyes and the pallor of death seemed to come upon her face. She opened them slowly.

"I may die, Bonnie, dear. If I do, my vow will have ended. You can do as you like thereafter. But, Bonnie, promise me that as long as I live, you will not obtrude yourself openly into Raymond's circle."

"I promise, Mother," I said lowly.

She took my hand and gripped it. The pressure relaxed. I looked into her face. She was gone from me forever.

After grief had been softened by time, I debated with myself as to how to contact my father. It would hardly do, I thought to travel to his home in Eden. I did not even know if he still lived there. My inquiries would arouse curiosity. Certainly, it would be difficult to see him without running into Coranne. Eventually, I decided to write a letter. In it I stated briefly but plainly who I was and where I could be found. Surely a private letter would not be opened by anyone but himself. To make sure, I typed the address to hide my feminine handwriting. If I could not go to him, perhaps he could answer my letter if ... .

Yes, if. That was now my fear. Would he acknowledge the letter at all? Would he claim me, even if it were maneuvered secretly?

I waited expectantly, yet doubtfully, for two months. I received no answer nor did my letter return. It couldn't because I had purposely left off my return address. Then I sent another containing the same information and only adding that I had sent the first one two months back.

Two weeks later, the postman brought me a letter postmarked Eden. I tore it open hastily and nervously. It read:

"I received your letter a few days ago. Can I begin to express the surprise or the emotion with which I read your letter? Surely, it is like a word from the dead. I have not told my wife. Do we need to? At my first opportunity I shall come to visit you. Yours with love. Raymond O."

Short, but it gave me unspeakable joy. At last, word from my father! That night, I shared its contents with Louis.

Now I listened with abated breath every strange footstep on the porch and wondered if it were my father's. They were either salesmen or people inquiring the location of other houses.

A month went by. Then one morning a tall, quiet, self-possessed man of middle age knocked at the door. I saw him through the window as he came up. Could it be he? May hand trembled as I turned the doorknob.

"Does Bonnie Widner live here?" he asked.

"Yes," I replied tremulously.

"This is she to whom I am speaking, I suppose?"

I answered 'yes'.

"My daughter," he cried, stretching out his arms.

I fell into his arms, murmuring "Father, Father, at last, after so long."

Later, I said, "My first letter must have been lost, Father."

"Perhaps," he replied, a little dubiously. "I rather think, though, it was read and destroyed without my getting a chance to read it. A letter addressed as you say yours was, could hardly have failed to reach me. I received the second one all right."

"Who could have destroyed it?" I asked.

"You see Coranne is a little jealous," he explained. "I have no doubt she read and tore it up."

"You mean she did not know about me?" I asked surprised.

"No, not until she got hold of your letter. That is, as far as I know. I had never told her anything."

"How did you manage to get away then?" I pursued. I wanted to know how Coranne felt toward me. That might depend upon whether I got to see father very often.

"I told her the plain facts," he said. "She didn't seem to like my past record. You know it all happened when we were supposedly engaged. I told her I was going to Windmer to see you. She told me to go ahead, but that she didn't believe she would go. It helped me a good deal for her to decide that way because I would have had to hire someone to stay home and take care of the stock."

"You mean you live on a farm?" I asked.

"Yes. We have a little 14 acre farm five miles from Eden."

Joy and enthusiasm mounted as father related his work on the farm. For sometime I had been wanting to leave the crowded city of Windmer and find a little place in the country. Maybe father could help Louis and me find one.

Father was to stay with us five days. I broached the subject the third morning. He agreed that it would be a fine thing. When I intimated that perhaps he knew a place somewhere near Eden, his enthusiasm fell. I noticed it instantly. Why?

The day of parting came. "Bonnie, I want you and Louis and the children to plan to visit us next summer," (it was then winter) said Father, lingering long with us on the station platform.

"Would you really like for us to? Do you think Coranne would welcome a visit?" I asked doubtfully.

"Forget her. She's all right. Of course I mean it. Come see us next summer. Ever in Eden?"

I said 'no'.

"It's a great little place," he said. "Lots of hills, valleys, rocks and rivers. Lots of history around, too. I will show you all when you come down."

"I would like to very much, Dad," I said familiarly.

"Only one thing," he said warningly. "If anyone asks, just say you are old friends from Windmer. That will be all that is necessary."

I pondered over that statement when he was gone. Would father refuse to recognize me publicly as his daughter? Surely, that was what he meant when he said "friends from Windmer."

More and more, as the weeks sped on, did I wish to be recognized as a real daughter, to have a real father. Archie was gone, Mother was gone, I had no parents to whom I could turn for parental love, help or advice. I was not disappointed in Louis, for he was all a young husband should be, but, oh that longing, that utter sense of forlornness which I felt, in a world in which there could be none of that love for me, unless, unless, Raymond Oaker would claim me before all the world and we could love openly and unabashed. Fate seemingly had dealt hard with me. I was still young, only 22, still a girl.

We managed to save up $50.00 by the time July rolled around. We boarded a train at Windmer one night and the next afternoon reached Eden. We hired a taxi to carry us out to Father's place.

Father greeted us joyfully and romped around with our three little boys. Coranne was very friendly, though at times she seemed reserved. I came to learn that it was more her nature to be so than because she did not welcome us. But it would be hard, I thought, ever to consider her in the light of a mother. She and father had no children.

We stayed two weeks. We had a wonderful time wandering about the small but luxuriant farm. We visited all the interesting spots in the country. We saw few of Father's kinsmen. He seemed to avoid them. Only one exception did he make. That was his aged mother. I talked with her several times. It was somewhat embarrassing to answer some of her personal questions and it required a good deal of my agility of mind to answer them without compromising Father. Of him always I considered. If he did not wish to have me known as his daughter, I would not be the one to betray him. We were introduced as "some old friends of Windmer." It seemed to pass with everyone.

One night, as we chanced to be sitting alone on the porch, I ventured to ask, "Dad, don't you want me to be known as your daughter? Just explain, I won't push you, nor will I think the less of you if you do not, why you do not or cannot."

He took my hand in his. "We cannot always do as we would like, dear. Convention, society, neighbors, kinfolks, won't let us. Maybe you haven't found that out yet, but it's true and especially in a narrow, puritanical community like this. I have a certain position here, one that binds me as you would never believe. If I were to confess to anything, or do anything that would shock the bigoted opinions of this community, I would have to be a much braver man than I now am to stand up under it. I am a church member, have been for years and am supposed to have led a very straight life. So I have, I maintain. I am up for deacon now. I feel that I am worthy of the office. True, I regret some things that happened long ago, but that has been atoned for. But my people, I fear ..."

"You mean you are sorry that I was ever born, that you ever met me?" I faltered.

"No, no, Bonnie," he said vehemently. "Never that. I mean perhaps I never should have married anyone except Winifred Gaines, your mother."

"But she refused you, didn't she?"

"Why? Because she thought my position demanded it. I could have thrown aside all that and having convinced her thereby, she would have accepted me. But now ..."

"You would not even tell your mother?" I asked. "Surely, she would understand. She would not hold it against you, her own sons. Why don't you, dad? Then, truly I could feel that I had a grandmother. Won't you."

Father shook his head slowly. "No, Bonnie, I am afraid to. She thinks I am perfect. She has her ways set. Further, she is getting old. I would not want to be the one to disturb her thoughts in her calm old age."

Coranne came out to announce supper, Louis and the boys came up and over conversation eased. I knew my father as never before. Oh, how many loving parents and children are thus separated by traditional convention, so cruel, so merciless

Our two weeks coming to a close, we returned to Windmer. Louis had no steady work that fall and times were pretty hard with us. We just managed to keep in food, pay the rent and buy the most necessary clothing. Never once did I seriously meditate calling on father for help. Where the money would be found in case any of us feel sick, I dared not think.

Louis was driving an old delivery truck during the Christmas rush. The streets were slick and dangerous. He had advised the manager of the second-rate store to equip the machine for slick roadways, but he had deferred it, saying there was not time and to go on.

The inevitable happened. In turning a corner, the truck slid crazily and crashed into the path of a passing car. The truck was overturned and Louis was pinned underneath it. He was taken out, crushed and bleeding. He died in the hospital the following morning.

I cannot convey my sorrow and anxiety. Everytime I try, I break down. Only one who has lived through such a tragedy can imagine my feelings. What were the children and I to do? Was this the time to call on Father?

The little insurance Louis carried barely covered the funeral expenses. Happily, in this time of need, a good woman was found to care for the boys and the house for her living while I looked for work. I was soon fortunate in finding a secretarial job. My high school typing now stood me in good stead, although I had not been able to graduate.

I wrote to Father and told him about Louis. I assured him that I was getting along very well, though I would not be able to save up any money for a long time. He replied by return mail, expressing his sympathy and assuring me that if at any time I needed help, to drop him a letter and a check would follow at once. In my heart I thanked him. He added, in a post script, that he would send me money to visit him when I got my summer vacation.

Another summer two-weeks came. I had not been able to save enough money for the trip. I wanted so much to see Father again, that I wrote, unashamed, for the required amount. I was in his home again.

On the 4th of July, we drove to Spring Hills, a rocky little state park about 30 miles from Eden. We took our lunch, prepared to enjoy the day there. A celebration was to be staged and there was much also of natural beauty and interest to see. Father had told me that he was favorably considering revealing the truth to Grandmother on this day, since she seemed in an unusual convivial mood. We expected to see few or none of Father's folks this far from home. If Grandmother was told and took the situation serenely, I could call it one of my happiest holidays.

At noon we spread the lunch on the soft grass near a little spring, which was excellent mineral water to drink. We were sitting around after lunch when a party of Father's kinsmen passed by, stopped and addressed a few words to us. I had never seen them before, but no move was made to introduce me.

We strolled to the upper end of the little park, that is, Father, Grandmother and I. Coranne stayed with the boys. We found a neat little cleft in the rocks and seated ourselves. Grandmother was alive to the novelty and beauty of the situation.

It was then that Father revealed who I really was. Grandmother took me in her arms and kissed me. "I didn't know I had a granddaughter from Raymond's side of the family," she said laughing. "I am certainly glad to know you, dear." She kissed me again. How happy I was!

Later in the afternoon we ran into Father's sister and her husband. I strolled over to the little soft drink concession with them. Father was not with us. We had just finished out drinks when three acquaintances stepped up. "Meet my friends Mr. and Mrs. Olen Dennis and their son, Jack," Father's sister announced. "Mrs. Widner of Windmer, old friends of Raymond and Coranne."

They greeted me cordially. I shook hands with the father and mother and looked up into Jack's face as I clasped his hand. I was struck forcibly by his fine appearance. He must have been 25, not large, but slight and gracefully proportioned. His hair was black, running far across and down his temples, his grey eyes looked out from under curving, heavy dark brows. Intelligence and sincerity shone forth in every look.

I thought about Jack many times that afternoon. I couldn't seem to erase his face from my mind. So it was that night and the next and succeeding days. I tried to appear disinterested when I inquired more about him from father and Coranne. Little, by little, I learned the main facts about his life. He was a student, a traveler and a teacher. He was unmarried. I will not confess that I began to love Jack even at first sight, but I must admit that my heart beat more quickly every time his name was mentioned.

I saw my third cousin only once before I left for Windmer.

My good woman married that fall, leaving me again with the three boys and no chance to work. I finally found another woman, but she charged for the work, which left me with a bare margin. I kept getting behind with the grocery bill and saw no chance to get an even start again. At least I asked for $40.00 of Father to clear my bill. Then, by the strictest economy, I managed to avoid running up another grocery bill.

Then I received a letter from Father. In it, he said, "Dearest Bonnie, I don't know exactly how nor when, but apparently our secret has leaked out. Who guessed it and betrayed us I do not know for sure, but I can make a pretty close guess. Gossip is growing around me. I am rather sorry for Mother, because she thinks it necessary to hide the truth at all costs. She is constantly hiding under a hypocritical cloak and I feel like it is worrying her and her conscience considerably, perhaps more than I can imagine. It seems the story has been pieced together little by little. Of course, no one has questioned me. Such propriety, on the other hand, is worse on my peace of mind than open accusation. Don't worry, dear, for I feel as it will all come out well in the end. What have we to be anxious for, except to have a chaff under restraint? Kiss the kiddies for me. Your loving father, R.O."

This letter worried me considerably. To be let down at his age and in his formerly upright, gossip-free position was no little thing. Added to this was my own struggle for a livelihood against great odds. Overwork, worry and inadequate food lowered my resistance. The weather was changeable and sometimes I would come in wet and tired. I was forced to take to the bed with a severe cold, which developed into pneumonia. I was dangerously ill and for a brief time, my life hung in the balance. Aunt Emma was living in another state happily married. A few friends came in.

I posted a letter to Father informing him of my plight. Almost before the letter had had time to reach him, it seemed, he was at my bedside, imploring me to forget all worry and concentrate on getting well. I struggled to do so, but I was anxious to learn of any developments about us in Eden.

"I don't believe I have told you, Bonnie, about the recent addition to our family."

I pricked up my ears and heart beat fast. "Did I have a little sister or brother?"

"Coranne has practically adopted her sister's little baby. It was on a bottle anyway and there were so many children that she could well afford to give up the care of one. After all the baby is only a mile from its real parents. You know," continued father puzzled, "it's a funny thing. Never before did Coranne manifest any desire for a baby, but now she is crazy about it."

"Is there still gossip?" I asked.

"Yes." Father looked sternly at the bare walls. Then he rose quickly and faced me resolutely. "You know what I am going to do? Just as soon as you are able, I am going to take you home, you, the boys and all for good.

"But Dad..." I remonstrated.

"To the devil with all of them Bonnie. I don't care what they say or think. They can fire me as deacon or anything else, that's what I am going to do. You are my daughter, you need help, I love you, that is reason enough, plenty. Too long already I have delayed. Now get well quick and we will have the time of our lives when we get home."

How can I express now, after the interval of these years, my extreme happiness. The utter joy of it all lifted a burden from off my soul that had been crushing my spirits down gradually and imperceptibly. From that moment, I mended rapidly and with in a week was able to board the train of my own strength.

We realized the gossip was thick. Raymond Oaker had brought home a woman, the same one whom had been seen twice before. It was almost flaunted in our faces. One could see the strange look that came into the eyes of those whom we met. Happily, Father did not wait long for his grand gesture. He called a large party the first Saturday night. Local musicians were invited. Cakes and refreshments brought by friends and neighbors supplemented Coranne's supply. Whispered conversations occurred outside. Frequent glances were cast at me. I bore it all as reservedly as I could. What did it mean? Were the people here to insult Father and me and for that matter, Coranne? The attempts to restrain the gossip were farcical.

Then Father stepped into the center of the room and held his hand up for quiet. "Friends and neighbors and kinsmen. I have an important introduction to make tonight. After the introduction, I wish every one of you would give her the glad hand of friendship, for she is to remain with us a long time." He pointed to me. "Meet my daughter, my own daughter, my own little girl, Bonnie Oaker."

I was smothered in a tangle of hands and women's kisses such as I had never before experienced. Such expressions of joy and friendship made me deeply conscious of the mistake that father, I or someone had made. From that night on, I took my place as the recognized daughter of Raymond Oaker.

There is not much more to tell. Our family was happy and the immediate kinsmen were relieved, none more so than Grandmother. A tension had been relaxed throughout the whole community.

Six months later I married Jack Dennis who lived nearly. Life's desires for me have been more than satisfied. I am terribly happy, happy in that I have a real, loving father; a home for my growing boys and a great lover like Jack Dennis.

—1930s

Kid Stuff

Hiking To New Columbia

It was on a bright Friday morning in the summer of 1922 that I arose early, ate breakfast and packed my knapsack with a small lunch. I soon came to my cousin's house and from here we started about nine o'clock. We made fast time and was at Enterprise School in a little while. After passing a few houses we came to the "bottoms" and walked a good while until we came to the road that goes from Round Knob to New Columbia. Here we got a drink and proceeded on our way until we came to the first dredge ditch. Here we stopped and got out our fishing lines and ate our dinner while we fished. We caught one catfish and got several bites. In about three miles we came to another dredge ditch. Here we got a drink at a house and caught another catfish.

New Columbia was now only about a half mile ahead. As we went up the bluff the rocks were on every side. Having come almost to the top, we turned off into a little opening and picked out a place for our camp. Here we found a spring with an iron pipe leading to a water trough. The water was constantly running into the trough, so we could stick our cups over the pipe and get a cold drink. We hid our blankets and things behind a dead tree and went on to the little town of New Columbia. It was only about a quarter of a mile so we soon got there.

New Columbia is a little town of about 150 or 200 people. They have a schoolhouse and three stores. They have no post office but get their mail from Big Bay, a small town east. Being thirsty we asked if they had any ice cream or cold drinks and were told they wouldn't have any until late in the evening. Not having much left for supper, we bought some sausage, crackers and cookies. We went back to our camp and having nothing to do we decided to see some of the big rocks. Accordingly, we passed through a small thicket and came upon a little spring with a rock bottom. We went on and came upon the highest point where we could view the country for several miles. We tried to locate where we lived but without success, it being too far away.

After exploring around for about an hour or so, we went back to New Columbia and decided to walk down the road apiece. On our way we saw an old church house and on a little farther we came upon a picnic grove. We went over where some men were barbecuing four pigs and two sheep. The next day being Saturday, they were to have a picnic lasting all day and part of the night. It was getting late as we went back and stopped to get some cream and cold drinks. A fellow named Hart went with us to our camp. He lived three miles away and begged us to stay all night with him, but we refused.

As soon as we came to our camp we started to build a fireplace to cook on. While Joe was doing this I went up to Mr. Mann Bonifield's and asked him if we could get into his barn if it got to raining. He said 'Yes,' and wanted us to stay all night with him and family. (It turned out that he knew Joe's family fairly well). We declined his offer. I went back to camp and found Joe had the stove ready and a large club to drive away any dog that might come around. We cooked our meal, which consisted of two eggs, cookies, raw tomatoes, crackers, sausage and fish. Yum!

Lover's Leap, New Columbia

Yum! I can almost taste that meal now. The spring being close by, we could get a drink any time. After supper we washed the skillet and spoons and Joe wanted to go back to the picnic grove. I didn't, so we built up the fire and I read a story that Joe had written. A few minutes later Mr. Bonifield's son came to water his horse and asked us again to come up and stay overnight with them, but we had our heads set to stay out.

It had not been dark long before Mr. Bonifield and his boy came down and stayed awhile. After they had gone we gathered more wood and I took the first watch, which I did until the moon came up. I excitedly awakened Joe and exclaimed: "The moon is coming up in the north!" He laughed and said that I was only turned around. We re-built the fire and I laid down, leaving Joe to keep the second watch.

It must have been 'way in the night when I awoke. The fire was out and it was cold. Joe had fallen asleep and I awakened him. We discovered that someone must have come and put the fire out, for we had put a long stick of wood in the fire earlier. We found the stick lying off to one side. Perhaps Mr. Bonifield had silently come and pulled the stick out as a fire safety measure. We re-built the fire and both of us went asleep, after first having changed sides with one another. We were lying on the ground with rocks under us as big as one's hand.

End of term, my Mt. Pleasant School

At last a red glow showed that the sun was about to rise. I had two fried eggs before Joe got up and I had a job getting him up. He made some cornbread, or tried to, for he put too much water in it and it would not cook. We fried some of the left-over sausage and ate it with the "cornbread."

After packing our things up we pulled out. We walked fast for three hours, taking the short route. We were tired, hungry and thirsty.

But we were well pleased with our first overnighter and 16-mile hike.

–Age 13

First Diaries (selected)

Nov. 8, 1921: I joined the Lone Scouts of America. Sent a story to a paper to publish. It was no count.

Nov. 21, 1921: The state of Illinois is going to give Marshall Foch of the French army $100 in honor of him. Each county is supposed to give one cent for each school. Hattie Barrett got the number so she has to pay one cent.

March 10, 1922: Started collecting stamps with 10 Mexico.

Nov. 3, 1922: Showing increase of stamp collection. 624 stamps, 87 different countries and 17 different stamp companies.

March 28, 1923: School out and received my diploma of promotion to 8th grade. Average 95.3%, best in school.

April 12, 1923: Sent off for ukulele strings and an ocarina.

June 12, 1923: Went fishing in Massac Creek. Didn't catch any. Water too high. Got three fish and one turtle at John's Pond.

Aug. 2, 1923: Baby is one month old today (Pauline).

Aug. 14, 1923: Threshed oats this morning. I made 50 cents at Deans yesterday pitching wheat.

Jan. 23., 1924: Sold old watch to G.C. for 25 cents, a pistol and knife.

Jan. 27, 1924: Sunday. Joe C. and I drove horse and buggy all day and went to Choat and Joppa. We also went to Choat tonight and played music when we got home.

Feb. 29, 1924: Went to Kozy Theater which showed *Man without a Country*.

April 2, 1924: Sold peas at Round Knob and received $100. Uncle Merit planted potatoes.

June 27, 1925: Had short contribution published in *Prairie Farmer* magazine, entitled "Winning the Degrees." (Lone Scouts).

July 12, 1925: John W., Bob, Lloyd and I went to Deaconville, Choat and church this Sunday night.

—Ages 12-13

Doggerel Lines

I know a man who in his slumbers
Knows and dreams about his numbers.
Whose daily work is that of a drummer,
Selling accessories to the skilled plumber.

There was a boy who lost his ball
And he was very small.
He tripped himself and got a fall,
So he at once began to bawl.

I know a bird whose name is sparrow;
He flew down and lighted on a harrow.
A little boy killed it with his bow and arrow
And hauled it home in a wheelbarrow.

There was a black-haired Jew,
Whose name I remember was Andrew.
He ran a restaurant on Kentucky Avenue.
He sold fish, ham sandwiches and oyster stew.

A man of Metropolis named Taylor Wentzell
Sat in his meat shop with a pretty red pencil.
All the products he sold he labeled and stenciled.
He bought seven hogs from Luna Linson.

     —Age 12

High School
And First
Year College

A La Thoreau (Journals)

Sept. 22, 1926: Dad is cutting and staking peas. Autumn is here, with its rich harvest of legumes, fruits and best of all it brings the hickory nut season when many an enjoyable hour can be spent roaming and exploring the woods and the bottom lands between our house and the New Columbia hills. Then, if ever, can we get in communion with nature; the squirrels frisking about hunting for their supply of nuts and flocks of crows winging their way o'er wood and field to some ultimate goal. Alas! How little we really know about birds. Why do they do this and that? Much is an unsolved mystery. Do they have a plan, an instinct to impel them to hunt for food? Their flight, as we watch them, should inspire people to get out and hunt for opportunities. I believe birds give a thought as to the morrow. If they do not, then like humans, their hopes of raising a family, means of sustenance and a bright future and happy life are lost.

Oct. 14, 1926: It is not the good fortune of many people to possess the writing ability of a Washington Irving or Fenimore Cooper. I, myself, must go on faithfully with my acquisition of knowledge and endeavor to develop my personality and powers of expression. I believe it will be a great aid to me if I will teach school a few years to discover my deficiencies and to get a practical logical view of life, and at no other place can a person learn human nature and psychology better than in the schoolroom.

But it is not prudent to sketch one's destiny too minutely. Circumstances will change the course of events. It is sufficient for adolescents to forge along with energy in increased intelligence. However, everyone should have his ideal clearly before his vision so that it will be a constant source of inspiration.

Oct. 16, 1926: We hulled peas for J.M. today. The hay is very tough and vinery and tasks one's strength to handle. We began late in the day but I had with me my little copy of *Songs of Labor* and until the work began I read J.G. Whittier's poems. I find him especially interesting in his manner of depicting rural life and scenes.

Oct. 24, 1926: Cold, windy, rainy; only 10 degrees above freezing. An ideal day for indoor study and deep thought. Oncoming winter incites me to give vent to my thoughts, simple though they may be, The lustrous leaves have been shedding, their original green having taken up through the cambium layer the precious food of the trees and leaving in its wake many different colored leaves: red, green, yellow (of which color ranging from the brightest orange to the lightest of yellowish shades); some parti-colored; some already fallen and turning brown; a few still dark green, the last survivors of the wind and frost. All these taken in combination and viewed from a somewhat distant hillock, appear as so many various and beautiful forms, as viewed from a kaleidoscope. On certain days like this I find myself in a somewhat pensive mood and find it difficult to eradicate that "restless and long-ing feeling," as Longfellow describes it.

Oct. 31, 1926: Sunday. I did a great deal of hiking and exploring in the woods. I commenced by taking a ramble along the course of Rocky Branch, a creek which flows near our house. Later, strolling along the road which was bound on one side by a weedy fence row and on the other by a bare field which had recently been cut of its legumes, I drew in several deep breaths of the crisp morning air, surveyed the general aspect of nature's autumnal garb and inwardly rejoiced in my exist-ence. Oaks, rearing their colossal trunks into the air, are taking on a various array of colors. Green yet predominated because they are the hardiest trees and are always the last to change color and fall. Here and there, however, a leaf has turned to a rich crimson. Elm, ash and cot-tonwood do not make a radical change of color; nor does the elm readily shed its leaves. But the ash after a few frosts begin to fall rapidly and are soon bare. Maples at this time are far along in their deciduous state but owing to the great number and to the smallness of their leaves gives the illusion that there may be a great many left on the tree at this time. Maples have their share of admirers and there is no other tree which receives so much commendation for lawn purposes.

In the course of my ramble I came upon one species of vine, simi-lar to the saw-briar but without briars or stickers, and which interested me very much. The plant was smooth-trunked varying from two to five feet in length, intertwined around the surrounding vegetation and with leaves of a rich cream color.

Attached at the base of the leaf bud, pendant, was an acim-form cluster of flat-shaped structures, upright, and radiating in three differ-ent directions. There were seven of these and inside each, one to two brown seeds.

Nov. 7. 1926: A bright, sunshiny day. Winter birds flitting about. I left the house early and walked northerly across fields of corn until I reached a wagon lane. I found a suitable spot and kindled a fire for the morning was crisp, for, well-clothed as I was, a fire would feel good for one of the reasons I had come thence, which was to read, meditate, soliloquize and maybe write. My book was Holmes' *Professor of the Breakfast Table*.

Why all this inutile raking, scraping for money and worldly gain? Why do we become lost in exhausting struggles for material things? Is it myopia? Or omniscience? Few can tell. Not long hence ere the final outcome when the body is cast into Erebus or lifted to the firmament of bliss. My leafy bower overhead; the rustling, incessant falling of the leaves; the gentle, intumescent breeze murmuring through the corridors of stately forms confound me. I am overcome, subdued, and am content with my mundane affairs. Only let me feel nature's omniparous spirit.

Nov. 20, 1926: We gathered corn today. Very crisp air. Everything covered with frosty crystals which, when reflected by the rays of early red sun, shone with a brilliancy exceeding that of diamonds. The frozen ground is not without the effects of the lesions: miniature upheavals over the surface of the corn hills caused by the expanding frost gave it the appearance of a glacier sheet, similar to those viewed in picture books.

Dec. 25, 1926: This has been a most disagreeable day for outdoor activities. Sleet early increased in volume; then snow was added. By four o'clock ice was over everything and turning colder with bitter wind. Trees bent over with the weight. However, this a beautiful, distinctive scene, what with everything with the oxaline crystals.

Dec. 26, 1926: I took a cross-country walk. Fence rows with dead berry stalks, the unharvested fruit now sear and hanging like so many pendant capsules, icy, transparent. I passed a honeysuckle hedge. Each little green leaf was completely encased by ice. To the north hung a brownish haze. Concentrated spots of moisture therein being touched by the sun seemed like little pink shells along a rocky water course.

Jan. 2, 1927: Sunday. I took a short walk this morning, passing along the course of our creek. The pools of water had a thin coating of ice and in some places where the stream was running, no ice at all. The main part of the thaw occurred two days ago when the snow, sleet and the greater part of the ice melted and was carried down the many rills and rivulets to this large creek. Today much of the water had run out, leaving weeds and other material swept level with the bed of the stream. I heard the cheery note of a bird and lifting my eyes to the height of an oak tree, I discovered that it was a cardinal red bird. Afar off, I heard the faint notes of a field lark, a common bird here and one which stays with us usually all winter. Gazing into the deeper pools, which appeared a deep blue or even black, and noting the sprigs of dead grass, gently moving to and fro, I indulged in idle fancy and imagined I saw little elves swimming about in the pool. This circumstance recalled to my memory the book *Water Babies* by Charles Kingsley, which I read twice when I was about 10 years old. It is a fascinating little book for children and even yet I secure a transient enjoyment in giving free choice to my irrational notions. Around a bend in the creek I observed half-way upon the side of the bank a beautiful bunch of moss. Upon a space two feet square the moss grew, some of the plants in a dormant state; others with capsules, and still others in the process of reproduction, but all abnormally large and with extraordinary large fronds, as it were. The large fronds were almost as large as ferns.

Jan. 21, 1927: It has rained every day this week with no indication of a let up. Rocky Branch, fed by many rills, streams and little waterfalls, was flowing swiftly to a depth of two or three feet, tumbling, rolling, plashing over the rocks in a frenetic journey to the Ohio River. I was drawn by the sound of a waterfall which I soon approached. It was almost five feet high and made an almost sheer drop. It was a singular scene.

March 13, 1927: The day dawns bright and cheery. It rained nearly all night. My brother and I took a walk by way of the pond. It was full and crystal clear. Some frogs croaked. The pond is surrounded by willows and vegetation, which gave to the water a brilliant hue. I delighted in gazing into the depths and to watch the oscillations of the rays of sunlight upon the surface. We went into the woods and along the creek which murmured and babbled its way along. The rocks and pebbles are of different kinds and colors and I felt as if I were walking over treasures of precious stones: opals, onyx, agate, chalcedony, turquoise and pearls, all lying at my feet and neigh as beautiful as I imagined the real ones would be. A series of cascades came into view. I happened to have the poems of Wordsworth, Keats and Shelley with me and searching the volume came upon Wordsworth's *The Fountain*. The scenes in the poem were similar to my present situation for I, too, was now sitting beneath a tree, not his oak, but my honey locust tree. What a coincidence! Today we saw juncos and our first daisy.

April 3, 1927: I observed a brown thrasher this morning in the woods and another in the afternoon in an apple tree, and other birds. Most apple trees are in full bloom. Such a sweet odor can scarce be found. Cherries also are beginning to come out but with a fainter odor than apples. The pears have lost their white blossoms and are being supplanted by leaves. Sassafras blooms have a stimulating aroma and are difficult to surpass in penetrating power. The lilacs are exquisite masses of Persian lilac and makes one feel he is in a Japanese garden. Lilacs in bloom are much too lovely for description. In the yard is also a kind of spirea which is putting forth its small, light-green leaves which, when in bloom of its miniature roses, pure white, will stand out prominently against the background of slender branches and solid masses of luxurious leaves. April is living true to its Latin name of Aperire, which means "to open," or the bursting of the buds.

May 1, 1927: In the afternoon I took Swedenborg's *Divine Love and Wisdom*, a book which has interested me for its philosophy and especially since I was to be alone and could more fully feel the import of the text, I seated myself under an arbor of trees right at the edge of the creek bank. Water lay directly under me; slow-moving, pure blue, clear. Tree branches dipped into the water and, gently moving to and fro the leaves, gave to it a drapery effect. Various kinds of birds kept me company and threatened to divert me from Swedenborg. I thus remained in the woods for about an hour.

June 20, 1927: I plowed hard all day in a field of stumps. Stumps in new ground are really something to contend with and get a person fatigued if anything will. Added, it was a very hot and sultry day.

June 21, 1927: Every year about the month of June it seems as if my interests fail. I cannot seem to concentrate for long periods of reading. Now I think I have discovered the reason, after a little personal analysis. It is this: With the advent of spring and early summer there comes into my system a spirit known as "wanderlust." It is neigh universal. However futile is that spirit many have it, especially boys. Visions of the open road lie before one. Only travel books interest me now.

July 20, 1927: While at rest this afternoon in the field I saw a drama which would have interested Mr. Thoreau and his nature disciples. A large spider was at the entrance of its web home, while a few inches away I observed a green grasshopper which had become entangled in the spider's meshes. A few moments later the spider gave a quick jump and seized the hopper and pulled it to the entrance of its circular web. The spider set about killing its victim apparently by sucking upon the hopper's head. At this moment, to secure more action, I spat into the web, nearly hitting the two creatures. The spider instantly dived into its circular web, leaving the hopper free.

Metropolis Community High School, student 1924-28.

The spider did not soon re-appear and when it did the victim had escaped. By interrupting this near tragedy I perhaps missed seeing something in nature. Thoreau would have stayed with the creatures all day, just as he watched "the battle of the ants" among the chips.

Aug. 9, 1927: Worked all day and finished laying by corn. This year corn is many weeks late, as is everything else (a wet spring). It seems strange to be plowing corn in August and with no roasting ears.

Aug. 15, 1927: Monday. I began a job which will hold me for all the week, potato-digging.

Aug. 21, 1927: Sunday. I visited my grandparents. During the World War (1917-19) we lived with them. Today I strolled over the old farm reviewing in my mind the many scenes of those days.

The scenery from the barn-lot is remarkable. The country for miles around can be observed in one sweep of the vision: north for eight or 10 miles; south for 10 or 12 miles, across the Ohio River into the uplands of Kentucky. Twice I viewed the panorama, morning and afternoon, attempting to comprehend the vast expanse. I had a half-wild desire to fly over those blue-green valleys and hills in an airplane!

—Selected

In Chemistry

The hardest study of all the year
Is chemistry;
Yet there are days we hold most dear
In chemistry.

It is a class of love, I'd say
Is chemistry.
For there's sweet Professor Runyan every day
In chemistry.

And then a girl I love is there
In chemistry.
Indeed! 'tis not a day of despair -
Not chemistry.

Classmates we love and acids of all kinds
In chemistry;
Right proudly I indite these lines
In chemistry.—1927

Rainy Day's Excuse

O what a misty, cloudy day,
The trees and shrubs are dripping.
The eaves of houses running water,
And leaves of grass with moisture dipping.

Above we see the misty blanket:
Below we see the plashy mud.
The streams and branches swiftly flowing
From frequent fall of vapory scud.

All day we sit around the fire,
And list to children's empty prattle;
Or read with subtle interest
Of great campaigns and clashing battle.

We are content o'en though the sun
Does not its orb display;
For we know that many times
We all possess our gloomy day!—*Republican Herald* 1927

To Depressed Man

Lost worldly man, what makes thee fear
Love's luminous light, and cause to leer
On airy life of Lydian men,
When thou, as they, art steeped in sin?

Rise up and make thine own Etude!
Rise up and wake from silent lassitude!
Time's flying, life's dying, still close, still close;
Take Love, court Love, take enthrallment, enthuses!—1927

My Lost Wig

I tell you folks I've lost my hair;
I've searched so long that I declare
'Tis hard to learn where went it.
I search o'er hills, o'er vales and lea;
I frankly say it puzzles me.

The house is turned all up and down
From cellar up; not yet 'tis found.
Pa tries hard to learn where went it;
But seek he may, with greatest care,
He does not find the wig of hair.
It must be found! My Sunday wig
I wear to church, at dance and jig;
But search I may I cannot learn where it went.
After sundown, that night at eight,
I end my search and false hair's fate.

Near rosy sunrise, toward the noon,
The crows cawed noisily and boon.
I then believed I knew where went it.
Perched on high, on a scarecrow fair,
Hung my precious wig of hair!

Seeing 'twas caused by innocent ma
(Who placed my wig in an old apple tree)
My old man gave a loud guffaw.—1926

On Longfellow's Birthday

'Tis said that people tired of reading,
Reading from the ponderous masters,
Drop 'side the easy cushioned chair,
And wish for simple, comforting masters
Turning the leaves of an old and worn volume,
The toiler rests with cheerful heart.
Thanks tonight for Longfellow's words.
The worker possesses ? - Utopian heart!—1927

The Spirit of Christmas Eve

It was upon the Christmas night,
When all the candles glowing white,
Shed out their tremulous sparking light.
The cedar tree, its emerald branches,
Yielding low from toys enhances
The joyful spirit of Christmas Eve.

Perched on high a tinsel star,
Emblem of the Eastern Star
That summoned the shepherds from afar.
Cornucopias, garlands, red, white and green
Embellish the tree with shimmering sheen,
Spreading the spirit of Christmas Eve.

Lovely dolls, teddy bears, story books galore,
Filled with legends, children's lore.
Recalls again the joys of yore.
Enters old Santa with a bound,
Completing the spirit of Christmas Eve.—*Republican Herald* 1926

Thanksgiving Day

Many years hence our Pilgrim parents
Gave thanks to God, the first to commence
A custom, observed by ancestors, both early and late,
Of thanking God for food in the plate.

Thanksgiving Day spells for the turkey
A quick, hard blow and a finished futurity.
And dumplings, pumpkin pies and cornmeal cakes
Complete the day's menu which the appetite takes.

Indoors is all cheer; outside is animation.
This November day is Spring's competition.
The winter birds, the woods and streams,
Reminds us of summer's sunny sheen.

'Midst the saw briars bright and ruddy,
Flit the juncos black and sooty.
The rise and fall of the wind 'round them
Swings the weeds in rocking rhythm.

To end the day well, let us give thanks
That all of our fortunes are as merciful as He thinks.
The Muses are serene, are good company;
Let them in your soul on this Thanksgiving Day.—1926

A Lovers' Night

The night is bright, outside is cold,
The earth with frost as ne'er been seen.
The starry sky so white and bold,
Shines with eminence as God's great scene.

Old Orion's belt, as white as day;
The Pole Star's faint and twinkling light,
Shining from Cuba to Baffin's Bay;
Guides the wanderer's steps aright.

The mobile moon its silvery disk,
Emits beautiful, soft beams;
Falls on lovers, moonbeam kist,
And true to life it almost seems.—1926

My Girl

Her cheeks were so rosy,
Her lips were so red,
That upon her face
My eyes I fed.

I looked again.
Down fell her eyes
And murmured low,
"You're wondrous wise."

Says I "such placid
Beauty as is thine,
Invites my soul to say
'You're mine'."—1926

Thoughts on a Beautiful Day

Just another one of those beautiful days.
Time goes on, a mysterious vision;
No beginning, no end, like endless bays
That wind in and out but find no conclusion.

This day is gone; God extendeth it not.
This day is His, is yours, is mine.
Then let us work and plan and plot
And not away our strength to pine.—*Republican Herald* 1926

Our City - Metropolis

(With apologies to George Van Walters)

Now south of St. Louis two degrees or more
Is the Ohio River - on Metropolis shore -
A city you'll find - though not a cosmopolis -
Bearing the cognomen, city of Metropolis.
In twain this river doth the North and South divide.
This city's near the center and on the northern side.
Here for pork and produce the farmer finds a mart.
The people, too, in traffic, think themselves quite smart.
Think of this, historians, in your new addition,
For this is thought to be a great omission
That a city of six thousand seems to lack even a cursory notice,
Even as Fort Massac.—*Republican Herald* 1930

Thoughts on Autumn and Winter

Oh! Noble autumn thou art come
And with you brought the golden rod.
And shocks of corn, the farmers' feed,
Are turning sear and brown as sod.

But not long thus you shall subsist,
When winter with its sweeping wind,
Shall rob the trees of lustrous leaves,
And upon the flowers great wrath expend.

Though destructively great in thy autumnal state,
Thou art not without transient joy:
The fireside nook, the pleasant book,
While, 'mongest hills skating, the country boy.—*Republican Her-
ald* 1926

The School Clock

The big school clock without pretense
Reposes on the schoolhouse wall.
What moral value has this machine
Which marks the periods one and all?

As period after period passes on
And the day resigns to night,
Opportunity comes, appeals and goes,
And soon is lost to sight.

Oh, pupil, stop and think awhile
Of the lesson of the clock;
A lot of time remains to you
And life's secrets may unlock.—1928

New Year's Day

Old Father Time has deemed it right
To blow out the fire of last year's light.
He's ushered in on this gray dawn
The beginning of January, its suit to don
Of bleak and wind-swept meadow lands.
Break his rule? Thou couldest not last
Forever and Eternity; the human race in its form
Does not the Great God's division of Time scorn.—1928

Washington Irving

When Washington Irving was a small boy his parents made a journey to Washington, D.C. and had George Washington to bestow upon his namesake a blessing. George Washington bears the pseudonym "the father of his country," while Irving is often called "the father of American literature" from his unique and more Americanized mode of writing. Formerly, the writers in the original colonies wrote to teach a moral or were of a religious character. Irving invented humor into his writings, which came as a delightful surprise to people on both sides of the Atlantic who now, for the first occasion, gave American people the credit of writing something which could be called literature, suitable to the people's taste.

As a youth, Irving roamed the woods, visited Dutch inhabitants and thereby gained an insight into their peculiarities and modes of living that enabled him to write to best advantage. Irving's works may be divided into two types: stories and tales and biographies and histories.

The Knickerbocker's History of New York was his first work. The tale or history of New York contains some of the most wholesome humor to be found in many days and is full of history, romance, sentiment and exaggerations. The description of Wouter Van Twiller, the official weight of the Dutch scales, Hudson's' men wearing five jackets and six pairs of breeches are to a great extent hyperboles, but their value is not decreased by that. Rather, it is a necessary element in order to carry out the purpose for which Irving intended: to embody the traditions of his city in an amusing form.

A few years later, while residing in England, Irving wrote several short sketches and tales which he combined into a volume called *The Sketch Book*. There are several good essays upon English subjects in this books, but he is chiefly known and remembered by his two short stories *Legend of Sleepy Hollow* and *Rip Van Winkle*. In the first few paragraphs of these two books or stories is contained descriptions more of the disposition of essays' but this gradually blends into the active phase of the story. Before the reader is aware, he will be reading both description and plot-making with great interest. Irving shows unusual ability to portray odd and unnatural characters and throughout, his stories are highly colored with over-statements.

There is another book which is worthy of note in this group of his writings, It is *Tales of the Alhambra*. He traveled through Spain extensively and actually lived in that old Moorish castle. The tales are highly imaginative but not always impossible and he succeeds in creating an atmosphere which places us in a conducive attitude to discover the mode of living of the inhabitants and their superstitions.

The second type of Irving's writings was history and biography. While residing in Spain as Minister, he unearthed many old documents and records and by putting into practice his fluent pen, produced *Life and Voyages of Columbus*. He put into this work his utmost skill and no other person has ever presented the ideals, ambitions and human aspects of Columbus in better form. *The Conquest of Granada* is a penetrating account of the conquest by Ferdinand and Isabella over the Moors. The book is highly romantic and has much warfare, but is told in such a manner as to give to the reader an imaginary scene of revelry. In the biographies *Oliver Goldsmith* and *Life of George Washington*, Irving shows an intimate acquaintance with the conditions of their lives and with his generous attitude says that we should take into consideration their deficiencies.

—1928

Reflections On "THANATOPSIS"

This poem of Bryant's is an elegy or descriptive essay of death. No other poem has been written on death on a scale of such vastness as this one. As you walk through the woods with Bryant, you enjoy nature and see her clothed in her most beautiful costumes, her deathless silence, calm and perfect in her inanimate surroundings, and it has upon you the effect of being in contact with the omnipotent power.

But as you behold and meditate on this infinite sphere of the spiritual world, there comes another still voice. In a few days, comparatively, the beholder shall not view this scene, for death will be forthcoming. But even at this warning and death as a subsequent, it is not such a terrible fate. For you shall lie down in company with thousands of others - great men, sages, philosophers, and the masters of old - and be in the best company desired. Eternal rest shall be forthcoming and permanent in his deep, warm bed of Mother Earth.

Death is an insignificant and frivolous termination if we observe matters calmly and give our attention to ethereal nature.

—1927

Mr. Williams' Views

We, as workers upon a new phase of school work, can feel greater assurance and confidence in ourselves when we get an opinion of recommendation from the Board of Education itself. The board has received the proposal of a school paper with favor from the time of its first appearance; the members are free and sincere in saying that they believe it will be an asset and a success.

Mr. W.W. Williams, president of the board, is of the opinion that there is only one way of the paper making a success: that is the securing of advertisements. When interviewed, his first question was: will the paper be a liability or an asset?

To make it an asset he would lay especial stress upon this phase of the work, because it is through advertisements, and they only, that a newspaper can live. Our boys, who act in the capacity of business managers, should seek an interview with every business concern in the city, regard each one as a possibility, and then stay after them until they are persuaded to advertise. The success of the paper hinges upon the amount of advertisement.

Mr. Williams is of the further opinion that a school paper is much more appropriate, practicable and beneficial than an annual. An annual, although it has many good qualities, cannot possibly reflect the school work, the school spirit, in its most intimate light. There is something artificial, refined, about an annual which one will not find in a school review.

As to our applying to the board for help, Mr. Williams gave his word that we should not find the board, as a whole, or as individuals, lacking in that respect; they will give us all the help they can. Views from the other members of the board will be given from time to time.

—1928, as an associate editor.

Sad And Forlorn

One cold winter day, as I was riding a streetcar in Paducah, I happened upon a scene that struck me as unusual.

I saw in the streetcar a large, middle-aged man coarsely dressed, and of rather a forbidding face. He was seated in a corner and gave an impression of surly ill nature. A little thin, weazened lad of not more than six or seven, with pinched features and a starved look, came in and took a seat next to the man.

There was nothing to indicate that the two knew each other and the boy's air showed plainly enough that they did not. But when the poor fellow blew on his small, dirty fists, in a vain attempt to warm them, the big surly-looking man put out a great hand, not much cleaner, took the boy's blue fingers between his palms and held them there to warm them. His grim face hardly changed expression, but the kindliness of the act, and the queer look of astonishment and pleasure in the child's face, made the incident good to see.

—1926

Enjoyment Of Wealth

"Wealth is not his that has it but his that enjoys it." This unique proverb, formulated by the ingenious and logical Benjamin Franklin, brings to my memory a story I once heard told when I was only a small boy, and which illustrates the maxim admirably to my way of thinking.

As this is a contrast between two altogether different individuals in both purpose and thought, I will narrate the conditions in both of their lives, leaving the reader to judge for himself the truth of the original maxim.

A certain middle-aged man in a large city owned an office building, several lots and a large apartment house from which he derived a very comfortable living. This man also owned a fine home and grounds in the suburb, luxuriously furnished; a fine library in which in his leisure hours he could read and study and come into communion with the great field of literature and art. Beautiful pictures adorned the walls of every room, which gave to the interior an atmosphere of cheerfulness and inspiration. In this condition he passed the most fruitful years of his existence in the enjoyment of his wealth.

To cite the other case: A man of middle-age, living in one of our northern cities of Illinois, owned a large wholesale grain and lumber concern. He also lived in a large house, but his premises were not suggestive of a good attitude toward keeping them in good condition. The interior of the house was cold, bare of all luxuries and destitute of all unnecessary decorations. No books, no pictures, nothing to divert one's attention from the cares of the day. No wonder, when he came in at the close of the day, he threw himself on the bed and fell asleep as quickly as possible, so that he might arise early to begin the raking, scraping, scrimping of more wealth.

He had accumulated a considerable fortune in his business, at the expense of cheating other people when possible, and by skillful financing and scheming. Those duties required so much of his time and energy that no leisure was available in which to devote a portion of it to literature, a knowledge of which will elevate the human intelligence to a higher and loftier appreciation of life and its incorporeal aspect. Nor did he take the time to assume any civic responsibilities. He was unsought and unloved, except possibly by his wife, who had the same desires as he.

—1927

Abraham Lincoln - The Man

Lincoln!
The man of men supreme.
Lincoln!
Thy thoughtful brow does o'er the stream

Of civil strife gaze long to glean
A passage out of war's desolation,
And saving of our Christian nation,
Lincoln!

Lincoln!
O hallowed art thy name.
Lincoln!
The nation thrills at thy just fame
Rise up once more o noble heart!
Old Honest Abe thou art embalmed
With admiration in our hearts,
Lincoln!

One name comes up in all minds, embalmed in all hearts, that must have the supreme place in our glory and in our national honor: that name is Abraham Lincoln. In this age we look with admiration at his uncompromising honesty; and well we may, for this saved us.

Fancy yourself roaming through a wild region amidst unsurveyed forests and rank vegetation, frequented with bears and other wild animals. Glancing, through a vista in the trees, place in the center of this scene a tall, strong country boy, wielding an ax with amazing facility; and, while resting, take from his buckskin pocket a copy-book, and commit a passage to memory. If this sylvan scene can be conceived, then we have a vivid outline for the conditions of Lincoln's early life, the boy who was destined to be future president of the nation.

His early environment - the unbroken forest far from the restraints of organized l ··· the difficulties and struggles against poverty, and the elements - how he labored against the unsubdued forces of nature - all are an explanation of his liberality, modesty, charity and sympathy in later life and his training in self-denial, patience and industry.

Throughout his entire career he possessed an intense hatred, not for slave holders, but for the institution of slavery. He early consecrated himself to the one pursuit of eradicating it.

As the years passed, Lincoln became a lawyer and a politician. His growing experience and acquaintances brought him influence in local and state politics. He became to be valued as a sagacious advisor. His advancement from postmaster to president was neither accidental nor easy. He met with many bitter disappointments, and there intervened fully 30 years of toil, study and self-denial. Every real success was balanced by seeming failures.

At last, after 30 years of endeavor, the people chose "Honest Old Abe" to carry them through the fearful night of war. When all was dread before us, when generals were defeated and not a ray of hope shone for our cause; then we looked to Lincoln for help. He stood like a rock before the storm, brave and self-restrained, as a man in whom, as Emerson says "Valor consists in the power of self-recovery." His forcible speech, plain common sense and benevolence made him the wonder of all ages, bringing him to the proscenium of national and world-wide fame.

Lincoln is radiant with all the great virtues, and these will continue to radiate as the ages look back into history. His achievements are many: he saved the nation in the perils of unparalleled civil war; he brought the states into cohesion as no other man could have done; as a philanthropist, he gave liberty to one race and salvation to another; a commander, he was untainted with blood; and as a ruler in the vortices and desperate events of war, he was untarnished with crime; as a man, he has emitted no adverse word of passion, no malicious thoughts, no deception, act of jealousy, nor design of egotistical ambition. The great emancipator thus perfected was placed in these troubled years to make beautiful all that is good and just in our nation, and to present to all future generations the divine idea of free government.

Patriotism, that essential element of a glorious nation, cannot be better propagated and extended than by studying and commemorating the accomplishments of our great men. The Sandwich Islander believes the strength of the person he kills passes into his own body. So also, when patriotism dies, the nation dies, and its resources actually pass to other peoples with strength, vitality and principles of life.

Washington and Lincoln are our twin heroes, and these two have been christened as twin stars in the firmament of our national fame. It is not too much to say that away down in the future - through the gentle, intumescent tides of peace; through the obstreperous streams of warring strife - that the generations looking this way shall see the President as the supreme figure in this vortex of history.

> —entered in an essay prize contest
> in 1927, but won no prize.

An Idle Hour With Dave

This was Dave's third year in high school. Looking back at the past, through his year as a freshman and a stranger to the new life amongst many boys and girls of his own age and through his sopho-more year and the gradual assimilation of some definite ideas, he thought how he had been a fool; how he had drifted along in this misunderstanding. Life, that great element, was now surging through his veins. Knowledge, conception, personality were developing, and as he sat in his comfortable arm chair beside the murmuring, singing fireside, he was conscious of a great many inexpressible and undefinable emotions.

The night was cold. A light snow had fallen during the evening and the wind whistled around the corners of the house. It swept down the chimney with a vortical motion, only to be buffeted against the bricks and die away. The azure flames leaped up with an intumescent motion, occasionally interrupted by consoling crepitations of the woody fuel. What more could bespeak a harmonious coziness?

Is Dave in love? Of that we think so. Note how he closes his eyes with that inexpressibly sweet drooping of the eyelids. Those silken lashes, those magnificent eyebrows - perfect, flowing, raven-black, invidiously distinctive worthy of any lad's envy; the smile playing about his tempting lips; the perfect contour of his face; an invulnerable personality.

Who is this sweetheart of his reveries? Is he at last to succumb to a petty love? Let us see. There is Verla A__, a beautiful, graceful girl, with a face as tempting as a freshly picked peach. She *is* a pretty girl. Not unusually so, but with a peculiar charm all her own. Her even, thick brows are expressive. We could easily fall in love with her.

Then there is Margaret W__. What a different type! She is a young slip of a girl whose large, elegant, soft, black, gazelle eyes have captured more than one unsuspecting lad. She is not beautiful, but gay and ensnaring. Can it be that Dave has yielded to that insatiable longing for an idol, characterized in the stree-walker lad? No, we scarcely think so. Does his countenance indicate any ignoble design?

Does Dave sleep or is he only deep in thought? Meditation? It must be, for his features change. The entire panorama of his school life is unfolded before him, as if each face were viewed through a kaleido-scope: every boy, every girl, heightened with the remembrances of many days spent together in the schoolroom; bathing in the fountains of knowledge; the many little words, the sly coquetry with girls in study hours; the sweet recollections of words with bright-eyed, flaxon-haired, blonde maidens; of infatuating maidens of a freshness excelling that of the morning breeze of beautiful sunrise.

Dave sees through all this haze of happy reminiscences, sees through the ocellated view of relevant states of mind, and arises from his chair. Perhaps he is a little more asleep than awake, but he has secured the idea of *omnium-gatherum*, a variety of things experienced. It is more firmly transfixed than ever in his mind. It was not a love dream at all, but only a wholesome soliloquy on fellowman!

—1928

The History Of Strawberries

The common wild strawberry which is found throughout Europe and North America is *Fragaria Virginians* and this was the first species brought under cultivation in the early part of the Seventh Century. It is a native of the temperate regions of both hemispheres as well as mountain districts in warmer climes.

We first find mention of the plant in the accounts of Americus Vespusci, who shortly following the discovery of America by Columbus, made a voyage to the new world and returned to Europe, giving account of his discoveries including the botanical accounts of various new plants. He gave a simple description of the strawberry which bore small, fleshy fruit berries.

In 1620 the Pilgrims made their first settlement in America. In the summer following their arrival, the colonists found many acres of the wild plant thriving upon the rocky hillsides and bearing luscious red fruit. The Indians introduced them in their cultural methods by teaching them how to transplant and cultivate it. We find from old accounts by the governors of the different colonies that the Indians were skillful in strawberry growing and were very fond of the fruit. They often gathered around the council fire on summer nights and had festivals of venison and native dishes of strawberries. Then could we find

"The aged chiefs come sit around,
And talk of deer and hunt and hound;
While simmers low, as a young brave's flute
The wild red berry's fulsome fruit."

By 1800 berries were grown by white settler individuals and did not increase in importance until 34 years later. Indeed, the whole industry has been developed since the introduction in 1834 of the Hovey strawberry, a variety which originated in Massachusetts. Later, other species were introduced. From these species, crossed and re-crossed in various manners, have sprung the vast numbers of different varieties enumerated in catalogues whose characteristics are so inextricably blended that the attempt to trace their parentage or to follow their lineage has become impossible. The varieties of strawberries have been developed and evolved through long experiments and the crossing of various types until they have been, by gradual and imperceptible degrees, conveyed to the present standard of excellence.

In 1834 strawberries suddenly sprang into prominence as a new important crop. There are two reasons for the slow development of this crop anterior to the year 1834. First: improper methods of handling. The crop was looked upon as a side-line, from which only a few meals were obtained. This is synonymous to the perishability of this small fruit. The people in the pioneer days did not have efficient methods for preservation of it. Second: Poor cultural methods. Tobacco and potatoes (two native crops) were immediately chosen as suitable crops and quickly reached a commercial status. Everyone smoked (?) and potatoes soon became the dependent crop of Ireland. Consequently, cultural methods were improved while the strawberry remained an insignificant crop.

In southeastern Missouri, northern Arkansas, western Tennessee and Kentucky, Florida and in Southern Illinois lies our principal interest.

These regions furnish the northern markets with quantities of berries every year. By the year 1895 many farmers owned as many as one to five acres of berries and employed pickers, packers and haulers, paying them a fixed sum per quart. Packing sheds were constructed, the berries packed and either taken to the local market or shipped to northern districts. Florida started commercial at Plant City in 1889. From 1922 to 1925 the total number of quarts produced were 10,500,000 with a value of $3,000,000 which shows the importance of the crop.

From 1909 up until 1917 we find the acreage remaining at a standstill of 143,045 acres with an annual value of $18,000,000 for the entire United States, according to the U.S. Census. It evidently appeared to the growers that the zenith of strawberry culture had been reached. At this period also a rot disease was introduced through shipment of plants which caused some loss to growers. This disease was described by Stevens in 1915. In 1917 the acreage decreased to 109,510 acres and in 1918 to 83,820 acres.

The decrease was partly due to the stirring and critical events of the World War. In 1919 there were 119,395 acres reported. From 1920 to 1922 the production of berries increased from 8,000 carloads to 18,000 carloads in the two year's duration.

The varieties at the present time vary in the most remarkable degree in size, color, flavor, shape, degree of fertility season of ripening and perishability so that the grower has wide opportunity of finding a ready market for his berries.

Today the increasing demand in the city market for good berries has caused a general movement to creep in in which the farmer begins to awaken to the possibilities of strawberry growing. The business is destined to increase in importance. The advance in prices, opportunities of good freight service - both must serve as an impetus. Berry associations are organized and cooperative marketing associations are developed for the profitable management of monetary affairs, and modern methods of cultivation and propagation. This plant is receiving the attention it deserves, financially and agriculturally.

—first prize in contest sponsored
by the Metropolis Rotary Club, 1927.

Our Earliest Tradition - De Soto

Just 50 years after the discovery of America the intrepid Spanish explorer De Soto, according to tradition, visited the present site of Fort Massac and occupied it as a base for his operations during one winter. It is a tradition which has always clung to the name Fort Massac. The veracity of this is doubtful, however. There is bound to be opposition when an old story or tradition is exploded or disclaimed. But historical facts are not far wrong and from a more or less close study of De Soto and his wanderings, this subject is seen in the correct light.

De Soto set out with 570 men and 223 horses in May 1539, from Havana, Cuba. His object was to discover gold and to take over all new lands in the name of the King of Spain. He first set foot on the new continent in what is now Florida.

From the very first he carried things on in a high-handed manner, making war on the Indians and making servants of what Indians he captured. His men were without morals and the incorrigible outlawry of his men was a great cause of later hindrances and hardships. At every place he met Indians, he made battle, killing, robbing and plundering them without reason and, thus, he soon came to have them as enemies all over the south.

De Soto's route led through Florida, Georgia and up as far as the southern slope of the Appalachian Mountains. Finding no gold or precious jewels or rich fabled cities and becoming discouraged and constantly harassed by hostile Indians he re-traced his way southward again to the junction of the Tombigbee and Alabama rivers to a place called Mawvila or Nawvilla, where a very fierce battle was fought. In this battle there were heavy losses both among the Indians and the Spaniards.

Meanwhile, the army was constantly diminishing in size and the men were becoming more discouraged every day. A mutiny was formed against De Soto that they might go back home. De Soto discovered, the design and immediately led them northward, so deceiving his own men that they thought they were going southward to the coast and to their homes.

The route now lay across the present state of Mississippi and after several weeks of toil, they discovered the Mississippi River rolling in majestic solemnity on its journey to the Gulf.

De Soto, when he gazed upon that vast stream, remained unmoved and is said to have remarked of it later: "The river now went very strongly in those parts; for it was nearly half a league broad, and 16 fathoms deep, and very furious, and ran with a great current; and on both sides there were so many Indians, and our power was not now so great, but that we need to help ourselves rather by flight than by force."

The first care was to build boats which took a full month and it can be seen that De Soto, already wearied by months of toil and encounters with Indians greeted the appearance of any impediment in his course with extreme disfavor. The Mississippi was crossed at or near the present site of Memphis and after crossing into Arkansas, they took a northerly course, crossing into Missouri and going up as far as the present side of New Madrid.

Historians agree that he went this far north but now the idea of his continuing northward as far as Fort Massac is mere conjecture. It is unlikely that De Soto, after having once crossed the Mississippi with so much toil and inconvenience, would go still farther northward inevitably encountering it again. It is unreasonable to think that he would again cross the Father of Waters, which was dangerous as well as requiring weeks of labor to build boats and also the Ohio River just for winter encampment. The Indians had given no encouragement of finding gold or fabled cities farther north. Hence, it must be concluded that De Soto, after wintering in the vicinity of New Madrid, and with a prayer of forgiveness on his lips for all the misfortune which he had brought upon his followers, died, leaving this place as the farthest point traveled northward.

That the ruins found about the Fort Massac eminence before 1700 are an indication of the early occupancy by De Soto, can be disproved when we learn of the opinions of the later French and when we hear what Father Mermet has to say when he visited the site in 1702.

He says there were signs to indicate that some sort of fortification had at one time been built. Father Mermet remarked that the ruins, although indicating a long age, were probably not those of De Soto's supposed fort but of the Indians who, recognizing the importance of the eminence, established some sort of a fortification in the last half of the 17th century.

Thus, although we would like to claim this tradition as fact, doubtful and conjectural it remains in history.

—Republication Herald, April 1928.

First Impressions Of Bradley

A traveler usually carries with him many associations of the places visited on his itinerary. These associations may be favorable or unfavorable. One city may be very pleasing to him, while another may carry with its name very adverse criticism. In almost every case the first impressions are quickly received and permanently retained.

But it was not thus in my case. A good while ago I decided upon Bradley as the college I would attend. Although I was impressed with the many advantages cited in its bulletin, I formed the idea that it was just a little aristocratic, both in manner and spirit. It was my prevailing objection for a good while. I saw it (through its bulletin and brochures) as a large bunch of athletic stars, triumphing over its neighbors or as a lot of fraternity men and sorority women.

Those ideas have vanished! One week at Bradley, and my whole opinion of Bradley college life has changed; it cannot be assailed.

Two days before the school opened I passed along its shady avenues, viewing the institution where I had decided to attend for four years. The first thing that struck me was the beautiful athletic field to the north of the gymnasium - perfectly level, in excellent condition. I viewed the gymnasium with interest, noting its exterior architecture, its size and its landscaping. South of the gymnasium just across the boulevard, I noted a still larger athletic field, its adequate size, good condition and its equipment. It struck me as being ideal and an excellent place for collegiate meets.

What interested me most was Bradley Hall, with its imposing front-

Bradley Polytechnic Institute, student 1928-30.

age, ivy-clad, the verdant campus and the general atmosphere of the entire grounds. To the north stretched the campus until at a line of shrubbery it stopped. Just a little farther stood the Weather Bureau Building of the U.S. Department of Agriculture. This struck me as being an ideal situation for such a station and as being a particularly valuable neighbor to Bradley. But back to Bradley Hall.

The size and architecture of Bradley Hall impressed me considerably. It possessed an air of importance and learning, an institution that anyone would be curious to inspect or to attend.

The Horology Building next attracted my attention. From across the avenue I could see students at work on both the first and second floors. The large clock upon the tower I thought certainly appropriate for such an adjunct of the college. It gave to it a certain enviable individuality.

Passing on down the avenue, or Institute Place, I observed respectively the Bradley Book Store, the cafeteria building and the Manual Arts Building. These last buildings, as well as the gymnasium and Horology, are scattered over the college grounds in such a manner that they do not present a conglomeration of buildings, crowded together in order to save space, but as a little community, no department being so far from the main building (the Hall) as to cause inconvenience. In this I saw the symbol of freedom of learning opportunities, which is now beginning to realize itself, even in my first few days at Bradley. In the long and leisurely drive down Institute Place, and the walk from Bradley Hall to Manual Arts, the College of Music, or to the gymnasium, I saw further still the symbol of freedom and liberalism of learning.

Those were my first impressions, as I walked along and as I walked away. But I still considered it a bit aristocratic. I had seen only the seat of the college life and not the actual life.

Monday was my first day at Bradley as a student. I altered my opinion slightly. Wednesday, still more. By Friday night I had broken the rule of the pure traveler - I had changed my impressions - and I saw now that it was not nearly as aristocratic a place as my own high school the first time I attended.

At Bradley everyone seemed to be singularly friendly, especially the freshmen. But they are usually more cordial, however, for they, know no one and are eager to confide their little troubles to other ones in like trouble. No loquacious or boisterous talking just because it is the first day or days of school, but quiet conversation upon such subjects as their college curriculum.

Thus, my first impressions have been abridged so that Bradley, to me, is synonymous to a quiet and conscientious learning.

—September 1928

The Advantages of Loafing

I sometimes think that the man who indulges in a certain amount of loafing is really benefited by it. Again, I see men who show all too plainly the ill effects of spending their time thusly.

There are two kinds of loafing. First, the common kind, which we see in the village store and around the city "hangouts." Secondly, the rare philosophical kind which we seldom, if ever, see.

It is the second type of which I wish to speak. He is the really valuable man. By this time you will have suspected my definition of "loafer." By "loafing" I mean intelligent loafing - not simply idling away time. A more or less definite purpose characterizes the true and useful loafer. Loafing, you know, oftentimes appears to be what it is not.

We now come to a consideration of some of the advantages of loafing. It may provide the person some needed rest and recreation. The person may be suffering from petty worry or from the tensions of a "fast life." Loafing enables the person to sit by and laugh at the seemingly-useless struggle of man with mundane affairs. It affords an opportunity to philosophize and reflect upon life's serious problems. And loafing has often provided us with some very good poets and writers.

Think of the authors, who in their youth were considered as idlers and dreamers. Robert Louis Stevenson shirked his school work and spent all the time he could out in the country, loafing. Francois Villon was not only a loafer but "respectable robber and housebreaker." Today he holds a good position in the minds of the French. Our own Thoreau was considered "queer" and not overly industrious. What was Edgar Allen Poe but a material failure?

Personally, upon more than one occasion, I have derived benefit from a period of loafing, short period though it was. I have picked up much information of a useful kind and I am certain that I have become possessed of an equanimity I would not otherwise have gotten.

—1930

Caricature Of A Bradley Celebrity

This particular celebrity on the Bradley campus has great celerity of thought; his mind is in a constant turmoil of ambitious thoughts; he is the prince of Bradley's Order of Fiddle-Faddles. No person in years has so graced the Worthy Order as this renowned Prince of Nonsense. Not long ago he served on a committee with admirable regard to the mystic doctrines of Quietism. With wonderful attention to the art of stammering, he presented to us the results of his work.

Not only is he a prince among the Royal Order of Fiddle-Faddles, but also because of his striking beauty and magnetic power, he has become a sheik, with all the power over women that a Mohammedan donkey has over a Turkish queen. He is omnilucent: Bradley women willingly pay homage to so noted a jabberer and resfactor that they may escape the attention of some greater respirator.

The secret of his remarkable success in the society circles of both sexes lies in his very close adherence to a trusty pal, who is both a fastidious speaker and dresser. Now, there is nothing wrong in a liberal cohesion of two elements of the same or like kind. A necessary force unites molecules of the same material; but one would ask our celebrity to take a more practical interpretation of Emerson's sententious "Hitch your wagon to a star." I am afraid to mention this maxim to celebrated masher of the Royal Order for fear that he will once again burst out in an unspeakable ecstasy of tongue.

Let us watch the renowned Prince of Fiddle-Faddles. We have the destiny of a coming leader of coeds and a genius of the easy art of jabbering in our hands. The responsibility is entirely ours. So much for our psitologist.

—1929

Travel

◖

Cuba - Pearl of the Antilles

Immediately after school closed in April 1931, I prepared to take a trip which would out-do any previous ones of mine and would take me to a foreign land. I planned on visiting Cuba, the romantic island of the West Indies.

The trip was of one month's duration during which time I traveled over 4,000 miles through Kentucky, Tennessee, Mississippi, Louisiana, Alabama, Georgia, Florida, Virginia and West Virginia and the provinces of Pinar del Rio and Havana in Cuba. Except for the 100 miles of water across the Florida Strait, I hitch-hiked practically the entire distance.

Announcement of a trip to Cuba was received by my friends with misgivings as to the safety of such a trip. Revolution was to be expected anytime, especially since the relations between President Machado and the Cuban people had been strained for many months.

My determination to see Cuba; to bathe myself for a few days in her romantic atmosphere, over-ruled all dire beliefs. Two days after school closed I took to the open road, bound for New Orleans, the Southland and most satisfying, to the land of age-old dreams.

Vicksburg I could not miss. The Civil War meant just a little more to me after a survey of the famous battleground.

Through Louisiana my thoughts were on Evangeline and Gabriel and of their long search through mossy labyrinths of bayous. Capacious Canal Street; sequestered Jackson Square; the foreign atmosphere of the old French market, Vieux Carre; old Absinthe House; Chartres Street, all were dramas in this dream trip of mine come true. Of the two, inspiration and knowledge, I lived for the former. To me, New Orleans was France, all Louisiana was French and I was living back in the days of Bienville.

The journey from New Orleans to Jacksonville, FL was one pleasure after another. Not least was the railroad trip across one end of Lake Pontchatrain, resembling the later passage over the Florida Keys. The Gulf Coast cities are winter resorts for Northerners. Many means are used to attract visitors, the wonder being that anyone desiring to winter along the coast could ever decided which city to choose, all are so charmingly ideal.

The Swanee River was a reminder of "Old Folks at Home," as well as good fishing, when a fellow traveler spoke of it from experience. The St. Johns River stamps Jacksonville upon my mind. Miami, a playground for the North.

The expectation of seeing Cuba keyed me into the highest state of anticipation, as the train sped over key after key in that long line extending from the Florida mainland to Key West. I can think of no single day in my life that can compare with the type of eye thrills I got in that half-day ride across the Keys. Such a trip illuminated those little dots on our Florida map as nothing else could. Among the silent thrills is seeing the first tropical water; the immense mangrove wastes; the little hop from key to key and eventually Key West, our southernmost city.

All was astir at Key West, as passengers left the train and boarded the steamer, to be another thrill source. Boys swam along the starboard begging in a foreign tongue for coins to dive after. A number of pennies cast simultaneously overboard sent them all downward like scared fish into the dirty-looking depths.

This, mingled with a feeling not quite of vague fear but of curiosity and unexpectancy of what lay beyond in that exotic, vaunted city over the horizon, gave me a sensation Irving must have experienced in his story "The Voyage."

High noon found us far from shore, with dinner served on board. A saloon at one end attracted many persons, now free from the yoke of Prohibition; the ocean scenery, others. The appearance of the Gulf Stream was announced by a deeper blue, as the ship sped on its way to Cuba, "Pearl of the Antilles".

Heretofore, a general air of rest had prevailed over the ship. Some were even asleep. The sun had neared the western horizon and the sixth hour aboard had come when a first view of Havana was announced. At once all was astir. The top deck was soon crowded, glasses were trained forward, the low lying shore was reconnoitered and El Moro was frequently spoken out.

Upon rushing from the ship into the crowded custom house, La Aduana, we were greeted by a bi-lingual company, Spanish alternating with English and English with Spanish, as some Americans stood bewildered at the exhibit of staccato Spanish.

A quaint room at a native hotel, secured at half-price, when I insisted that I already had reservations at another hotel; a short walk along the Prado and I slept contentedly, after one wonderful day in the semi-tropics.

The following morning, in my room opposite the National Cuban Capitol, I was awakened from a deep sleep by the chattering of many street urchins, the calling of peddlers and the swift passage of automobiles along the Prado (avenue).

Whereas some 35 years ago Havana was shunned by travelers and yellow fever stalked the city, today it is visited by thousands and boasts a healthy, well-kept, thriving city of over half a million people. The $16,000,000 Capitol, although out of proportion to the republic's riches, is the pride of the loyal Havanans. It well illustrates their love of display for its own sake.

By a meandering route, I found the American Consul. Through his aid I secured a room with Cuban people in the Vedado, a suburb of Havana where, in my comparatively short stay, I hoped to increase my knowledge of Spanish. I never met people more cordial, understanding and interesting than those on Calle 19, Vedado.

To Americans Havana *is* Cuba. It is true that one can see much typical of Cuba. The language, customs, food and dress are Cuban. However, to really know Cuba one must travel from the city many miles. There is El Moro Castle, Cabanas Fortress, La Playa Bathing Beach, El Gran Casino where one may woo the goddess of chance, the ancient cathedral, where the bones of Columbus were supposed to have rested at one time. There are the many native shops. But to know Cuba is to journey down her length; to view the tobacco fields of the *vuelto abajo* in Pinar del Rio province; to see how absolutely blissful the native *Cubano* is in his poverty, amidst a land of high natural and plenty.

Though my feelings toward Havana were those of Joseph Hergesheimer in his *San Cristobal de la Havana*, I soon began to feel for open spaces. With a dream already fulfilled, I was now ready for the Cuba that lay nearby.

I was fortunate in making the acquaintance of an American on board ship, who had brought his automobile across with him. We arranged for a long drive to the west of Havana, into Pinar del Rio province (the *vuelto abajo*) and the finest tobacco producing region in the world.

To stop at roadside inns, converse with the people as opportunity afforded and to linger in

El Maceo Statue, Havana, Cuba.

Peddlers at Guanajay, Cuba.

the larger towns is to learn much. I exulted in my Spanish, meager though it was. With it every Cuban boy was my victim. The camera is a never-failing means to entice the boys as well as adults. Whether the Cuban ingratiates every tourist as his victim for a piece of money or whether his is sincere suavity, one cannot always tell but the fact remains that they are outwardly courteous.

Strange to say, but I was to see the first mountains of my life in western Cuba, the low-lying range of the Rosario and Organos appearing on our way between Guanajay and Artemesa.

The Central Highway of Cuba is much the same as our roads in Illinois. Constructed of the finest materials, the roadbed is equal to any in the States. Much of the way is lined by royal palms, bamboo, little banana patches and an occasional thatched hut. I came to learn the ti-ti and poinciana tress almost by sight.

The drive back to Havana, followed by a visit to La Playa Beach and the *Capitolio* brought my brief but adventure-filled sojourn to a close.

Although I was to see, in this trip of over 4,000 miles, much to charm the eye, nothing compared with my Cuban episode. Florida's playgrounds were delightful, Lookout Mountain was sublime almost to reverence; the mountains of eastern Tennessee and the Virginias were irresistible in their appeal, but the memory which will longest live is of Havana's adroit hospitality, its never-slumbering gaiety, 'a vision,' as Hergessheimer called her, 'in blanched satin with flowers in her hair.'

A trip to Cuba was a realization of a dream long ago experienced. It was a dream come true in a tropical land, made romantic by the Spanish. With great reluctance I bid *hasta manana* to Cuba.

As I saw the low shores of Cuba fade from view and disappear entirely, she was translated to me as not only the Pearl of the Antilles, but my pearl of memory securely locked within me, to be a never-ending storehouse of delightful memories.

—Prize winner in "Travel Contest" of
Instructor magazine, 1931.

Through Mexico on High School Spanish

"*Viajer es Aprender*," I once read in a Mexican newspaper column, "To travel is to learn" and although my term as teacher had expired and I was free from mental work, I began my Mexican adventure with the sentiment of that maxim in my heart and soul to the utmost.

As a departure from the ordinary tourist routes and because of my interest in Latin America, I decided upon Mexico for the summer vacation. Mexico had been pictured to me in its worst aspect. Even though I believed that Mexicans had virtues, opinions of other people who, however, had never been there and of course did not know and the meager accounts in our school geographies, made me skeptical as to the safety of a trip through the Republic. In my case, desire overruled reason and I went.

I entered Mexico by way of Nuevo Laredo, going thence to Monterrey, Saltillo and San Luis Potosi. From the time I neared Monterrey until I left the Republic, I never was out of sight of mountains. They were omnipresent but the thrill in viewing their blue, serrated bulks never decreased, rather my love for them increased.

My means of travel were various. Bus travel is popular in Mexico where there are roads. The busses are always loaded with some hanging on the side. It was not uncommon to have as fellow-passengers parrots, chickens, dogs, pigs and I expected any time to see a calf or donkey loaded in. There is not much comfort in Mexican busses.

I rode the Mexican National Railways during much of my trip. I found it a very efficient, courteous and comfortable line. A glance into the second-class cars, however, revealed such scenes as are in a bus. Baggage of enormous size, dirty, ill-smelling peons and hard seats characterize second-class accommodations.

Following my plan, I stopped off for a day or two in the largest cities, bathing in the easy-going, pleasure-loving atmosphere of the

Mexicans. At Monterrey a fine band played while the younger set promenaded.

I walked from Monterrey to Saltillo some 50 miles and traveled incognito. At this time of the year, May, the aspect of the country was dry and barren indeed. Only the fantastic, saw-toothed peaks saved the walk from drudgery. Great lumbering ox-carts passed me; men riding burros seemingly smaller than the riders; a stop for a drink of water in a road-side adobe hut, these and other incidents put me in closer contact with the Mexico I desired to know.

At Saltillo I was surprised and charmed by the number of old-time, horse-drawn carriages. Here I boarded the train again. I stopped two days at quiet San Luis Potosi. Its market was so interesting that I visited it several times a day.

I was now below the Tropic of Cancer and at noon it was hot. At night, however, due to the elevation (almost a mile), a coat was welcome. This is true of all plateau Mexico. After a night's repose, one feels doubly refreshed.

For the Fifth of May I was in Queretaro, the Opal City. This was the anniversary of the Mexican victory over the French in 1867. Except for the display of flags, there were no holiday demonstrations. In Mexico City there is more celebration. I walked up a little hill just outside the city and viewed the spot where Emperor Maxmillan was executed.

It was a night's ride into Mexico City from Queretaro. Everyone calls it "Mexico" or "Mejico," leaving the "city" off in conversation. I spent two enjoyable weeks in and around the capital. I made it my base from which several of my trips and excursions radiated. Putting up at a boarding house, I got much for my money and was in congenial company. It was distinctively Mexican but with my smattering of high school Spanish, I was soon on intimate terms with almost all the people.

I carried with me a letter of introduction. With that, in Mexico, one can very easily get into Mexico's best families. I was allowed scarcely an hour to myself while in the Capital. A young man from the Engineering School was my constant companion, with two or three others walking with me arm in arm. Such display of affection I never saw among new-found American friends but it was to seem common before I left the country. Though there is much formality, one comes to like it, especially when you know it is sincere.

One soon becomes impressed in traveling through Mexico without a guide and upon one's own resources with the politeness and helpfulness of the average Mexican.

One morning in the capital, I was desiring to visit the Pyramids of San Juan Teotihuacan, 28 miles north. Not knowing just how to get there by bus, I directed a simple inquiry to a public typist in the shade of an alcove. Before I left him, he had quit his work, walked a block with me and given all the information he could. Upon another day in the city of Guadalajara while in the Cathedral, I asked of a bystander if it were possible to see certain pictures within the baptistry. He took me in to see the priest and although the pictures were not there, he was instrumental in my seeing others of lesser note. Nor did I lose him until I had climbed the Cathedral tower, inspected the city museum and aided in carrying my baggage to the rail station.

On other time in Uruapan, down in the coffee country, I was trying to get information relative to a bus running to Los Reyes. A shopkeeper ceased his small task in the store, sent out a boy for information and acted as interpreter himself. I believe he would have been oblivious to customers until he had me satisfied. These few instances I think will prove one character trait of the Mexicans.

It is not possible to see everything of note in the Valley of Mexico within two weeks. I saw the Pyramids of San Juan Teotihuacan; the famous "floating gardens" of Xochimilco; La Villa, the most poplar religious shrine in the retire Republic; the Forest and Castle of Chapultepec; the National Museum and other public buildings and walked down the fine Paseo de la Reforma where several imposing statues may be seen. I heard one many say, who has traveled widely, that Mexico was the "best" city in the world. If by the word "best: he meant in interest, contrasts, beauty, health, courtesy and the many other attributes of an ideal city, I could wish to see no better city.

One of my letters of introduction was the means of my staying a week with the Hernandez family in Puebla. It is 80 miles east of the capital and is sometimes known as the Church City of Mexico, from its 300-odd churches. I enjoyed a week of amazing hospitality here. I lost account of how many Mexicans of the better class I met. I saw my first and only bullfight in

Bullfight, Puebla, Mexico

Floating Gardens of Xochimilco, Mexico

Lake Chapala, Mexico

Puebla. It made a sickening, pitying impression upon me. Near Puebla, I inspected the church-crowned Pyramid of Cholula.

Returning to the capital, I made the round-trip to the Pacific coast city of Acapulco by bus. No railroad yet enters that city. Crossing the States of Morelos and Guerrero, one sees some of the most wonderful mountain scenery in all Mexico. It is a great cacti-covered, dry and mountainous region. The road is a great credit to the people. The short curves, precipices and changing panoramas leaves the eye no chance for quiet.

At Chilpancingo, capital of Guerrero State, another letter of introduction afforded me the pleasure of meeting Senor Molino, superintendent of the Guerrero State Schools. I was shown through the city school. Night sessions were the most interesting. Children and adults were in the same class learning to read and write. It is a most encouraging sign for Mexico when the poor peon class come for miles around begging to be taught. During class time I was considerably surprised to see the director of the school light a cigarette, followed likewise by the music instructor who smoked while teaching and playing the mandolin. What would happen if an Illinois teacher smoked in class!

From the capital again, I made a brief excursion to the volcano Popocatepetl. Going horseback, the two guides and I spent a miserable night in a makeshift of a tent a short distance from perpetual snow. Sunday morning we ascended over half-way (15,000 feet) but due to the snow being so slushy and with poor foot gear, we did not continue to the crater.

Continuing west from Mexico City, I visited in close succession Lake Patzcuaro, its shores lined by Tarascan Indian Villages; Morelia;

a wonderful sunshiny city; Uruapan; north to Penjamo; thence west to Lake Chapala, the largest lake in Mexico. A fine swim left me with the feeling that I should like to live in Chapala always. The Falls of San Juancatlan were nearby, but due to the dry season being present, the sight was not so impressive. They are called "The Niagara of Mexico" and are some 70 feet high.

There were so many places I visited where I would have liked to while away a few days or weeks, that I can mention only a few: San Luis Potosi, so quiet and somnolent; Puebla; Taxco, in Guerrero; Uruapan; Patzcuaro; Lake Chapala; the west coast cities and Hermosillo; not to mention cosmopolitan Mexico City. Though often exaggerated, let me not fail to give due credit to the beauty and picturesqueness of many Mexican cities. It is true there is much squalid poverty and uncleanliness, but when seen with proper perspective, their charm cannot be given enough praise.

To me the high points of the trip were the ascent of Popocatepetl; Acapulco, the unexpectancy of the trip lending much to its pleasure; El Salto, a village near the "Falls" which seemed the farthest from home, most Mexicanized place I visited; Puebla and its hospitality and lastly Chapala. Remote and off the beaten American tourist path, I felt entirely emancipated from the workaday world.

In Mexico one will find the most modern often beside the most primitive. It is this contract which affords so many pleasant surprises. The natives were sources of constant interest as were also the markets.

Perhaps the greatest benefit derived from my Mexican journey was the dispellment of an illusion or belief concerning this exotic country. In geography class we were told that no good came from Mexico; that is was wild, half-civilized, turbulent, revolutionary and not safe to visit. Now I can say that such is not altogether true.

I think we have been prone to under estimate the Mexican character. I traveled in various ways and some remote places, but was never "knifed in the back." With the help of Domiduca, the sweet and gentle goddess, who watches over our coming home, I was delivered safety in Arizona. I think, since I have observed Mexico firsthand, that it is a nation worthy of respect and visit. She will always have a warm place in my heart. I love Mexico, I love her language, her blue mountains, her people and I hope some day to feel again her gentle breezes, her warm atmosphere and her cordiality.

—Prize winner in "Travel Contest" of
Instructor magazine, 1932.

Letter from Mexico

Guadalajara, Jalisco, Mexico
May 30, 1932

The Republican Herald
Metropolis, IL

Dear Editor:

Having been used to reading the *Republican Herald* every week, it seems like an age that I have been in Mexico and the weekly news not available. If I had a copy at this moment I think I would stop where the paper found me and read every word from cover to cover without looking up.

I have been in the Republic of Mexico a little over a month and I thought that some perhaps would be interested in just a few things about Mexico. Please excuse the personal element.

I entered the Republic via Nuevo Laredo, going thence to Monterrey, Saltillo and San Luis Potosi. My means of locomotion were various and have been during the time I have been here. Bus travel is popular where there are roads and the busses are always loaded with some hanging on the side. It was not uncommon to have for fellow passengers parrots, chickens, dogs, pigs and I expected any time to see a calf or donkey loaded in. There is not much comfort in Mexican busses.

From San Luis Potosi I went to Queretaro, Mexico City, Puebla and to the Pacific coast town of Acapulco where the temperature made me hunt the gracious shade of the plaza very early in the morning, there to remain until late evening.

At Chilpancengo, in the state of Guerrero, I had the pleasure of meeting Señor Molino, superintendent of the Guerrero schools. I was shown through the school. Night sessions are the most interesting. Children and adults are in the same class learning to read and write. It is a most encouraging sign for Mexico when the peon class come for miles around begging to be taught. During class time I was considerably surprised to see the director of the school light a cigarette, followed likewise by the music instructor who smoked while teaching and playing the mandolin. What would happen if an Illinois teacher smoked in class!

From Mexico City I made a brief excursion to the volcano Popocatepetl. Going horseback, we spent a miserable night a short distance from perpetual snow in a make-shift of a tent. Sunday morning we ascended over half way up (15,000 feet) but due to the snow being so slushy and with poor foot gear, we did not continue to the crater.

Morelia is noted for being a fine breeding place for fleas. I got acquainted with none but I did have a battle with a mosquito in Acapulco where they abound. I visited in close succession Lakes Patzcuaro and Chapala, the latter being the largest lake in Mexico. A fine swim left me with the feeling that I would like to live in Chapala always. The falls of San Juancatlan are nearby but due to the dry season begin still present, the sight was not so impressive. They are called "The Niagara of Mexico" being some 70 feet high.

In Mexico one will find the most modern beside the most primitive. The natives were sources of constant interest as were also the markets. I think we are prone to under estimate the Mexican character. I traveled by bus, rail, afoot in company with Mexicans in remote places and horseback and I have not yet been "knifed in the back" by a Mexican. I think, since I have observed and learned them first-hand, that they are a nation and a people worth of respect. Mexico is certainly a country worth visiting.

I hoped I have not overtaxed the patience of anyone reading this. I would like to see some of our people take a similar trip and arrive at the same conclusion as I have concerning Mexico; not least, of learning just how much one appreciates the good old local paper which brings the news each week.

Sincerely, your reader,
G. Wilburn May

"This Is The Forest Primeval" - Acadia

I set out June 19 with the desire and determination of reaching Acadia and the Evangeline country if the funds scrupulously saved during a term of school would admit it. Although as the crow flies the village of Grand Pré is not far as California, my circuitous route made the distance seem much greater than what it was.

Expectations formed through previous reading and study at home were so far surpassed that I am tempted perforce to extol at once the beauties of Acadia, New Brunswick and the lovely Metapedia Valley. But there were so many places I enjoyed that to pass them by would do an injustice.

Certainly, I received the thrill and triumph of my life when I set foot within the Century of Progress Exposition in Chicago, knowing that contained within it was the Past, Present and Future in many lines of endeavor. A gala scene, a world of enchantment, unfolded before my eyes an entire day. The exhibits told an absorbing story of triumph over the forces of nature. Industries showed me the evolution of their products; agriculture portrayed to me its history; humanity's progress from the old traditions to the beneficent effects of scientific discovery in ways of doing things - combating disease, living conditions, travel, education, building, religion's contributions to progress and many important movements along recreational, economical, criminal justice and other cultural lines. The buildings struck me as being truly original in form. The Travel and Transport Building, windowless and with sky-hung dome, pleased me most. In design it seemed to me the most daring and original innovation of the entire Exposition to observe the newest in transportation; then compare with the older; to study the largest Canadian map in the world; to pass through the Royal Scot; these features alone gave to the trip its full value. The Federal and States Pavilion interested me a close second.

I followed the well-kept King's Highway to Toronto where the Canadian National Exhibition was to be held in August and September. The scenery along the shore line was beguiling. I slept one night within hearing distance of the gentle, lapping Lake Ontario. As evening drew on and the countryside became subdued with the lengthening shadows, I felt that its memory must be enhanced by a night along its moonlit shores.

The insular labyrinth of the Thousand Islands is my Elysium. Someone has said of them, "This sylvan maze suggests a multitude of gorgeous jewels studding a shield of turquoise blue." Nearby, I visited the city of Kingston and old Fort Frontenac.

My entrance into Ottawa marked the realization of a long desire: to visit the capitals (and capitols) of our three greatest neighbors, Canada, Cuba and Mexico. A most wonderful view lies under the eye, viewed from the clock tower of the House of Parliament. The sinuous course of the noble Ottawa River vied with the city along its banks for my attention. I was meditating from my vantage point, that here, even as late as the Revolutionary War, Ottawa was a wilderness, the river itself being the sole and practical route for the furs of the Hurons and Algonquins. The government edifice itself is imposing in architecture. The library impressed me with its order, quiet and elegance.

I was first struck with the provincial French character of this part of Canada upon entering Montreal. One night enabled me to secure a vivid, if hasty, impression of the metropolis, the largest in Canada. I strolled along St. James Street. Notre Dame Church, facing the Place d' Armes, is a replica of that in Paris. I found "Old Montreal" tucked away near the St. Lawrence River. Mount Royal loomed behind the city. Many statues and groups in the public square gave it a distinctive French atmosphere. Immediately, I compared Montreal with the Vieux Carré of New Orleans. The following day the "Lower Town" of Quebec also was to remind me of our southern city.

Quebec! What memories that name conjures up! It seems to me that Columbus could not have scanned the vast expanse of sea for a sign of land with more avid eye than I as I neared that historic city. Many have repeated, "No traveler can forget the view which greets him of Quebec." No such writer as I can portray Quebec worthily. It is a city of various parts. The 350 feet of almost sheer height is possessing. Church and state have remains upon its summit. No only that, but is base is grilled with a live and by no means unprogressive city. My best view of Quebec was from St. Levis, across the river. Quebec is practically an ocean port for the salt of the Atlantic penetrates the St. Lawrence within 21 miles of the city. Travelers agree that the grandeur of Quebec lies, first, in the gift of God, its situation; second, in the work of man - its stately terrace and imposing citadel.

I found Quebec one of the queerest cities in which to get around that I ever saw. Situated on cliffs (Upper Town) and up the valley of the River, St. Charles and the Cape Diamond littoral (Lower Town), the streets circle around in order to arrive at the two sections, making it difficult for one, a stranger, to keep his bearings. Mountain Hill is the most frequented thoroughfare between the two sections. It is very circuitous. "Break-Neck Stairs" is the most direct route for pedestrians.

To me, Lower Quebec was not beautiful. It was a labyrinth of lanes, dingy houses and squalor. It is practical but picturesque and replete with France. The characteristic vehicle is the caléche, a two-wheeled affair drawn by one horse. I admired the Upper Town most. Quebec's finest buildings are the world-famous hostelry Chateau Frontenac and the cannon-belted Citadel, which covers 40 acres, I was told.

Seen from a height at night and in deep quiet, historic memories swept over me and since, as Stoddard says, all history is little more than magnified biography, I called to mind the mighty dead connected with the place: Frontenac; Laval, the priest; Wolfe, Montcalm, Cartier,

Montgomery and the founder of Quebec, Champlain, whose monument is on Dufferin Terrace.

Northeast, along the south shore of the St. Lawrence, lay my route through a country preeminently French-Canadian. My eyes scanned the shore and the constantly-changing landscape to my right. This was the land of the "habitant," the rural people. Even a cursory view indicated feudal vestiges. The farms have been in the same family often for several generations. The fields have little frontage along the way, but extend many rods back. Here I saw a lazy windmill, there a white-washed stone manor. The habitants have quiet, tree-embowered streets in the little villages; small, steep-roofed, wooden houses in their villages and a church that would do justice to a town three times it size. The habitant has changed under modern conditions but I saw oxen, the old road-side, French oven and ancient houses that still possess the distinctive French atmosphere.

The scenic splendors of this unspoiled land increased as I neared Rimouski. On my left the calm St. Lawrence stretched to an unseen shore; on my right arose, across the intervening fields of the habitants, the tree-covered Notre Dame Mountains. Arriving in Rimouski for the evening meal, I was treated with a courtesy that defied belief.

It was at St. Flavie that the railroad turned south, leaving the Gaspé Peninsula to the left and having reached the divide, entered the lovely Matapedia Valley. It was then that I entered what I am pleased to call "The forest primeval." To me the forest primeval (though not what it was in the time that the events of Evangeline transpired, nor even in Longfellow's day) includes all Maritime Canada, eastern Quebec and the state of Maine. Forests of balsam, fir, black and white spruce, pine, hemlock, cedar, tamarack, birch, oak and ash clothe the hills and mountains with verdure. Down the tracks or along the highway they form borders to vistas of unparalleled beauty. The forest was one of the most pleasing features and will longest and most vividly characterize the entire trip.

Lake Matapedia is a most entrancing body of water. Val Brilliant, Salmon Lake, Assametquaghan and Matapedia are little villages nestling among scenic hills. The road hugged the hill-bordered Matapedia River. There was room enough only for railroad, highway and river. Rising as it does from the lake, I was able to follow the Matapedia River from its source to its mouth in ever-widening breadth, even into Matapedia Bay and from there into the Chaleurs Bay. The latter is aptly called the "Mediterranean of North American." Its many bays are bounded by beautiful beaches, their peerless beauty accompanied by rare scenery.

I remained overnight in Bathurst, New Brunswick. The entire province is an incomparable fishing ground. The next day I passed through what seemed an endless forest. Newcastle, Moncton, Amherst, Truro and Halifax came by stages, the scenery diminishing none in beauty and picturesqueness. A peculiar natural feature was experienced near Amherst when crossing the narrow isthmus, when ocean fogs enveloped everything and cold began to be felt by the passengers. Before one enters Truro a most pleasing country is Folleigh near Folleigh Lake, Folleigh Mountain and along the Folleigh River.

Half of my journey was now completed for I was in Acadia. I spent a few hours in Halifax before continuing to Grand Pré. The beauty and security of Halifax harbor are world famous. The citadel approaches 300 feet in height. The view along the shore of the inner basic attracted me most.

Evangeline is truly the Flower of American romance. How much more is the story appreciated after a visit to the scene of that fateful Sept. 5, 1755. Approximately 2,000 souls were exiled; almost 700 buildings including the church were destroyed; thousands of domestic animals confiscated. It was September 10 that Gabriel and Evangeline were separated and spent the rest of their lives with the consuming desire to meet one another again.

The present people have imagination and archeological enterprise enough to indicate places mentioned in the story. The dikes, willows and apple trees are surer relics. The tremendous tides of the Bay of Fundy are still kept out by the dikes. As I surveyed the countryside I saw that Longfellow's description was adequate and in no way inaccurate.

The Dominion Atlantic Evangeline Park borders the railroad and is maintained by it for the public. A road leads upward a short distance to Grand Pré Post Office. Still farther along, one enters the main highway.

Harbor of Halifax, Nova Scotia

I entered the well-kept park to spend many minutes in quiet survey. On the east side is the site of the Acadian Church of St. Charles 1687-1755. Going westward, I saw Evangeline's Well, the Burying Grounds, the very old, decrepit Acadian willows and the Chapel Yard where Winslow's troops were encamped in 1755.

Near the center of Memorial Park is the Acadian Memorial Hall erected in 1922 by the Acadian National Society. Within 3 feet of the hall is part of the millstone of the original Acadian Community Grist Mill, found on the Dominion property. This stone is French granite, Brought over from France by the Acadians.

On the west side of Memorial Hall is the site of Priest's House and Winslow's headquarters. To the front (south) of the Hall is the Acadian Road to the diked meadows and to the church. The status of Evangeline (of a dark, almost black color, caused by the elements) is in front and south of the Hall some 50 yards. It is a remarkable statue in that when viewed from the left side you see buoyant youth and happiness; but from the right side she is seen as a mature woman, lagging in step, heartbroken and discouraged.

I visited Grand Pré in the early morning.

"Peace seemed to reign upon earth and the heart of the ocean,
Was for a moment consoled. All sounds were in harmony
blended."

The birds were singing, cocks crowed, sheep were bleating, the sun shone brightly through a few fleecy cirrus clouds stretched overhead and domestic work was going on tranquilly. The apple trees had only recently shed their white bridal dress. There was a cool, salty tang of the sea, touched by a delicate aroma of balsam and pine.

Along the shores of Fundy Bay this inviting country continued. There was Acadia University in Wolfville; the old fort in Annapolis Royal, much of the fortification plans remaining extant and Digby Basin. The American and British flags few in Digby on Dominion Day. I stayed with people on Prince Williams Street who showered hospitality upon me. It was in the "Gap" on the *Princess Helene* that I bade good-bye to Digby. Soon we were tossing about in the rough Bay of Fundy, watching the shores of Nova Scotia fade into blue indistinct. So assured a place in my affections has Acadia secured that it is my wish that I may return.

I must place my praise upon the state of Maine as well as New Brunswick and Nova Scotia. Booth Tarkington once said of Maine: "To my mind Maine is the most beautiful state we have in this country, but even more appealing is its homeliness. It is easier for a stranger to feel at home in Maine that in almost any other place I ever knew." He voices my sentiments precisely. The view along the way of rivers, sequestered lakes and forest-clad hills was altogether too fleeting. The Penobscot, Kennebec and Piscataqua were beguiling as well as being historic. Portland had a beauty all its own.

The historical associations of Boston; the towering architectural giants of New York City; Philadelphia, our second national capital; Baltimore and the old Fort McHenry and Providence, where I particularly enjoyed myself, made more vivid the realization of the greatness of our Eastern States. Not least in scenic beauty was the ride over the mountains of Pennsylvania into Pittsburgh.

Last, but by no means least, was Washington. If no thrill of pride and patriotism sweeps over the countryman as he views Washington Monument, the Capitol, the Lincoln Memorial and the various other government edifices, that American's heart is indeed dead. The few hours were not enough to fully satisfy the consuming desire, which I had always had, to see our nation's capital.

It is always difficult to synthesize one's experiences of a trip into an inclusive summary. Time, reflection and recurrent memory enhance the values and joys. However, I must make the attempt. In the light of my experiences, the Century of Progress Exposition was Progress in epitome. The lovely forests dominate in my thoughts of New Brunswick and Maine. Courtesy, subdued beauty and peace characterize Acadia. And finally Washington should be the desired and legitimate goal of every person in this great nation of ours.

—Prize winner in the "Travel Contest" of
Instructor magazine, 1933.

Summering In Queensland's Winter

Why do I want to visit Queensland? The old saw "Birds of a feather flock together" might well be applied to us teachers. I want to visit Queensland chiefly because I want to meet an old teacher-friend in Ipswich whom I have never seen, but we have corresponded for years.

I would steam the 18 miles up the river and anchor in the heart of Brisbane. I would proceed at once to my old friend's home. We would talk professional a while. I am sure I would be interested to learn about the educational system of the state.

Of course we would hurry back to downtown Brisbane, "the garden city of Australia," where we would visit the Queen's Garden, profligate with colors in rare abandon. We would take the Jacaranda Drive to New Farm Park. Queensland! I want to see her rich pastures, farms, rich lands and deserts; the various phases of sheep-raising work; the fishers of Coolangatta, the veritable fairyland of the scrub; tall trees laden with rich orchids; exotic plant life, moss-grown rock ferns and palms; Australia's monarchs of the forest. I want to get a glimpse of the "Far West," so much different from coastal Queensland; where rivers are only strings of water holes and ribbons of sand; where the coolibah and swamp gum live on; where the Leichhardt River flows.

I shall jest at Queensland's winter, where the winter wears the guise of spring. But short days and chilly westerly winds swirling through the streets may change my conception. At Southport I shall winter-surf and sun myself in the land-locked haven where ocean, bay and river meet. I shall feel the mystic spell of the sea. The nearby mountain resorts of Tamborine and Springbrook will beguile me.

With my congenial friend ever with me, we shall visit Raining Falls in National Park, at Binna Burra, where we shall see the waterfall's delicate veil. Rockhampton Gardens, Tully Falls, Barron Gorge, Glasshouse Mountains, the new university of Queensland, the palm-lined roadway of Eungella Range and the curious Egg Rock formation in Upper Nerang Valley - all will be seen. At Redlands I shall see strawberries ripening from June to December. From my interest in the fruit (I grow them) I would like to see how Queensland grows them.

As the winter draws to a close (and my summer), I shall see, rather hurriedly, Sydney with its maze of water passages, rock quarries, Fellmonger Shops, the winding streets, reminiscent of Boston and the famous Domain Park. I might get to run over to Jenolan Caves, across the Blue Mountains, where I would be in a scenic sanctuary. Last of all I would want to visit Canberra, a capital city made to order.

Would I enjoy such a summer? Better than anything else I can think of.

—Received Honorable Mention in
Instructor magazine contest, 1940.

What My Travels Have Meant To Me As An Individual And As A Teacher

"The world belongs to him who has seen it." While this aphorism may not be literally true, yet anyone who has returned from a journey must feel that it is applicable to him in some degree. Cultural benefits merge into or overlap practical, classroom and community values.

Everything which I intend to say, though couched in the third person, has definite application to me. As Bacon advises, I have seen churches, monuments, walls and fortifications, havens, harbors, ruins, libraries, colleges, shipping, houses and gardens of state and pleasure near great cities, armories, exchanges, warehouses and other things memorable in the places where I have traveled. These things alone are cultural and cause one to feel the world is his own. We may have read but "the reality will burst on us like a revelation."

I have never traveled abroad but I have learned much of the real life, thought and customs of our neighbors: Cuba, Canada, Mexico and of our own country. I see the "habitant" on the St. Lawrence; the plodding Cuban and Mexican peon; the sheep herder high on the slopes of Popocatepetl; and I can more nearly approach his outlook on life. Illusions have been dispelled. Distorted perspectives have been righted and mental pictures cleared or sharpened. I have a deeper interest and warmer sympathy for the people of those places mentioned and I hope for the peoples of other countries that I later may visit. This love for other countries is much needed in the present desire for universal peace. If everyone traveled and gained love for the places and peoples one saw, we would, have no wars. There must be a personal contact to know, understand and love other nations.

This broad and sympathetic understanding relates to natural phenomena as well. The attitudes and materials gained enables us to look on with a many-sided understanding. Strange lands foreign shops, schools, streets, theaters, homes and the exotic atmosphere of certain places make it necessary that we have this quality. It prevents undue local egotism. Once I thought my Ohio River was the widest in a world because I had always lived on its shores and seen no other.

Literary characters seem to live by my having visited literary scenes. Western novels glow with descriptions of the West that I have seen. Tom Sawyer lives for me in Hannibal, Mo. Evangeline is as real as any Joan of Arc heroine. Mexico City conjures up what seem true memories of Wallace's Fair God; the brown people I saw there were figures in the story. The eastern States are a veritable mine of literary associations.

Another value of travel is the realization of dreams and desires which, if never realized, might lead to a travel "inferiority complex" and thus hinder the teacher's proper mental development. All of us, who have a consuming desire to see the world, must of necessity have this complex to some extent. I shall have it until I have seen the six continents. But since seeing four countries on only one continent, my complex has been dispelled appreciably.

History has been stamped deeper in my memory. The Battle above the Clouds is more real after a climb up Lookout Mountain. The Vicksburg Battle ground impresses one. I have visualized Grant and Jackson in their homes. I have walked with Lincoln in Springfield, Old Salem, Hodgenville, Washington and other places within his own Illinois, New Orleans, Montreal, Quebec and Acadia recall the French. I have viewed the overcoming natural difficulties of the Westward Movement. I visited the scene of one of those tragedies, the Donner party in California where the snow fell upon them a score of feet in depth. Havana is famous for its harbor alone. The bones of Columbus are supposed at one time to have reposed in the Cathedral. I viewed the monument erected in memory of the destruction of the Maine. I felt myself on sacred historical ground in Massachusetts, Rhode Island, Connecticut, New York and the cities of Washington and Philadelphia. Cortez, the conqueror of Mexico, was in my memory in the Capital and in Cuernavaca. The Great Pyramid of Egypt could hardly be more impressive than the Pyramid of the Sun in Mexico. It is an ancient, prehistoric relic. I have seen in fancy the Mound Builders of the Ohio and Mississippi valleys while surveying their works. The Lewistown Mounds and Burial Grounds in Illinois gave me my first view of prehistoric remains.

A visit to any of these places has a practical as well as a cultural value. In general, one's horizon is broadened, historically, socially geographically and ethically. One returns home with a distinct sense of fulfillment, achievement and triumph.

When one crosses our southern border into mañana land, a very valuable trait is either manifested or found lacking in the visitor: self-adaptation. There is good discipline in this adaptation to the accommodations to the country through which one is traveling.

Transportation will perhaps not be as good across the Rio Grande, nor in other countries; food is prepared and served in a different manner; the food itself is new; money must be exchanged and its use learned; conduct must be and will be conditioned; even dress will change, due either to style, seasons, attitude or prevailing weather conditions. More in rural Cuba and Mexico will this power of adaptation be called into action.

So much for the increased cultural background. For the teacher, the industries, people and current life should make for personal powers in the classroom. I can make a greater appeal with what I have learned of the commercial and industrial life of our great American cities of Canada, Mexico, Cuba and the various sections of our own country. Relating my experiences with the aid of post cards, photographs and travel literature for opening exercises, gets the pupil to school on time to avoid missing what I have to say or show in the way of souvenirs. I bring to the classroom coins, books in Spanish, a Mexican serape, pressed flowers, postage stamps and other things to show the children. Not only do they take great delight in the relation of my experiences, but also they are amused by my Spanish readings. In grammar I try to get them to understand English construction by contrast with the Spanish.

With the exception of the Ozarks, I have traveled over the entire Evangeline country: Nova Scotia, Louisiana, Arkansas, Michigan the Ohio and Mississippi valleys and Philadelphia. This has given me a deeper interest in the story, a greater vividness, an interest which can be transferred more easily to the children in their reading.

An unusual appeal may be made, in my own case, when the Florida Keys (of which children in general have only a hazy idea), the Great American Desert (after having crossed it, along with Great Salt Lake), the sand dunes of southern California and the serrated mountains of Mexico, are colored by personal experience. None of my school children have ever seen the ocean and few of the parents; hence, the sea and the sights have become more real to them. I give work based upon my trips and up and down Illinois, over the home county and in the various states of the Union in which I have traveled. I wish the children, along with me, to feel more fully the sentiment of that fine song *America the Beautiful*.

Community contacts have been widened and enriched. I have met people who wanted to talk with me about my travels. People in the community become more conversant. I addressed a county teachers' meeting for 45 minutes on Cuba and Mexico. I do not think I am conceited nor vain when I say it was listened to with undivided attention. This receiving sincere attention over the community aided in dispelling that already mentioned inferiority complex, which I customarily have among people. In this instance a superiority complex was more comforting, if not more worthy than the former state of mind.

The practical value of travel in the way of financial return does not always obtain. I have received no promotion nor increase in salary, but I will not be surprised that in later years the travel experiences, excepting misfortune, will, in part, bring this to pass. However, I do think that this travel experience, emphasized in my application for a school, had great weight in my securing the school.

One of the major reasons for traveling, especially among teachers, is for pleasure itself. I have always had strength and good health. Nothing could improve perceptibly either one. But it is the spirit that most often needs regaining. Following a trip I take on a new zeal; I am buoyant; I am exhilarated after a vigorous and attentive seeking for some of the better things of life.

Paradoxical as it may seem, one of the greatest pleasures of travel is the return. Home has beckoned to me on every trip. With Wordsworth, not until then did I know what love I bore "to thee."

I have obtained viewpoints of other peoples upon America. A Canadian up in Quebec gave me the British view on the war debts; a Mexican of the middle class told me the bullfight was a more humane sport than the American prize fight. Other peoples cause us to re-examine our own customs.

Another practical value is contact with people within the locality one travels. There are the Mormons in Utah, the Quakers in Philadelphia, the mountaineers of Tennessee, the hospitality of old Kentucky, a particular priest in Quebec whom I met, the fisherman in Maritime Canada and the peon in Mexico I talked with. Men in many walks of life (even a radical I W W) I have conversed with and secured ideas that perhaps I never would have gotten at home.

One of the most novel and practical experiences I ever had was a visit to the Federal School in Chipancingo, Guerrero, Mexico. My conception of a vitalized school was measurably increased.

Travel enables one to follow current events with more understanding and appreciation. To cite an instance: the Cuban Revolution in August (1931) of this year meant more to me after having been in Havana, trod its ground and heard the people even two years before, half-secretly denounce President Machado.

A last value derived from traveling 3,000 miles through Mexico, a value which I do not wish to overlook, was improvement in the Spanish language. It is an idiom adulterated with the patois of the various people. I think I improved my use of the language.

As I have intimated, these practical values merge into increased community contacts, a more vitalized classroom and ultimately into some of the phases of an enriched culture.

Anticipation, realization and recollection are all these phases of any journey, one scarcely to be listed over the other in importance. Through my ramblings I have come as near as I ever expect to get, or would wish, to drama, romance, glamour and mystery. Things seen on a hasty journey are often rediscovered in later years. Pictures we have taken, our souvenirs and our memories, rich and cherished, afford an inexhaustible delight. With Kirke White I can say: "My fond heart reverts to daydreams of the summer gone."

—Received Honorable Mention in
Instructor magazine, 1950.

'Hanging Loose' In Hawaii

Fortified by travel folders and James Michner's *Hawaii*, the wife and I boarded the plane at Peoria at 7:00 a.m. on a bright October day and, after a change to United Airlines at Chicago, we were on our way to Hawaii. We were booked for a two-week, four-island escorted tour, but we opted to take our meals on our own, always having preferred such freedom on other journeys when possible.

"The Enchanted Isles," "The Playground of the Pacific," especially Waikiki, were terms learned from early school days, this reality only now to verify what we had only imagined.

Hilo was our gateway to this fascinating land, where we put down at 1:30 p.m. Hilo time, same day, and put up at the Hilo Lagoon Hotel. Our efforts now were but to soften our superlatives in our conversation.

Hawaii has many faces and it depends upon who is asked the question as to the answers. A dozen different people are likely to give the same number of different opinions. May this be more than a pedestrian narrative, nor may it be overly ecstatic. It is hard, however, to restrain one's self when speaking of Hawaii and the difficulty rather increases as the years go by and nostalgia creeps in to color impressions.

The Big Island is known as "the volcano island" or "the orchid isle" and was our introduction to the wonderful chain of islands. We boarded a bus at the Lagoon Hotel for the day's excursion. The first thing our general tour director, Howard Yoshida, had said and Ken, our driver, repeated was the advice "hang loose" and "throw away your neckties."

Our first stop was in Volcano National Park, which is the island's biggest attraction and where we viewed the lava beds or fire pits of Kilauea Crater, steam, lava, sulfur, a faint picture of Dante's Hell. Still active, the last eruption was in November 1975. The crater rim drive was 11 miles. A boardwalk included the Thurston Lava Tube, which is

Rainbow Falls, Hilo, Hawaii

a tunnel through which once poured streams of fiery lava. Dead now and the outside area clothed in the lush, verdant growth of the fern forest. We paused at the Volcano House and the Visitor Center. I forebear to speak of the legend of Pele, goddess of the volcanoes; the first appearance of man on the islands; the later arrival of the haole or foreigner or, today, the "white man." Our previous reading and our guide related the history.

Returning, we stopped at Mauna Loa Orchid Gardens, where *leis* were being made. All along we saw sugar and pineapple fields, vegetables, bananas, cattle and much more. Flowers were in profusion; hibiscus, plumria, poinciana, birds of paradise, lehua, orchids and others were to meet our eyes on the four islands. We passed through a number of small towns, including Kalapana and Pahoa and Black Sands Beach. Finally, we saw the rainbows of Rainbow Falls, near Hilo. I thought of Minnehaha Falls in Minneapolis at the moment—some resemblance.

We took a 30 minute flight via Hawaiian Airlines to the Kona coast, skirting the slopes of Mauna Loa at 12,000 feet to get over the rain clouds, a rain which had plagued us during much of the morning. We lodged in King Kamehameha Hotel in the town of Kailua, on the coast and at the foot of Hualalai Mountain.

The Kona Coast is the Big Island's "classic charm spot." We walked along Alii Drive, the main street, pausing at the various shops, seeing the Huilea Summer Palace, the oldest church (Makuaikaua) and other things. There was a lazy, restful atmosphere about the town.

The hotel holds a *luau* (native feast) four nights weekly. All guests are welcome, but one goes attired casually in aloha shirts (men) and muumuus (women) dresses and *lei* around the neck. After the day's adventures the wife and I were too tired to go, besides having already eaten our supper on our own. This day was my 68th birthday.

The next day we took a cruise to the Captain Cook Memorial southward, on Kealakekua Bay, on the "Captain Cook VII," a glass-bottomed ship through which we viewed fish. A school of dolphins also amused us. High, rocky cliffs arose from Cook's monument, cliffs with holes or caves where the old Hawaiians secretly buried their dead. Here Cook was killed by the natives. This two hours at sea greatly pleased us.

Hawaii's unique Kona coffee is the result of a combination of favorable features. Kona is sheltered from the northeast trade winds by the towering mountains to the east and the town is usually calm, fanned by wispy, off-shore breezes and rather dry. Above 1200 feet lush vegetation appears. The soil is just right. This combination has given Kona a languid, timeless, tropical serenity in which the magnificent coffee has been cultivated for more than a century. Mark Twain said of it in 1866: "I think Kona coffee has a richer flavor than any other..." It is the only place in the United States where coffee is produced commercially. But the famous coffee alone would not support the economy.

As a *malihina* (newcomer) and a coffee drinker, the wife was one who could appreciate the high quality of Kona coffee. Later, at the Ala Mona Market in Honolulu, we had a can of Kona and a tray of tins of macadamia nuts shipped to our home. Not a drinker, I settled for cones of superb macadamia ice cream.

We made a 17-minute flight to the island of Maui, passing over the mountains and landing at Kahului airport near the town of Wailuku. Approaching Maui we saw from aloft the deserted Kahoolawe Island where the US Military set up target practice in the 1940s and a bit farther west, on our left, the pineapple island of Lanai, much of which is under the Dole Company control.

Maui, "the valley island," close to, if not first, the most popular of all the Hawaiian chain, "the very essence of Hawaii," is serviced by three airports, Kahului being the one most used. Mt. Haleakala (10,023 feet) and crater dominate the eastern part of Maui, 30 miles from Kahului. We did not visit Haleakala National Park but many tourists do so.

From the plane we boarded a bus at once and toured Wailuku and

Iao Needle, Maui, Hawaii

environs. The unique green-clad Iao Beedle is a curious peak 2,250 feet above the historic valley. The long drive continued across the neck of Maui and along the southwestern coast, through the towns of Maalaea, Kihei and Wailea. We saw much sugar cane, many flowers, strange trees and Japanese and Portuguese gardens, the sea in sight most of the way. The soil was red or gray and fertile. We backtracked and drove west on past Lahaina a few miles and put up at the Kaanapali Beach Hotel in the resort area on the sea. Here was the Whalers Village Museum and a shopping complex. In the evening we picked up coral on the beach. A late evening rainbow appeared on the mountainside, followed by a light, misty rain.

The birds (mynah ?) awakened us through the window and we readied for a full day in Lahaina.

Lahaina is a seaport town where Hawaiian royalty, lusty whalers and staid New England missionaries once made history. It is ideal for exploring. The town lies flat, clinging to the shoreline for two miles, but only four blocks deep. Mountains lie behind the city and offshore lies Lanai Island. Front Street is the principal thoroughfare, along which are located the Yacht Club, Brick Palace, the wharf, the Baldwin Home Museum, Whalers Market Place, the old courthouse and the venerable banyan tree which shades three-fourths of an acre. The old Prison House still stands on Prison Street.

We rode from the resort area to downtown Lahaina on the little Sugar Cane Train, the worlds smallest railroad, a replica of the 36-inch gauge road which used to haul sugar cane to the coast.

Lahaina! "always sunny," "west Maui's magic town," a city of 5,000 inhabitants, where Herman Melville, Robert Louis Stevenson, Mark Twain, Jack London and Somerset Maughan spent time and where today a host of movie and TV faces show up.

We walked and gawked all day, seeing various features of Lahaina and when exhausted sat under the ancient banyan tree and rested.

As I half dozed, the thought came that my first mandolin was made of koa wood, grown in Hawaii. But I also had read, perhaps in Michener, that koa were certain fishing grounds off the Lahaina coast. What was the connection? None as far as I could see.

Tired, napping and musing went together under the tree. Lahaina was like a lazy, little Mexican pueblo on a warm day. This languorous dreamy frame of mind was a subtle intoxicant, as if of mesmerism. Was the spell of Hawaii beginning to take over? I think the wife was also yielding to the spell of Lahaina, an effect without exertion.

The birds roosted next to our hotel lanai (balcony) and the booming ocean waves that night rather brought sleep quickly than as a delayer of sleep.

The view of Oahu island from the airplane was magnificent. Below us lay Honolulu, Waikiki and, of course, Diamond Head, the mountains behind the capital city and Pearl Harbor. We boarded our bus at the airport and toured the area until past four o'clock. Then we circled to the Punch Bowl, a dead volcanic crater in the foothills of the Koolau Mountains, with a panoramic view of matchless beauty to be enjoyed

Fern Grotto, Kauai, Hawaii

and never forgotten of Honolulu and Waikiki below. In the National Punchbowl Cemetery lie 27,000 bodies, including that of the famed Ernie Pyle.

Our hotel was the Hilton Hawaiian Village composed of three hi-rise sections, 17 stories high. Our room was number 678 in the Diamond Head wing where our view of the ocean was unfortunately restricted.

Waikiki is dubbed "the playground of the Pacific." We did not play in the usual sense: shows, bars, swimming, surfing, etc., but we did a lot of walking and seeing. The busiest streets are Kalakawa Avenue and the nearby Kappahula Avenue. Our tour director, Howard, took us aboard a bus the second day and we toured downtown Honolulu, with frequent pauses at choice spots. We ended at the Ala Moana Shopping Center located near the mouth of the Ala Wai Canal and which surrounds most of Waikiki. Here we made various purchases and the wife even bought a muumuu (probably unwearable in our rural home, community).

Followed our various rambles about Waikiki afoot. We walked toward Diamond Head, stopped in Kapaioani Park and ran through the nearby zoo. We viewed the free Kodak Hula Show, with music of a haunting, off-beat tempo. We retraced our way along Kalakaua Avenue and went into the colorful International Trade Center. Here we ate ice cream at Farell's Ice Cream Parlor with its gay, old-fashioned look. A bamboo shack rests 15 feet high in the spreading branches of a banyan tree. All so romantic to pass through this large market! I concluded my day by a brief swim at the beach. It was a long time that I had felt as well, though comfortably tired. Perhaps it was the swim.

Sunday morning we walked to Kewale Basin and boarded the *Adventurer,* a 3-deck boat, bound for Pearl Harbor. We threaded the winding bay, passing through the three locks and seeing the sites of several ships sunk by the Japanese on December 7, 1941 and at last got off the boat and stood on the famous *Arizona* Memorial. Returning, the *Adventurer* stood out farther and the rough billows frequently sprayed us. It was a very fine ride.

That night we attended services at the Waikiki Baptist Church, 424 Kuamoo Street, near the Ala Wai Canal. We ended the day with a pint of ice cream in our room. (Hawaiian ice cream beats Illinois cream all hollow!).

Wife and I "made" downtown next day afoot for over three hours.

Honolulu! "There is no place like it," say many people. "It is alone, a luscious charmer of a town," says the writer Eddie Sherman. Again, he exclaims: "warm, beautiful, wonderful Honolulu."

We saw the *Falls of Clyde,* an old 4-masted ship in the harbor and the adjacent Aloha Tower. We made a few blocks around Chinatown. Then to the group of buildings a bit east and inland away from the sea. Included is the state capitol. Congress at 10:04 a.m., March 18, 1959, officially passed the Hawaii Statehood Bill and a great celebration was quickly held in the city. It is a curious structure in that it sits on pylons in shallow water where fish dart about. Adjacent is the Ioian Palace of the early Hawaiian rulers. Adjacent also is the Judiciary or State Supreme Court with a "gold" statue of King Kamehameha I in front, Hawaii's greatest ruler. We saw other points of interest in this area. We walked back to Hotel Street, along King Street; ate fish and drank milkshakes at Woolworth's; took a bus to the Ala Moana Center and walked the mile back to our hotel. If this be only a pedestrian narrative, certainly it was a pedestrian tour.

Kauai is perhaps the most spectacular of the Hawaiian islands— beaches, deep valleys, canyons, great vistas, the wettest area on earth— "your single most urgent destination." Says William Meredith: "It is a place to live when you are reconciled to beauty and unafraid of time," and: "One is menaced only by surf and flowers and palm." The first Japanese in 1902 "saw the full grandeur of Hawaii." Known affectionately as "the garden island," the land is verdantly lush with roots in red soil. A map of Kauai resembles an emerald in contour. Thus, Ireland must share its name Emerald Isle.

It was a 30-minute flight to Kauai. Howard had the bus waiting and we went up the east coast to Wailua. Here we boarded a boat on the Wailua River, Hawaii's only navigable stream and proceeded to Fern Grotto, located amidst a jungle growth of tree ferns and other exotic foliage. Here native people played music and sang. Small but vigorous ferns draped the caverns entrance. Here, in this romantic setting many marriages are performed. The musicians rendered many songs of Hawaii as we slowly descended the river on the return. There were three hula dances by a good-looking, slim, brown-skinned young girl. Not being familiar with Hawaiian songs, I did not know the titles sung. They may have rendered *Hawaiian Wedding Song, Lovely Hula Hands, Blue Hawaii, Hawaiian War Chant* or any of numerous others and I forget if they announced the titles or not. I want to highlight that this day on the river was the best single feature for me of the entire Hawaii tour. Just so, I want to digress a bit upon Hawaiian music.

There are some 13 basic instruments (pipes, rattles, drums, etc.)

used in the hula dance but our boat group used only ukuleles and guitars, as well as I recall. "Music is the most famous face of Hawaii," says Bob Krauss. It has magic for many people because of its emotional impact. But how authentic is the music? Is it all phony? Take most any hillbilly howler, says Sherman, slow the beat, strain most of the noise out of it and you have it. Even so, back home in New York, this same music came back to him as a charming message. True, many Hawaiian songs were composed by outsiders. But the music is a joy to one who has tasted it. Possessing aloha shirts and muumuu skirts, good looks and infective smiles, the Hawaiian is born with a singing voice and ukuleles or guitars under their arms (Kane). These cherished melodies, whatever their origin, "passionate evocation of the islands," belong to Hawaii. Because the songs evoke "unashamed nostalgia," the Hawaiian breathe into them depths of emotion. Maybe that's the reason Hawaiians are natural musicians. I found them haunting, nostalgic, like *My Old Kentucky Home* and the other Stephen Foster songs.

Off the excursion boat, we bussed to visit the Opaikaa Falls, a thin stream but pretty. Next was Coconut Grove, the island's oldest coconut plantation and a pause at some ancient sacrificial rocks. The final stop was at our Beachboy Hotel, a fine landscaped place right on the reef-booming sea. From our lanai we could view the "Sleeping Giant" mountain, reminiscent of Mexico's sleeping lady profile of Mt. Iztaccihuatl.

The following day we went to Weimea Canyon under the jovial driver Billy Ouye. On our way to the mountains we saw much sugar cane, taro and rice. We saw the profile of Queen Victoria on a mountain. We passed through Koloa, Hanapepe, Poipu and Waimea. At Eleeie we looked into the deep gorge. We saw the Spouting Horn (crevices in the sea rock which sprays and makes a continual blowing noise). At last, at Weimea Canyon, we gazed into and across the awesome depths.

In the late afternoon at Beachboy we enjoyed a hula show on the lawn by a performing group, Hawaiians, New Zealanders and Tahitians. The little girl, 6 or 8 years old, took the cake for perfection and charm.

The next morning I took a four-mile walk to Wailua and paused at Pahaku Ho' Ohanau, an ancient sacrifice spot and the Birthstone Rock where a baby was placed for four days and, if surviving the test, would become king or chief. Returning, a misty rain threatened and I saw rainbows over the Sleeping Giant. The same day we saw another hula dance.

At 8:30 p.m. we flew to Honolulu and at the International Airport we bid *aloha* to Hawaii.

Just as one at day's end and lying in bed reviews the events of the day, so the returned traveler mentally repeats his adventures. For many days colorful Hawaii will be revisited. Those glamorous islands, that legendary paradise, the balmy airs and the breath of flowers will linger. If one did not find quite the romance one expected, it must be agreed that this amalgamation of peoples is something singularly intriguing. It is the secret of the charm. Truly, says Krauss, "Hawaii is more than a place to live; it is a *way* to live." My high spots were, in order: Fern Grotto, Lahaina and Kona, with the Kilauea Crater, Waikiki and Pearl Harbor trailing.

However all is said and done, I would not want to live in Hawaii permanently. Prices are very high for about every service or commodity. The sameness of temperature lacks the excitement of the change of seasons as in Illinois. Would not one become satiated with the exotic, carefree life? Retired, I would be under no necessity to work. Life must pall upon Hawaiians sometimes, as it does with the rest of us. One cannot live upon praise and beauty alone, daily and forever. On little Kauai would not claustrophobia became a possibility? But the beauty and spectacular contrasts and the many faces that greet one at every turn might prevent it; might transcend the hazard. Yeah, not altogether facetiously, there are coconuts that fall upon one's head! And there are other negatives to a permanent residence in the islands.

"There is a chain of islands,
Out in the deep blue sea,
Where the trade winds gently rustle,
Through the fern and Banyan tree." (Marshall Snow)
ALOHA!

—George (Keoki) W. May, July 1999

Motor Camping In Alaska

I was 75.

A visit to Alaska, the 49th state, was my dream for many years. The other states I had traveled over. However, questions arose. Although 75 is-and the wife was 72-not anymore considered really old, yet it is an age when consideration of driving the Alcan Highway demands some thinking about. Could I meet the physical demands of daily driving and camping out for six weeks and 10,000 miles? For those many years of dreaming, I had compared costs by air, ship and car. All seemed prohibitive to my means. Moreover, public transportation (plane, ship) offered mainly brief tours. Air travel certainly would pass over territory which one could not intimately see much of. I wanted close ups.

Then one day in early 1985 a brilliant idea flashed in my mind. I needed a new car anyway, the Volare having seen its best days. Why not buy a pick-up truck, install a slide-in camper and head out? Besides cutting the cost of the journey, I figured, by more than one-half, the cost outrageously asked by the travel agencies, we would still have a brand new truck upon our return.

From previous reading of books on Alaska and other literature, we sensed that the contrast between our two youngest states could scarcely be imagined greater anywhere in the nation, in size, the people, the scenery and in general character. We had not read Edna Ferber's *Ice Palace* (1950s) which had had some influence on Alaska's obtaining statehood; nor had James Michener's celebrated *Alaska* (1988) yet been published. I write these lines 14 years later. Time has wrought its work; details have dimmed, but pleasant memories (and photos) remain, some subtle, some sharp.

This account is not a re-hash of information gleaned from books, histories and travel folders, useful as they were (although a stray word or phrase may have crept in), but is 99.9 per cent a personal journal of what we saw and experienced.

We left for Alaska on June 20, 1985 and within a few days, via the Black Hills, crossed into Canada at Sweetwater, Mt. We spent two hours in Calgary and noted the changes since our visit in 1963.

Before we reached Edmonton, I became ill and suffered an anxious day or two there and beyond and we did not cover many miles. Must we give up the trip? One can imagine my conflicting thoughts. The second day I felt better and by the time we reached Dawson Creek, I was much better. At this place we faced the Alcan Highway, 1,523 miles in length, Route 1. On the camper we installed protective headlight lenses and a wire guard for the grill and exchanged our money ($100 US for Canada $135). We camped at Milo-o, just outside town.

It was with some trepidation that we took off next morning on the Alcan. We faced road construction, narrow roads, some gravel stretches and the infamous pot holes, all besides the stamina required for continuous driving and camping, other yet unseen possible hazards—all for several weeks.

Thus, we continued camping out every night, preparing two meals a day and dinner at restaurants. By letting my beard grow I saved time and trouble. I left it on until the following March and became quite a venerable fellow in appearance according to members of my family and friends; wife Hazel remained equivocal.

A day out of Dawson Creek, we passed through Fort Nelson and camped at Muncho Lake. The lake nestled among the snow-blotched Rocky Mountains. It is deep, 730 feet and 300 feet at points along the highway. The scenery all day was superb.

We entered Yukon Territory at Watson Lake and read the placards on the famous signpost, which visitors had begun during the construction of the Alaska Highway. Our PEORIA was posted but it was not our Peoria, IL; probably a Texas town. Then to Whitehorse for our first view of the Yukon River and other local attractions. We crossed into Alaska and within a few miles reached the first town, Northway. We encountered some road work this day: stones, dust, one stretch of 28 miles of construction, narrow roadbed and no shoulders. Tok was a road junction town. We camped at the public Delta Junction campground. Next morning at North Pole we paused at Santa Claus land. We had seen some farms and crossed rivers with backgrounds of low mountains. At last, Fairbanks and the end of the Alcan Highway. Thus far we had found the dangers of the road exaggerated.

Fairbanks lies on the flat valley of the Tanana River and on the banks of Chena River. The city is modern and is the seat of the University of Alaska. The city's role is as a service and supply point. The population is about 60,000. An interesting and important city, but, oh, those winters! It can be as cold as 60 below zero.

We enjoyed the day in Fairbanks for there are many attractions. We visited the Rampert Mall, entered shops, crossed the Chena River and toured the university campus. We camped at Norlite Camp on Peger Road and read and wrote our notes in good daylight at 11:00 p.m.

The reader may wonder why I speak so little of Fairbanks, Anchorage, Denali Park, the Kenai Peninsular, etc. I have abbreviated those place because most tourists who visit Alaska see those places very well. But Barrow, Chicken, Matanuska—many do not. They are unique and many writers fail to cover them or tourists to venture to the more out-of-the way places,

On the afternoon of July 6 we boarded a Markair 737 jet for Barrow 330 miles north of the Arctic Circle and the northernmost town in Alaska. At 30,000 feet we viewed the Yukon River, the Endicot Mountains, the Brooks Range and the vast tundra beyond and put down at Barrow about 4:00 p.m. With its 3,000 people, it looked like a frontier town. We were whisked to the "Top of the World Hotel" situated on the Arctic Ocean and within a rock's throw of the ice pack shore.

But first, at the airport, we saw the Wiley Post-Will Rogers Memorial. Followed the famous blanket toss, which Michener so well describes (page 198 ff.). The Eskimos there make special walrus blankets with rope handles so that one can almost be tossed out of sight. During the bus tour we witnessed a native ceremonial dance and saw Eskimo crafts. Installed in our comfortable room at the hotel, we strolled about the dusty streets, dodging the many three-wheel vehicles and ate out at Sam and Lee's restaurant.

We continued our walk in the cold wind, but the sky was clear and the sun still shone, as it did all night for at Barrow the blatant sun remains up all 24 hours for 80 days. There were no paved streets or sidewalks. The buildings were nondescript, many mere huts.

And yet Barrow, the largest Inupiat Eskimo settlement in Alaska, is modern in various ways. There is a newspaper, Channel 13 (KBRW) TV station, daily jet flights, 10 churches, a $70 million dollar high school, a hospital and other amenities for good "city living." Still the extreme winter cold creates problems of water supply, sewage, unemployment, etc. in addition to the long sunless winter through which some people develop depression, ending in crime, booze or suicide. Only one ship comes in per year, in June. This single supply ship (with plane cargo) and distance equal high prices for just about everything. House rent $1,000 a month, pizza pies $35. But wages are high. We were told that a maid could make $40,000 a year. And, says Edna Ferber, "Polar Barrow has become inured to tourists."

Nowhere in Alaska are the contrasts in nature, history and culture more vivid than at Barrow: no trees, no gardens, but grass where undisturbed, first sighted by white men in 1826, earliest people the Eskimo and still dominant. Barrow has assumed the role of regional center of all phases of life on the North Slope of Alaska.

Barrow has had a great role in missionary work. In 1885 a trading post was set up by Charles Brower and the same year the Reverend Sheldon Jackson (Presbyterian) began his work. An ecumenical plan was devised whereby the mission field was partitioned out, a wise plan.

Typical house, Barrow, Alaska

During the bus tour next day of "Where the

Whalebone at Mattie's Cafe, Barrow

world ends" (Michener) we saw the Naval Arctic Research Laboratory, 10 miles east up the coast. There in 1952 the DEW line was set up. Nearby is the "farthest North American flag," Milepost, a totem pole and "the farthest north toilet." From there we bussed back downtown and saw a skin boat and two huge standing whalebones. Dinner at Mattie's Cafe (we took reindeer soup). After lunch we ran to the large fresh water lake, bordered by grass. It was breezy and cold, even with the parkas which had been loaned us. (It was 35° of the morning when I checked the thermometer at a church).

At four o'clock we took the return flight to Fairbanks and received our Markair certificate, certifying we had crossed the Arctic Circle to 67° 30' North Latitude.

I have painted a faint picture of the Barrow region. Edna Ferber (*Ice Palace*) has her Birdie ask Thor Storm: "What's a young girl want to see Barrow for?" Then Thor answers: "A strange thing is going on in that Eskimo village. It's a workshop full of scientists, engineers and Air Force Men." Despite the harsh region, climate, alcohol, etc., Barrow carries happily on. The summer sun doesn't set; baseball is played at midnight. Ferber seems to feel that the people are on the whole happy; they're always laughing; they just feel good. Maybe it's the long daylight, violet rays, the magnetic pole, or isotopes. So what Barrow lacks is made up by its unique climate, topography, people, culture and the stark beauty of the tundra. There is a mystique, esoteric. Certainly, the high point of our six-week's trip.

In Fairbanks we found our car intact parked at the International

Airport. We spent the night at Tanana Valley campground, across the east side of the Chena River. Another early visit to shops in the morning and we faced toward Denali National Park, 121 miles south on the George Parks Highway. The Alaska Railroad paralleled the highway from Fairbanks to Seward, about 500 miles.

Among the beautiful flowers of Alaska, many of which line the highways, is the ubiquitous fireweed. The blazing magenta pink (some are red, some white) is hard to miss. It is to Alaska what the golden rod is to Illinois. It gets its name because it tends to spring up so rapidly on burned over land. Besides its beauty it can double as greens and the dried leaves brewed for tea. The plant is a tasty source of C and A vitamins. In our travels over Canada we have seen it as far east as Ontario. It is an appropriate floral emblem of the Yukon.

We had to camp at Lynx Camp, near the celebrated great park because one has to be early at the Riley Creek Information Center, by 11:00 a.m., to get a campsite and it was now 4:00 p.m. in the afternoon. The camp was forested and good but the price was stiff, $12. The wife saw a moose and calf wandering at the rear of our camp while I was on a stroll.

We arose early to catch the shuttle bus at Riley Creek Center at 8:30. Use of the bus is now being required to keep the great private automobile traffic off the one road into Denali National Park. No cars beyond Savage River, 12 miles out, except with a camping permit and other restrictions.

Our campsite secured, we boarded the shuttle bus and rode all day to Wonder Lake and return, covering about 200 miles, free of cost. The bus driver was obliging and stopped any time a passenger wanted to photograph an animal he spied. The scenery and some of the road curves, etc. was breath-taking. We paused at Eleison Visitors Center to lunch out of our own sacks. It was a merry crowd. We saw golden bear, moose, sheep, elk, caribou, ducks, muskrat and squirrel.

At Wonder Lake (end of the road proper) we gazed

Denali National Park

across the McKinley River flats to Mt. McKinley, 33 miles as the crow flies. The summit of this highest peak in North America (20,320 feet) was obscured this day. In fact, the chance of seeing it is only about four days out of a month.

We arrived back at our Savage camp past seven o'clock. At 10:30 I picked a few tunes on the mandolin, wrote up the journal, sun still up. We were worn out but happy. High point No.2 for us.

The run down to Anchorage was pleasant. All morning we drove between mountain ranges with snow on them. We crossed the Sustina and Chultna rivers and several babbling brooks. We passed through Wailla and soon exited onto the Glenn Highway No.1 leading into Anchorage, where we parked for an hour to get the feel of this largest (204,000) Alaskan city.

Located between Knik Arm and Turnagain Arm (extensions of Cook Inlet) and with the backdrop of the nearby Chugach Mountains, Anchorage began as a tent city in 1914. Growth was rapid and it now equals any USA city in modernism. It was chosen as an All-America City in early 1985. We found there was too much to see and do to hope to cover as it deserved.

We headed south down the Seward Highway No.1 to the burgeoning and beautiful Kenai Peninsula. We drove along Turnagain Arm known for its very high tides and deadly quicksands. The scenery was spectacular. Near the end of the Arm lay Portage and its glacier, a sheer wall of ice 80 feet high rising three miles away from the waters of Portage Lake. Close by, we set up at the Walliway Campground. It was a lovely spot, wooded and surrounded by mountains. A small waterfall fell from a midget glacier across the brook beside our camp.

We took a branch road (Route 9) to Seward, on Resurrection Bay. In Seward we walked awhile and saw several of the more than 30 attractions. We backtracked to the Sterling Highway No.1 and veering south at Sodotna, the fishing capital of the Kenai Peninsula, we reached Homer. Jutting out for nearly five miles from the city is Homer Spit, a long, narrow gravel bar bustling with activity. Shops built on piling line the shoreline of Kachemak Bay with a fine view of the Kenai Mountains beyond it. We camped at the Homer Spit campground, right on the beach. A man sold us two large cooked crabs.

Next day, July 12, we retraced the way to Anchorage, stopped awhile and camped at Eagle River, 15 miles north. Rain fell all night. Continuing east on the Glenn Highway we came to the Matanuska area. This I had long wanted to see, from following its development in the

1930s and from the fact that I had farmed off and on for a good many years myself.

The Matanuska Valley area is the agricultural center of Alaska, spectacularly cradled by the Chugach and Talkeetna mountain ranges. In the Great Depression of the 1930s a most ambitious agrarian experiment began when North Central Plains farmers homesteaded Matanuska under the aegis of the Federal Government. There were early successes and failures. But with up to 20 hours of sunlight farm crops flourished. James Michener makes much of the story (begin page 787 and for many pages). He catches the spirit if not all the facts.

We visited the University of Alaska Experimental Farm. A girl guided us through the dairy barn, among the cows and calves, seeing and smelling the hay and other rations. Nearby were the test plots: fruits, vegetables, flowers. We saw plots of Sweetheart and Ozark strawberries. (We raised berries for years). Our third high point!

After a stop at Palmer for lunch and an oil change, fine scenery accompanied us as we drove along the paralleling Matanuska River. Cloud-shrouded mountains with some snow, lakes, valleys, forests and bare rocks and a fine view of Matanuska Glacier on the right and at various points along the road. But we had to watch the road: frost heaves, rocks, potholes and long stretches of narrow road without shoulders and some miles of construction.

We camped three miles beyond Glennallen at Dry Creek Camp, a state park. It was surrounded by spruce, bedecked with wild flowers and a nice camp except for voracious mosquitoes. Bears have repeatably been seen at this park.

At Glennallen Highway No. 1, we turned northeastward. We had a good view of Noyes Mountain (at 8,147 feet) near Mentasta Summit (2,434 feet). We reached Tok at one o'clock and set up camp at Sourdough Campground. Even though sprayed, mosquitoes were plentiful. Here I wrapped an old rug around the gas tank, advice that might be good in preparation for the Taylor Highway the next day, to Dawson City, 175 miles away. Hazel did laundry; I trimmed my beard for I was beginning to look like a bear. Then supper and a light rain.

We found the Taylor Highway surprisingly good, no complaints on our part. It was briefly rough at the start; the last half quite good, smooth, no shoulders, a few potholes always expected, some dust. We drove slowly. A shower, a rainbow, a miniature glacier or snow bank. We ate lunch "out of the wagon."

At Chicken, 67 miles from Tok, we stopped awhile. With only 37 inhabitants why should we pause there? Located on Fortymile Creek, a tributary of Fortymile River and named for the ptarmigan bird (chicken), it experienced the gold rush days and some mining is still done. Now there is an airfield, grocery, restaurant and gas station. Souvenirs are sold. This is the new part of Chicken.

We visited Chicken for a good reason; in fact, it was our intention before we left home. We had read the book *Tisha*, a told-to book by Robert Snecht in which Anne (Hobbs) Purdey was the relater or author, a story of the young teacher who in 1927 became the first teacher in this Chicken wilderness. "Tisha" was the Indian pupils name for "teacher". Among other problems as a newcomer ("cheechko") from Oregon, Anne had to combat racial prejudice. The white man did not want Indian children in Anne's school. But she prevailed over the school board and parental hostility. Her friendship with Fred Purdy, half Eskimo, raised eyebrows. He eased Anne over many problems. A mutual love developed but because of prejudice it was 10 years before they married, even though Anne taught only one term in Chicken and then moved to Eagle to teach. This true story is lively told, filled with warmth and love. Love for her pupils carried her over many hurdles. Anne was an indomitable woman and in the end usually got her way in a society which knew violence and death.

We took the half-mile lane north across the main highway to the home of Mrs. Purdy, now aged about 78 and talked with her for an hour. Her husband Fred deceased, a young Indian woman lived with her. Extremely friendly and talkative. Her autograph in our book *Tisha* reads: "To George and Hazel May. Happy landings from the gold land and the midnight sun. Chicken, AK, July 15, 1985. '*Tisha*' Anne Purdy. Whatever is lost among the years, let us keep Love. Its meaning never ends. Blessings always." Red letter event No. 4.

We were entranced with the superb mountain views along this "Top of the World" highway. We had not expected so much. Roads winding, traffic light. We crossed the Alaska-Yukon boundary at 4 p.m. No examination, no trouble. Another hour and we saw Dawson City and the swift Yukon River from the heights along the left bank. We set up camp at the West Dawson campground opposite the city. A free ferry crossed to Dawson City and we took it afoot before preparing our camp supper.

Dawson City! What pictures arise in our minds of the gold rush days! Once it was called "the Paris of the North." Today it is a modern town of under 1,000 people. Many of the old buildings remain and restored. We saw the post office with its unique facade, Mme. Tremblay's Dress Store, the museum, the Palace Grand Theater, the Red Feather Saloon, the old steamship KEMO and stopped at several arts and crafts shops. We went to the cabin of the once renowned poet Robert W. Service and to the Jack London cabin.

Upon departing down the Klondije Loop highway No. 2 we paused at once famous Bonanza Creek. Then gravel roads again. To the left the Ogilvie and to the right the Dawson Range arose. We camped at the Moose Creek Government campground. From Carmacks we had pavement on to Whitehorse. Almost every mile on this 324-mile run was of interest: rivers, lakes, mountains. Just before Whitehorse lay Lake Laberge, said to be second in size only to Lake Superior in North America.

Still on the Klondike Highway, we detoured the 99 miles south to Skagway, paralleled large Bennet Lake for miles and made it over the 3,290 foot White Pass. Superb scenery to Skagway. Along the 14-mile trail (the Chilkoot Trail) once toiled the gold seekers on the way to the Klondike fields. Once boisterous (Soapy Smith, etc.), this city of under 1,000 seemed to us quiet and staid. Tourists provide the movement and business. There are at least a dozen attractions for the tourist and a special Soapy Smith show runs all summer. There is a good view down Taiya Inlet, toward the Lynn Canal. Backtracking the 99 miles, we camped some miles east of Whitehorse at the Squango Lake Government camp. Mosquitoes were bad.

We wanted to take the new Cassier Highway No. 37 (459 miles) south to Hazelton (the end). But it occasioned us much thought before the decision. It might be a *tour de force* run: gravel dust, mud, construction? However, others had made it. Why not we with our new Dodge Ram.

We camped at Boya Lake in the still snowstreaked Cassier Mountains. Now in British Columbia, next morning we paused at Good Hope Lake, passed an Indian village, ran along Iskut River and enjoyed the splendid views of the coastal ranges on our right and those of the Skeena on our left and the fine view of the rushing Bell-Irving River.

We pulled out at the Bell II Limited (store, cafe, gas, etc.) and camped at no charge. We carried our wash water from the nearby Bell-Irving River. Here the wife's spirit slumped; perhaps the weeks of camp routine, the rough and dusty roads, mosquitoes or perhaps, a tinge of homesickness.

Next day we had 60 miles of gravel; dust from passing cars, of course. A light rain eased the strain for awhile. At Cranberry Junction a good paved road continued the rest of the day; in fact, to Spokane and all the way home. Our fears over the conditions in this quite isolated part of British Columbia ceased. We had met the challenge! Through

Old Hazelton and New Hazelton and we entered upon the Yellowhead Highway 16. On the Buckley River we saw the falls and the Indians fishing with spears. We paused in Prince George to buy gifts.

We left the Yellowhead at Tete Jaune Cache onto Route 5. At Merritt (just south of Kamloups) we ate fresh-frozen Cohoe salmon for supper but it was so windy and dusty we prepared it inside the camper.

Around Osoyoos next day we saw many acres of cherries, apricots, apples and grapes. At Greenwood the police stopped us for over speeding (40 m.p.h.) through the town but let us go with an admonition, seeing we were tourists. A mile south of Cascade we crossed into Washington state, USA. Spokane, Denver, Kansas City followed and we reached home August 1 at Metropolis, IL. Mileage 10,575; cost around $2,800. Mission accomplished!

POSTSCRIPTS—Says a letter to the editor of *Alaska* magazine (August 1984): "The first year up here is very difficult. Winter is long and jobs are scarce and the cost of living is high. January is a whole lot different than cruising the Inside Passage or driving the Alaska highway in July." Roads are seldom up to stateside standards but only one-fourth of residents live unconnected by road to the outside world. Some cry "stop the bulldozers"; "more roads" counter others. Tourists fuel the debate. Other arguments, pro and con. What may aid Alaska in dealing with its varied problems is that its people have gone there to a place "that tolerates their individuality, rewards their initiative and demands their courage" (David Broder, October 1986). Fleeting tourists like us never get to know the real Alaska.

Don't fail to take along the *Milepost* publication as you travel to Alaska, maps, pictures, notes galore. We highly praise it.

It was once in a lifetime experience but we have little desire to repeat it; certainly, we would not want to live there.

–November 1999

The Polar Bear Express

We were comfortably seated and prepared to hold this train down to Moosonee, on James Bay, Province of Ontario, 186 miles north.

It was July 24, 1985. We thought: what would your children or grandchildren give to take an all day ride on a vintage passenger train. Few such opportunities remain in these days of Amtrak. The wife and I were on just such a jaunt.

We had run from our home Metropolis, IL through Detroit, Toronto, North Bay, car-camping and had last night camped at Cameron Beach on Big Nellie Lake near Iroquois Falls, 24 miles south of Cochrane, our train boarding station. At Cameron I had swum in the lake. We had arrived in Cochrane early, to be greeted at the city gates by a huge polar bear statue.

This town of 5,000 sits in a region of timber where gold mining is still done. Wood pulp is a leading industry but hunting, fishing and trapping are also carried on and there is the important tourism business.

A Polar Bear Express ticket

Cochrane has the usual service industry: groceries, sports supplies, restaurants, drug store, four motels, etc. Although game is not plentiful, deer, the larger, ducks and geese abound and the town has several outfitter stores and fly-in services. The Railway and Pioneer Museum is located at the railway station for everyone to conveniently see, free.

We had found the famous Polar Bear Express with its No. 1510 diesel locomotive and a string of passenger coaches drawn up at the station museum and hopped aboard. (We had parked our camper in the adjoining parking lot also free). Often in school days I had pored over maps of the James Bay region and wondered what it was like. I was now about to see it.

This railroad, the Ontario Northland, is an 186-mile branch of the Canadian National Railway. It runs from Cochrane to Moosonee and is a 4-1/2 hour run. A round trip is scheduled daily except Fridays, June 25-September 5 (1985) and the cost is $34 a person (over age 65, $17, which we paid). It is billed as an unusual rail excursion through a naturalists delight. However, the name belies the reality. There are no polar bears or white fox around James Bay, for one has to go up the coast to Fort Churchill to find them.

Although there were many tourists aboard, the wife and I were well-seated in the coach, as I wrote earlier and next to a window so we could see the passing views well. Soon we were in the deep forest of spruce, poplar and tamarack. Little settlements slipped by-Larocque, Genier, Blount Chute, Gardiner, Workman, Wurtele, Maher and then Island Falls, where we crossed the large Abitibi River. There is a dam upriver and power is developed to run the Abitibi Mill.

For Fraserdale it is the end of the line, north. Only the railroad and Highway No. 807 (60 miles) give contact outside. (But there is always the canoe!). East three miles was another generator plant, the Abitibi Canyon. North, past two other settlements, was Otter Rapids and another hydroelectric installation. The next towns (?) were Coral, Onakawana and Moose River Crossing. We paralleled. the left bank of the Moose River the rest of the, way into Moosonee.

Between viewing the forest and river scenery, interspersed with some open spaces, I fell to reflection.

Geologic ages ago a so-called Great Shield was formed in this region. Upon it now is the Hudson Bay Lowland, the largest bog in the world. The soil is poorly drained and sterile. Lakes, bogs, canal-like streams, rivers intermix with forest areas. It is muskeg (sphagnum), moss-like growth which in time may form peat or lignite. Unusual rocks and some colorful fossils are often found. Poor soil and the cold and wet climate are causes of these conditions. Woe unto the stranger if he tries to traverse this terrain. Not only is there danger of becoming lost afoot or canoe likely, but he may get bogged down. One needs a good Cree Indian guide. The alternative is that a mistake could cost a life, warns the travel brochure. For the tourist, the thing boils down to sticking to the railroad, get a guide or fly in if this fascinating land is to be experienced safely.

Occasional stops were made that morning; perhaps to take on or throw off mail and cargo. I really don't recall whether old No. 1510 pulled boxcars or not. I would say that the Polar Bear Express was not an all-tourist enterprise for many commodities must be had at Moosonee and Moose Factory and the railroad was the best way to tap this isolated region.

Again, I mused. This road would seem to be a hobo's dream or horror. Beautiful country. But to be thrown off the train, a penniless Knight of the Road could be stranded, from a few miles to a settlement up to as many as 93 miles (one-half of the 186 miles). In spite of my hobo adventures as a young man, with some accompanied mishaps, I would not fancy trying this remote stretch.

It was actually hot as we walked the dusty, graveled streets of Moosonee, "Gateway to the Arctic." As it was well past noon, we lunched at the first food place before strolling along the Moosonee bank of the Moose River and the "downtown" waterfront.

Moosonee began as a fur trading post in 1903 but the place as we now know it was founded in 1932 with the coming of the railroad. At this mouth of James Bay, of which body of water we could see far down the river, tides five feet high lap the shoreline. There are 1,500 residents in the town on this flat land and extends as a strip one-half mile wide and two miles long along the rivers west bank. Moosonee is a frontier town in the tradition of all such towns. Old buildings stand near more solid modern structures. It was the jumping off place for prospectors, scientists, missionaries and military of the misty past.

Business is about the same kind as found in any small town but here especially are the native arts, crafts and gift shops. There are five churches, the Northern Lights Secondary School, a Hudson's Bay Store and a museum in Centennial Park. CHMO is the radio station. The Revillion Freres Museum is worth seeing. The James Bay Education Center is located here. A bank, a lodge, public restrooms, an old sawmill, a hospital and of course, the docks are among the features. Moosonee is governed by a seven man, appointive, Development Area Board.

We strolled unhurriedly, paused to rest a few times (much walking tires the wife) and kept our watches checked for return time. Many of our fellow tourists took the six-mile, large canoe rides to Moose Factory across the river. From the reports of returnees and a charge for the ride ($20 round-trip) we chose not to take the trip. Even so, a visit to Moose Factory could be worthwhile for there is much to see.

The French came to Moose Factory Island in 1668; the Hudson's Bay built Moose Fort in 1673. To push out the English intruders the French led an expedition against the Fort in which, in a battle on June 21, 1696 the English were caught by surprise. The English surrendered still in their night clothes without having fired a shot. Further attacks up coast ousted the English and the French took over the fur trade until the Treaty of Utrecht in 1715.

At the Moosonee-Moose Factory final reach of the river lie several islands: Charles, Sawpit, Butter, Bushy, Tidewater, Big Duck,

Old buildings contrast with the new, Moosonee.

Little Duck, Ship Sands, some others and of course, Moose Factory Island. The big 16 paddle canoes weave their way along Charles and Sawpit. Another cruise by a larger engine powered ship is made into James Bay itself and costs more. Moose Factory is the oldest English speaking settlement in Ontario.

At Moose Factory, population 1,775 one may see the General Hospital, St. Thomas Church, Centennial Museum, Hudson's Bay Post, an old blacksmith shop, an old fur press, the old cemetery, the Bannock Tepee, a native village, a general store, post office, eateries, etc.; in all some 30 attractions. Sine the area is 80 to 90 percent Cree Indian, native arts and crafts are readily purchased and is a supplementary occupation to hunting, fishing and guiding.

Thus, we leisurely breathed the pioneer air of this northern town and walking the half-mile back to the station, parked ourselves in a grassy, park-like area near to old No. 1510. I strolled down to a trestle under which flowed a little stream and amused myself with the pygmy life within it.

It was past five o'clock when we pulled out for Cochrane. The scenery reversed. In our coach we met up with a Christian Mission group from Brevard, NC; three young women, I believe and jolly tempered. Wife Hazel carried on an animated conversation with them. There was some singing, if I recall rightly. Rather tired and drowsy, I took a minor part in the exchange and I sat next to a window, alone, lethargic.

The Polar Bear Express reached Cochrane at 9:30 and by this time it was rather dark. A kilometer away we camped at the city-sponsored Drury Park for eight dollars. That was convenient, indeed, as it saved longer night driving. Nor did I know of a camp westward under 100 miles.

We arose late the next morning. We drove over Cochrane, provisioned and hit the road west on Trans-Canada Highway No. 11. This route runs through forest-river-lake country north of Lake Superior to Port Arthur. Then Duluth and home via Wisconsin. We enjoyed good scenery and good camping, especially at Lake Mary Louise situated on a peninsula extending into Lake Superior near Thunder Bay.

A boyhood dream and map at last made real!

–December 12, 1999

Bible Lands Diary

It was a morning flight into Rome from Paris on July 9, 1971. With our vicarious acquaintance with Rome we were prepared to appreciate the historic sites and the association with Christianity. I, myself (wife, a bit less), came into Rome hungry, as a man comes home to a big meal after a days hard labor, hungry for all that Rome stood for in history and culture, aye, for its very gods and goddesses of mythology. Same for Greece, where I continued the feast.

From the Cavelieri Hilton Hotel on the heights overlooking Rome like a map a wonder-

St. Peters, Rome

ful view spread out. Along the Appian Way and the Tiber River we had come from the airport by bus. From the hotel we could see the Vatican State, the Coliseum, Hadrian's Tomb and other things we were to see in the next two days. Vatican State and its Sistine Chapel complex was the first stop, the frescos of Michelangelo, St. Peters, the museum. Followed the catacombs, the Church of St. Peters in Chains, the Forum, the Arcs of Constantine, the Coliseum, Trevi Fountain and the Mammertine Prison.

On my own I took a three-hour hike via the streets of Trianfolo and Della Milizie to the sycamore lined Tiber River and made my way back by way of St. Peters and its souvenir stands. I entered several shops, observed the people and felt that I was seeing the more normal life of Rome's people.

Arrived at the Piraeus airport about 6 p.m., we were bussed to the King Minos Hotel in Athens. After a quick supper we went to the open air Dionysos Theater nearby where folk dancers performed. The emcee gave a welcome historical talk in three languages successively Greek, French, English, a feat in itself. How dramatic it seemed as I sat in the stone-tiered amphitheater and as the moon, Venus and Jupiter looked down upon us in this re-enactment of many songs and dances from various Grecian districts, Macedonia, Minian, etc. and the unusual music, large bodied mandolins, little clarinets, violins, drums and dulcimer-like instruments, the whole a delight!

In succession we toured the Parthenon and Acropolis, Mars Hill (where Paul preached to the Greeks) and upon which I scrambled to the summit and to Corinth, 60 miles south. We rode along the Sacred Way of Eleusian Mysteries, across the isthmus canal and to the modern

Corinth and the old Corinth ruins. Here we walked where Paul walked with Aquila and Priscilla. We saw the acropolis, the Agora, the Temple of Apollo, the Bema Seat in the forum where Paul was acquitted by the Tribunal Court and the fine little museum. Returning over the Eleusian Isthmus again, it was here we saw an old-time gypsy band go by with wagons (two-wheel carts) and a dog led by a rope tied to a cart.

In Athens I just had time for a quick lunch, a turn around Constitution Square (with its subway shops) and a post card mailing. It was too unfortunate that our time in "the Queen City of ancient Civilization" was so short. But a crumb is better than nothing.

July 12, we had a mid-afternoon flight on Middle East Airlines over the blue Mediterranean to Beirut and were driven like mad (watch your step, pedestrians; also, in all major Mid-East cities) to the palacial, 22-story Phoenicia Hotel, just a block from the sea. After a huge meal, wife Hazel heard Dr. Unmack's lecture on Bible history. These lectures and short religious services were held periodically these three weeks, of which I did not attend. My attitude was "get my sermons at home and see what I can now, my first and perhaps my last opportunity to experience the old world."

We toured Beirut and then took out east over the Lebanese Mountains on our way to Damascus, with much good scenery along the way. We sidetracked north to see the ruins of Baalbek and the spectacular temples of Jupiter, Bachus and Venus. Much of Lebanon is fertile and we saw much farming, some of the labor being done by animals treading the grain, winnowing and reaping by hand scythe. Bedouins in huts and herds of sheep and goats lent the flavor to the land.

Dinner at the Oriental Hotel and then we were led by our Syrian guide Mohammed (Eddie in English) into the Mosque of Omar. We trod the street called Straight of which Mark Twain quoted was the only facetious thing in the Bible, because the street was certainly winding. We saw the site of the house of Aninias where Paul

The Parthenon, Athens

recovered his sight after his conversion on the Damascus road and we saw the wall over which he was let down in a basket to escape the enemy. A walk through the bazaar was confusing but novel.

Political talk was taboo in Damascus we were told. And this was the only place in three week's travel where the people seemed to resent our presence. We saw many scowling faces, especially the youth.

After a sabra breakfast in Beirut we boarded a Cyprus Airline and put down at Nicosia 40 minutes later. Cyprus: the "Island of Love" (Aphrodite or Venus) with a rich history, a sort of cloak and dagger land in which Greek and Turk struggle for control, with the Turks outnumbered four to one. It seems strange that so much has been made of this little 3,500 square mile island.

We took a 40 minute drive to the ancient Salamie ruins stopping on the way at St. Barnabas Monastery where Paul preached on his first missionary journey with his companion Barnabas. We picked our way afoot over the stones of the Salamis ruins and marveled at the good condition of the tiers of seating of the amphitheater. As the day advanced, I was impressed with the Cypriot scene, at least in this part of the island. Neat, clean, friendly people, fertile and level fields, some mountains. John, our guide, said that often it did not rain for six months.

Famagusta the fabulous golden city, east of Nicosia and on the seacoast was our lunch stop, where we ate at a restaurant right on the fine beach. This is the new city (Varosha) adjoining the old city where there is much of the ancient to see. Fortified by lunch after much walking and with "White Lady" wine under my belt, I took a luxurious swim in the sea. (It was 95 degrees inland). Some of our group chose boating.

Back in Nicosia we ate supper on the roof garden of the Ekali Bar and Restaurant. It was just before sunset. A few clouds hung over the mountains. A pretty view, idyllic, lacking only music, I fell into a romantic mood and thoroughly enjoyed the evening.

It was 3 a.m. when we hit bed in Jerusalem after a late flight from Nicosia to Tel Aviv. Our St. George Hotel stood on Nabulas Road, just outside the city wall and we had arrived via bus tired and sleepy.

For many pilgrims a trip to the Holy Land is the highlight of their lives and they may be on a spiritual "high" when they enter Israel, especially at Christmas, Easter and the Jan. 1, 2000 AD millennium celebrations. Tour guides suggest five top pilgrimage sites: the Sea of Galilee, Meggido, Mount of Olives, the Garden Tomb, Masada and the Dead Sea. Three faiths share the Holy places as represented by the

Wailing Wall, the Dome of the Rock and the Mount of Olives in this "City of Peace".

Jerusalem! The most haunting of cities. It has never lost its fascination or significance. Israel is a tiny country but the setting of enormously important events of which center, most would agree, is Jerusalem. Situated on a ridge of the Judean hills, 30 miles from the great sea and above its level 2,000 feet, it has been fought over during 20 sieges and often destroyed. It was first settled by the Bronze Age Canaanites around 3,000 BC. Came Abraham to Mt. Moriah; came David 2,000 years later; came the Babylonian captivity (586 BC); it and the Second Temple were destroyed in 70 AD. Tempting as it is, I must not take the space to outline the subsequent history except that at last in 1948 Israel became free and sovereign.

July 15-As we set out by tour bus I regretted that the wife felt unable to go and a few others of our party because the tourists' nemesis diarrhea had struck. At Hebron we saw the tombs of Abraham, Isaac, Jacob and their wives. In Bethlehem we entered the Church of the Nativity and the grotto of Christ's birth; thence, to the "Fields of the Shepherds". The Judean hills were bare and rocky. Only terraces permit of farming. We saw many on donkeys, turbaned people, jars carried on head, all ancient, looking as in the time of Christ.

We were off to the Mount of Olives next morning, with wife Hazel along. We paused at the Ascension Chapel and walked down to the Garden of Gethsemane and the Basilica of the Agony; thence, down the Josaphat and Kedroan valleys, past cemeteries and ancient tombs to the Pool of Siloam.

Standing at the rugged stone Wailing Wall, with tufts of grass growing from the mud-filled crevices, I reflected: Here is all that remains of the Second Temple, a bit of rampart that encircled it. At this remnant of the Temple Mount I marveled at seeing the Jews tucking letters or prayers into the crevices. I pulled out one. How great a faith after all these centuries! After a 20 years' absence the Wall was again open after the victory in the 1967 Six Days' War.

We stopped at St. Peters Church where the high priest Caiaphas imprisoned Christ. We passed on to King David's Tomb on Mt. Zion, stopped at the Israeli Parliament building, viewed Hebrew University across the way and viewed some of the Dead Sea scrolls in the Shrine of the Book building. On the grounds also was a superb model of the Second Temple covering a space about the size of a croquet court.

After lunch at our St. George Hotel we rode to Bethany and saw the church and what was more pertinent the Tomb of Lazarus and the

Resurrection Cave which we entered, stooping. We were pestered by venders and beggars here and at other places quite frequently. (The cave hag demanded a fee).

We settled down for a longer drive over the Jericho Road. We paused at the site of the Good Samaritan episode and also saw remains of a Crusader tower. The Judean mountains were bare but beautiful in their way. Bedouin bands with their goats and sheep and tents or hovels appeared. We

Lazarus' Tomb, Bethany

stopped at Jericho, a very oasis, where the rows of palm trees and tantalizing orange groves gave forth the redolent scent of the subtropics. We dipped our fingers into Elisha's Spring and saw the nearby ancient ruins.

Retracing a few miles, we saw the old Essenes monastery. Here at Qumran were discovered the first Dead Sea Scrolls by an Arab boy Odh-Dhib ("the wolf") in 1947. Of the 11 caves later explored, cave No. four has been perhaps the most productive of other scrolls. The Essenes, religious zealots under the Jewish law and pre-dating Christ, made a last ditch stand in 73 AD after the fall of Jerusalem and committed mass homicide to avoid Roman conquest. This was at Masada, many miles south of Qumran, which we did not visit.

The Dead Sea was blue and calm and lay across from the Mountains of Moab even Mt. Nebo. I got my swim. The effect was absolutely fascinating. In this water, eight times saltier than the ocean and lying 1,290 feet below sea level, I had an unbelievable feeling of ease.

July 17-The Dome of the Rock is a most beautiful building. It sits on Mt. Moriah on the same spot as was the Jewish Second Temple but now next to Mecca, the most revered place of the Moslems. We entered, shoeless and saw the intricate mosaics. On this Second Temple spot occurred the pivotal struggle of the Jews against the Romans in 70 AD. The Jews, weakened by dissension among themselves, accompanied by mutual greed, hunger and slaughter, were finally defeated by the Emperor Vespasian and son Titus and the Temple completely destroyed, as foretold by Christ Himself and other prophets. The Jews had their own lack of cooperation to blame.

Josephus and his *History of the Jews* plus the Bible are the authorities for this event. He himself fought valiantly for the Jews in another city but somehow played little or no part at Jerusalem. He allied himself with Vespasian, posing as a prophet and has been considered by some to have acted the part of a traitor to his fellow Jews. I have found only one book which has novelized this event, G. A. Henty, a writer of many boys' books, in his *For the Temple*.

I drew off from our group and reflected. The 70 AD event has given rise to various doctrinal differences among the pre, post and a-millennium people (and the preterits). The preterits believe that Christ came in 70 AD to end the world (the end of the Jewish age) in punishment for the Jewish failure to repent. In the clouds, symbolically, a Spirit only, came He. For years there had been signs of his parousia (Second Coming). In 70 AD other signs appeared, a comet, earthquakes, strange lights at the altar, heavy gates opened of themselves, voices, a man running the streets crying "Woe, woe" but when beaten showed no resentment but cried on and other signs. Obviously if all these things happened then they do not apply to the view that these things are to occur in the distant future. So strengthened, the preterits believe that in 70 AD Christ actually set up His Kingdom, bolstered by the phrase "This (70 AD) generation" (Matthew 24:34). (A few days later our young driver several times that day on the Nazareth run declared the end of the world to come early in the 1980s. Thirty years later, his prediction of the Apocalypse has not taken place).

My unspoken thoughts were broken into by the command of our leader to march on. We went by the Pool of Bethsheba at St. Anne's Church. At the Fortress of San Antonia Christ took up the cross. We followed the Via Dolorosa by several of the 14 stations. As we walked we noted much of novelty and interest, black-dressed veiled women; hippies; black-bearded Greek priests; the calls of tradesmen; pesky boy salesmen getting under our feet, many races, colors, creeds and so on. Finally, a visit to the Church of the Holy Sepulcher where Christ may have been buried.

It was a short stroll from our hotel to the Tomb of the Rock (Calvary, "Place of the Skull," the "Garden Tomb") or Gordon's Tomb. Charles George Gordan was a British military man who later became a religious enthusiast and ascertained this place, rather than the Church of the Holy Sepulcher, as being the burial site of Christ. We had a communion service here fronting the tomb. The breeze was sighing through the large pine trees; doves were cooing; the garden itself. It was appropriate and impressive.

July 18-Sunday, we must leave Jerusalem and travel north. We bid farewell to our genial Arab boy bell-boy Assad Abusawy. He said his was a very poor family and that his desire was to get an education. (In September we mailed him a small check). Thirty years later, I wonder how Assad has fared.

We paused in Shiloh Valley where the Ark of the Covenant was kept at one time. Then followed terraced olive groves, occasional Bedouins, donkeys, sheep, goats, a camel. We drank out of Jacob's Well at Nablus. On the hill of Samaria lie the twin peaks of Mt. Elbal and Mt. Gerizim behind. Here Jesus spoke with the woman of Samaria. Into the Valley of Jazreel we passed where is Meggido, the place where Armageddon is to be fought. This valley is "the bread basket of Israel", level and fertile. We toiled up the huge butte (as we would say of our Far West), seeing the ancient wall, the gate, palace, temple, altar, stables, grain silos and the museum. We cautiously picked our way through the water tunnel. A little later we viewed Mt. Tabor, supposedly the Mount of Transfiguration. Then into Tiberias on the Sea of Galilee.

Our two parties of 91 on two busses, often traveling separately, were soon set down at the Galei Kinnereth Hotel facing right on the sea of this beautiful body of water 10 miles by six miles, blue and hazy mountains to the east, we had a splendid view from the balcony. Hazel

Bedouin woma, Valley of Shiloh

and I strolled an hour over Tiberias and most businesses were open. Later, I swam in water in water up to my neck 20 feet out. The cold and stones hurt my feet!

On Monday we drove north to Dan in the Golan Heights, one area involved in the Six Day's War. We saw plenty signs of the war: damaged buildings, destroyed war machines, bunkers, barb wire, a destroyed bridge, etc. Israeli soldiers were working, apparently on further fortifications or repairing machinery. I talked with one soldier. We saw several ghost towns. Near Caesarea Philippi we saw a Druse woman at work on the threshing floor. Mt. Hermon, snowcapped at the summit, loomed near. At its base gushed forth a stream feeding the Dan and Jordan rivers. The valley is extensive and fertile and despite long stretches of marsh grass, is well cultivated. As tourists, we were lucky to be allowed to visit this Golan Heights area.

We back-tracked to Capernaum on Galilee and examined its ruins.

We boarded a boat and crossed over to kibbutz Ien Gev where a sumptuous meal was served, a main dish being St. Peters fish, served whole with eyes and all. I am told that some diners also eat the eyes! The palm tree, oleander, pomegranate, almond and the luscious orange yield in their season.

The kibbutz is one Israeli way of life, the communal or collective community. Do the members like living on one? A spokesman says, "An olive tastes both sweet and sour. Bite an olive and you taste our lives. The newcomer who comes to like the taste of our olives will stay." Along the lower end of the sea is Ashdot Yacov Kibbutz. Begun in 1935 and consisting of sheep, goats, cattle, chickens, fish ponds, fodder, vegetables, grapes and other fruits and raised on 1,000 acres, the inhabitants number around 1,200. We drove along the kibbutz but did not stop.

Some of our party were rebaptized here in the Jordan River but I only awaited another dip in the sea when we reached Tiberias, a short 15 kilometers farther.

We climbed up the mountain to sea level, piloted by our merry driver Tony, a bridegroom of six months. Tony sang along the way and taught us one Israeli song. We paused first at Cana where Christ performed His first miracle. In Nazareth we saw the Church of the Annunciation, St. Joseph's Church and the Jewish synagogue. We passed through the bazaar (not equal to those of Damascus and Jerusalem). Only a lunch at Haifa before we climbed the long and steep road to Mt. Carmel. From here was a spectacular view of Haifa and the harbor. Here Elijah confounded the prophets of Baal with consuming fire. (I Kings 18:38).

The remainder of the day we drove along the seacoast. The highway was modern and nearing Tel Aviv, became a fast four-lane, quite like an American countryside. At Caesarea by the sea we studied the remains of a large Roman city: aqueduct, amphitheater, headless statues, the wall and moat. Nearing Tel Aviv we saw boy and girl soldiers waiting for suburban busses and some hitchhiking. At last into big, bustling Tel Aviv.

Early the following morning we drove over the narrow streets of southern Tel Aviv to the ancient port city of Jaffa. Younger (founded 1909), Tel Aviv has grown to 460,000 (1960) and has merged with Jaffa. Andrommeda's Rock juts out to form a protected harbor. We inspected the house of Simon the Tanner where Peter raised back to life the woman named Tabitha. Here and the rest of the day I felt weak and faintly but I held out, bless God. Much of Jaffa is modernized.

We cut across country and passed over the Valley of Elah, where David slew Goliath. We picked up a stone at David's Brook. Again, we reached the sea and followed the road to Askelon and looked over the Roman, Byzantine and Crusader ruins. The last stop was at Ashdot but military restrictions prevented our seeing very much except the harbor from afar.

After a 2 o'clock lunch in Tel Aviv the wife and I walked the streets, down the biggest street (Allenby), through the bazaar, some tree lined sidewalks, kiosks, some narrow streets, some subway shops, trying to get our fill of our last hours in the Holy Land.

Off at 7 o'clock a.m. for Lodi Airport. Aloft, Tel Aviv lay below us like a map even our Shalom Tower Hotel. We had to go first to Cyprus to connect with a Cairo flight because there was still ill feeling on the part of Egypt toward Israel. We waited at the Nicosia airport. Some looked over the souvenirs; others conversed or read.

We boarded the United Arab Line but the plane was Russian and in about two hours reached Cairo. A big, friendly Egyptian in a mini-bus drove five or six of us to downtown, pointing out points of interest-Nasser's home, Sadat's "White House," mosques, driving wildly all the while, tooting horn, barely missing cars and pedestrians. Wah!

I might mention here that we had purchased a week's extension onto our two weeks Bible Lands tour for Egypt, Switzerland and Paris; thus, it was anti-climatic and so accordingly I shorten this part so as to not detract too much from the Bible Lands theme.

We put up at the palacial Nile Hilton Hotel overlooking the Nile River on one side and the Egyptian Museum on another. Soon we boarded a *felucca* (sailboat) and skimmed over the Nile for half an hour, passing by the Holy Fountain in the center. After supper I strolled along the streets. What a pandemonium! Lying on the ground, eating, boarding crowded busses on the run, speeding cars and taxis, pedestrians jay-walking. I was amazed, almost frightened, worse than Rome.

We traveled to the ruins of Memphis and rode a camel a short way next to the three pyramids and of course, we viewed the Sphinx. Much other I omit, tombs, recent excavations, the fertile countryside. Later, Abidul our driver, took us to the Mosque of Omar, which we entered shoeless. We shopped for a few items in the teeming bazaar, cautiously aware to the geniality of the shopkeepers and their tricks. In the fine museum we heard a lecture, saw artifacts and the Tomb of King Tut. A letter from home concluded the busy day.

A reschedule put us back in Piraeus, Greece. It was not the fault of our director, Dr. Jake Boggs and although we grumbled at the delay, we made the best of it, at least I did. Knowing that we would be grounded all day until 11 p.m., I got an okay and hiked to a village seen over the horizon. No one spoke English; I needed a match to light my pipe and no one had one, nor cigars. For supper we were bussed to George's Steak House several miles up the coast and uniquely and romantically were served on the sidewalk under dim lights.

July 24-We reached Zurich via Swiss Air and at once boarded a bus for Interlacken where a tired, sleepy and disgruntled party hit the pillows of the Grand Victoria Jungfrau Hotel at 2 a.m.

The next day was spent traveling along Lake Thun to Neiderhorn Mountain where we rode the chair lift to the summit and drank in breath taking views.

July 26-We took the winding valley road which leads to the foot of the Jungfrau and Mt. Schiethorn. We took the cable cars up the latter, four changes or stations, to the summit, almost 10,000 feet. A spectacular view of the Jungfrau and in other directions greeted us. Hazel and I snowballed. A novelty was to lunch in the revolving restaurant. Both coming and going were delightful; great vistas, high and rocky walls, little waterfalls, farm houses, farmers making hay, glaciers, snowfields, even hotels.

Wife tired out, I strolled the Interlaken streets alone, window shopping and eating a sandwich and ice cream and idling along the pretty little Aar River. No doubt, Interlaken has what it takes to attract tourists, mountains, lakes, scenery, all-electric trains, frequent bus service, shops galore.

On the way back to Zurich (pop. 600,000 Switzerland's largest city), we lunched on Sarnen Lake under an outdoor canopy. We passed many chalets and farms. I was struck by the varied designs of the houses; no two seemed alike and the courtesy of the people. A mountain along beautiful Lake Lucerne resembled Saddleback Mountain in Monterrey, Mexico.

A thunderstorm while we flew over the Alps that night alarmed us for some moments-up, down, we dipped. But our Air France plane made it onto Orly Airport, Paris on time at 9 p.m.

Fulfillment of a dream! Although more elegant than Rome, Athens or Cairo, I experienced some irritating incidents. Maybe it was my impatience with Parisian ways.

Our city tour took us to the Eiffel Tower, Napoleons Tomb, Tuliers Gardens, the Sorbonne, the Luxembourg Gardens, the Grand Opera House. Notre Dame, the Louvre ("Venus de Milo", "Mona Lisa"), the Pantheon and of course, the Champs Elysees and the Arc de Triumphe. I took a three hour walk from our LeGrand Hotel back to Pont Neff, the famed Left Bank and along many other streets. Next morning Hazel accompanied me on another walk, window-gazing and buying a few trinkets.

July 29-We packed up our treasure trove, a hookah water pipe, a Cyprus handbag, an olive-wood bound *New Testament*, a Swiss wrist watch, Israeli cigars, books, color slides, post cards, miniature flags and other sundries. We passed customs with a minimum of red tape. A dim view of Lands End, England and we climbed to 35,000 feet.

New York! And a tour of the "Big Apple."

Was the trip up to expectations? Had I read and studied for six months in preparation and had so long dreamed about, been in vain? Partly, because three weeks were too brief to cover such a large area adequately. However, we got some of the feel of antiquity, history, literature and art as well as a picture of life in that part of the world today. Yes, the experience was worth the money, time and effort.

–Written January 2000

Iberian Impressions

Ignacio Oloque, Spanish writer, once said, "the first pleasure of the traveler in a foreign country is to sit in a cafe in the open air and watch life pass in front of him." Bob and I were sitting at a table on the sidewalk of Avenidado Libertad in Lisbon and leisurely sipping an orange drink.

"Well, Bob, we're here. What's ahead? Fulfillment or disillusion? Iberia - a land of romance and contradictions?'

"Who knows," replied son Bob.

"Will our preconceptions dissolve in the day-to-day realities? Has all our reading been in vain? Will it be Don Quixóte or El Cid?" I questioned.

"We come well prepared, I think," said Bob. "We both have studied Spanish in high school and college. We both have a real interest in Spain and Latin America, you dad, greater than I. And you've read a lot more than I have."

"Well, naturally, Bob, I am older."

"Are we going to see a bullfight?"

"I think not, Bob; at least, not I. The two I saw in Mexico years ago sickened me out. Michener in his *Mexico* lets Ledesma, a character, say 'Americans ought not to look at them'."

"Will we hear flamenco? *Malaguena* like it should be played?"

"Maybe, but what I'd like is to meet the gypsies of old George Borrow's *Bible in Spain, Lavengro and Zincali.*"

At this moment the sun dimmed and a gentle rain began to fall. Where the mosaic pavement had vied with patches of sunlight and shade formed by the dancing leaves of the tree-shaded avenue, the pattern faded. We hastened to the shelter of an alcove.

Just that morning, July 8, 1972, we had been set down in Lisbon at the Florida Hotel, opposite Pombol Circle, on a flight of a TAP 747 plane from New York for a two-week package tour of Portugal and Spain. It was to be my gift to son Bob upon his graduation from Western Illinois University back in June.

A petite lady had been our guide on a bus tour of the city during which our party saw the Tower of Belem, the Jeronomos Monastery, the National Coach Museum, the Arc of Triumph, the great suspension

Tower of Belem, Lisbon

bridge over the Tagus River, the soaring statue of Christ, the War Memorial, the cathedral and other points of interest.

In the afternoon Bob and I walked the length of Avenida do Libertad, one mile, to its terminus at Don Pedro IV Square where were many shops, tri-level streets and buildings. In this city of one million people, built like Rome on seven hills, there is too much for the tourist to see and do in a mere two days. Lisbon is still growing. But really, the life of a country is more interesting than the famous "must see" points.

The next morning we planned to walk awhile but I arose feeling faint, jet lag and loss of sleep, so Bob walked alone for a long time. By afternoon I was somewhat recovered from my indisposition and we took a long bus tour.

Sintra is set among misty, wooded heights. Here is a Moorish castle and the summer palace of the kings of Portugal and much else, a place, said Lord Byron in *Childe Harold*, that was a glorious Eden. Estorial is a high-class casino with golf grounds and hotels in the nearby fishing town of Csacais on the beach. It holds bullfights. It is a pleasant resort with many shops. Que Luz Palace concluded our tour of this part of the Costa do Sol.

We now left Lisbon for 12 days. Our tour bus ran north along the Tagus River and the big island. We ran through interesting rural villages and small cities like Franca de Zira, Alanquer and Caldas Da Rainha. We then veered northwest to the coast to the famous fishing town of Nazré. Once picturesque, it has been spoiled by a cluttering of beach tents, sales stands, high prices and great crowds of tourists. We stopped here awhile and I talked with some fishermen mending nets.

Just east of Batalha we ate lunch at Fatima, world famous center of pilgrimage. At this revered shrine our guide, who spoke five languages, told the story of the three little girls who in 1917 beheld the apparition of the Virgin Mary. We viewed the Basilica.

Seated again, we passed through eucalyptus and pine lands (for resin), by olive, fig and grape lands and seeing hand-cut wheat grain, quaint donkey carts and an occasional windmill.

We paused at Coimbra, a city set on hills along the Mondego River. The university is the oldest in Europe. I was particularly excited in the rare book room of the library, rows upon rows of books, rising to a high ceiling with a ladder for access. Here was written and sung by students, *April in Portugal*, a fado on folk song.

Finally, at the end of a 234 mile drive, we stopped at Urugerica and put up at the nearby sequestered rural hotel Canas do Senhorim near the Mondego River. The ride from Coimbra had been over high, steep,

Coimbra University, Coimbra, Portugal

forested mountains with narrow roads and sharp curves. Pleasant were the gardens about the hotel, grapes, pine trees, etc. We heard a peculiar species of frog, sounding like tinkles.

Off early the next morning, we passed through Guarda over the Sierra da Estrela, highest point in Portugal at 6,539 feet and with spectacular views and roads. We crossed into Spain at Vilar Formosa and soon went through the considerable city of Ciudad Rodrigo.

As I rode over the vast brown plain I had a chance to reflect upon Portugal thus far. I had found the people kindly, a "smiling land," as opposed to the more austere, silent Spanish, as we often stereotype them. The Portuguese, as I had read, were brave, docile, patient, courteous, possessed a keen sense of injury and insult but at the same time often dishonest with lax morals, superstitious yet devout Catholics, from the city people to those on the *quinta* (farm). To stand possible correction, these are words from a 1902 writer. Times may have changed and after all, I had been in Portugal only five days! However, through all Iberia, there seems to be one common axiom of life, "Never do today what you can put off to tomorrow." Mexico and mañana land are synonyms.

And now "land of the vine and olive, lovely Spain!" But "almost every Spaniard is a poet."

We crossed a vast, brown plain and saw olives, sheep, rock fences, people cutting grain by hand, donkeys pulling at a grinder, a few tractors. We had a fine dinner in Salamanca with the usual fish done in olive oil. I skipped the third course and spent the time looking around the Plaza Mayor. I entered the shops in the arcade, quadrangle Monestry Court and mailed cards home.

Salamanca has been compared to Athens and Rome for its elegant monuments, plazas, convents and palaces but its greatest lure is the university (1230-43) and it still operates. Plaza Mayor, the most beautiful in Europe and the two great cathedrals have their admirers, but Salamanca is rich in architecture and other art forms. It is a golden city of pladersque buildings, all wonderfully preserved. A peculiar golden limestone makes the structures unique. It is a compact city and opulent. Unamuno, the writer lived many years in this city. There is a statue of Lazarillo de Tormes, the writer of the first picaresque novel. Salamanca was a patron of Columbus amidst his troubles. We left Salamanca over the Roman bridge (200 BC) spanning the Tormes River. I was sorry the visit was so brief.

We passed over a region savage in aspect; dry, dusty, glaring with only a few farmers. We crossed over a pass between the Sierra de Gredos and Sierra de Guadarra which gave way to a wind-swept plateau littered with giant, grotesque boulders. We made a rest stop overlooking the ancient walled city of Avila a mile away; then through one of the nine gates into another age, The Medieval. Begun in 1090 AD, a "scent of the dim past hovered over the peculiarly garbed place." It was a walled Old Jerusalem. Equally renowned is that Santa Teresa was born and lived here, she the religious mystic and writer (1515-82) who headed the convent. She is the soul of the place today.

A few miles along, nearing Madrid, one of our teenage boys aboard became sick and we were delayed beside the new super highway for the cleanup. Too much and too rich a Salamanca dinner, all that olive oil and wine. Olive oil is almost universal in Iberia but many northerners do not like it and well so, for no other foodstuff known to man is as loaded with calories.

From a great distance and from a height we could see across a valley to Madrid, resting on a plateau of 2,373 feet. It is the highest capital in Europe. Its population of 2,624,000 is rapidly expanding and the streets never seem to be empty except in the afternoon lull and the city stays up late. Beloved by Madrileños for centuries, the center is the Puertadel Sol and the Prado, the mecca of many tourists whether much interested in art or not.

Lodged in the Grand Colon Hotel on Doctor Esquerdo Calle, Bob and I promptly took to the streets to see Puerta del Sol, the Royal Palace, The Cortes and the various squares, plazas, important streets, circles and fountains. We viewed the many stores and cafes and bucked the very busy traffic.

The following morning a local English speaking guide and a French speaking guide (our party had some French Canadians) accompanied us on a bus tour, covering some of the identical places Bob and I had made so laboriously the day before. We spent time in the Prado galleries. It has over 3,000 paintings, 800 of Spanish artists alone and 40 Murillos besides those of Velasquex, Borch, Goya, El Greco and others.

In the afternoon Bob and I took a five hour walk which took us over several main streets again, past shops and cafes and imbibed the life of the city. We mailed cards at the post office. At City Park we viewed the group statue of Cervantes, Don Quixóte, Sancho Panza and the horse Rozinante, down by the oft dried-up Manzanares River. We had to cross the spacious El Retiro Park (over 300 acres) to reach the hotel, a park worthy of many words. We ate heartily at the Nebraska Cafe (187 pesetas for two). I retired with tired and stiff shanks.

The two of us took an excursion bus the 40 miles to the ancient and one-time capital of Spain; the austere and magic center of spiritual and intellectual life of those days, perched insolently upon a high hill, rocks and steep and the Tajo River rolling three-quarters around it. But Toledo's one-time glory has departed.

We entered the city through the double-arched Puerta de Bisagra, built by Alfonso VI in the 11th century and with a double eagle shield near the top of the warm, orange-colored structure. A wall protected the north part of the city; the deep gorge of the river the rest of the city.

During the day we wandered freely over the busy main streets made up of many tourists like ourselves. Bob and I walked across the Puente de San Martin bridge where we got a fine general view of Toledo and returned by the old Roman Puente de Alcántara bridge near a restored castle. We saw the Alcazar, Lady Carmen Church, the cathedral, the Synagogue del Transito, El Greco's house and other features. We lunched at the Hostal de Cardenal, built into the old city wall with a delightful court. Resuming our stroll, we stopped at Santo Tomé Church where we viewed El Greco's "The Burial of Count Orgaz." We listened to a short lecture on the great artist.

Souvenir buying was in order and as Bob and I were resting on a stone ledge along the narrow street, a cry went up, "Reagan!" A car passed by and we saw the California governor who was vacationing in Spain.

We reluctantly boarded the bus for Madrid for we had been fascinated by the narrow, crooked streets and sights of this old walled city.

Our tour party headed for Cordoba the next morning. It was a region of barren, rocky and dry tableland where rain seldom falls, although we saw wheat, olives, sunflowers and chickpeas growing on the red soil There were a few windmills and alfalfa grew under irrigation.

We were now in Andalusia and in the heart of La Mancha country.

We made a rest top in Puerta Lapice at the La Venta Don Quixóte store where the famous knight was recognized by its various wares for sale. As one who enjoyed reading of the tortuous career of the windmill fighter, I fully relished this rare chance to see the country. Don Quixóte has been staged and filmed of which latter I have seen *The Adventures of Don Quixóte* and *The Man of La Mancha*," both 1973.

Through Manzanares, over the Sierra Morena (where in a defile in George Borrow's day robbers held out), lunch at La Carolina at Hotel Perdiz (with its zoo, swim pool and trees), Linares and into the rich valley of the Guadalquiver River (with fields of cotton, corn and sugar cane) we rolled into Cordoba.

From our Grand Capitan Hotel, Bob and I walked to the chief sights. The Mesquita, a mosque converted to a church, dominates the city. Inside is a labyrinth of columns and arches, some 850, the arches red and white like peppermint candy. Bob climbed the tall bell tower near to the beautiful Patio de los Naranjos. We inspected the Alcazar and strode to the Moorish bridge over the Guadalquiver whose stone arches rest on pylons laid down before Seneca was born in a house by the river.

Cordoba has a statue of Seneca the elder. Other features we missed for lack of time: three museums, plazas, city gates, palaces, cafes and shops and other. Cordoba deserves more time. A letter from home at the hotel closed our day.

The route led southeast through Espeyo and Alcaudate over productive land, wheat, chickpeas, sugar beets, olives, small Spanish melons, tobacco, cotton, sunflowers and cordas. We saw salt flats and pyramids of salt from the saline ground soil. Into the snow-streaked Sierra Nevadas and we entered famed Granada, resting on three hills. I could now relive Washington Irving's *Tales of the Alhambra,* for the Alhambra is the pearl and magnet of this last stronghold of the Moors.

From our Melia Hotel we bussed to that exquisite Moorish palace. My account must be brief, only the high spots. We entered the Court of Justice and proceeded to the Hall

The Alhambra, Granada

of the Ambassadores and the Comares Tower; then the King's Gallery and to the Court of Lions (my choice feature of the whole palace). We passed by many patios, arches and cupolas, lavishly colored and adorned with wood, plaster and tiles. A kaleidoscope of flowers lined the walkways. We saw pools of water. We saw the room where Irving lived and wrote his book.

Across the valley we toured the Generalife, summer palace of the Moorish kings and surrounded by extensive gardens. Here was an incomparable view of Granada and on the right stretched away to the distant vega (plain) and the snowy Sierra Nevadas from across the Darro River and directly across the Albaicin caves of the gypsies.

Many tourists view gypsies through romantic eyes and I suppose I am one. But many writers speak of these Sacre Monte cave denizens as dirty beggars who cozen gifts from tourists. One does hear the guitars, tambourines and castanets from across the river sometimes; perhaps a *zambra* staged for tourists who are safer if they go only as a group. Beggars are still in Spain but they must not be as impertinent or impudent as they once were for neither Bob or I were ever approached for an alms.

We saw other sights in downtown Granada. Next to the huge cathedral is the Capilla Real (Royal Chapel) where we saw the tombs of Ferdinand and Isabella, with they handling the charter for Columbus' voyage. Alone that night I trod various streets and had a short conversation with two girls who initiated it by asking the time of day. Putas? Who knows? I was later on a narrow street with one-way traffic whizzing by. A man on the sidewalk gave me a sudden push as I stood on the curb. "*Cuidado*," he said. "They (the cars) will hit you." Tired, I rested in Plaza Nueva. A new moon shone. All about even at this hour life teemed. It was fit that Granada was called the "Dove's Nest." Here I digested the impressions of the day and mused on El Cid, the Lusiads, Irving, Cervantes, Richard Ford (early guidebook writer), George Borrow, Harry Franck (*Four Months Afoot in Spain),* yes, even on our modern James Michener (*Iberia*). I was tempted to agree with the sentiment of a poet:

"Quien no ha vista Granada, no ha vista nada."
("He who has not seen Granada has seen nothing.")

We left for Malaga on the Mediterranean coast at 8 o'clock. We noted many wheat fields on which the stubble burned, a voluntary, but to me, a bad practice. Old time threshing floors trod by donkeys and men appeared amid the dense smoke from the fields. Other crops were growing and there was the ever-present olive. We climbed ever higher and paused at Colmenar in the Almijara Mountains for lunch; stratified rocks, tunnels, spectacular views succeeded; then up the Malaga Mountains to the steep Cuesta de la Reina from where we had breath-taking views of the sea and Malaga.

Our bus passed through Malaga and continued another 10 miles to the burgeoning resort town of Torremolinos, one of Europe's leading playgrounds. At this town of 6,000 begins the real Costa del Sol and continuing west to beyond Gibraltar.

Our hotel, the Riviera, one among many, was a high-rise along the beach. It was part of the Melia chain. Jose Melia, born in Valencia in 1911, was well educated; worked in England; then back to Valencia and established the Melia Travel Agency. He eventually also operated many busses and hotels. He moved to Madrid in 1957. So this was our second Melia "home". Although the Riviera had its own fine pool, Bob and I chose the sea. Almost to the day a year before (1971) I had swum in the eastern end of the Mediterranean at Famagusta, Cyprus.

After a dinner, which included squid and sturgeon, we two walked several miles to the outskirts of Malaga. That night Bob and some of our group went to a discotheque.

Next day was Sunday, July 16. Bob and I took a bus into Malaga (15 pesetas each) where we enjoyed a quiet day in this pleasant port city of lovely villas. Malaga averages 324 days of sunshine in the year. We strolled over many streets and alley ways which had a charm of their own. Many shops were closed. We walked through the shady Paseo del Parque, to the Plaza de la Marina with its fountain and cafes to the Alcazaba (Moorish fortress), to the cathedral and stepped in and along the Calle Marquis de Lorious. We skipped the two or three museums. We learned that Picasso was born here. We saw the dry Guadalmadins River. Sipping a coke and a Cruzcampo beer at a sidewalk cafe, two *señoritas* asked for a cigarette light. (I exulted on this trip in my Spanish cigars).

Time magazine (Dec. 11, 1972) said Spain was enjoying prosperity at a price, inflation one percent per month, rising food prices, some protests and demonstrations, rapid change with the pain of adjustment to a new political era, grossly over-build concrete jungles ("Miami Beach East"), traffic-choked streets, crime, drugs and unemployment.

We followed the Costa del Sol westward to Cadiz, through Marabella and Las Lines and from a distance saw the Rock of Gibraltar across from Algeciras. The air was too dim to see across to Africa. We took lunch at Tarifa at the Mesón Restaurant. Cattle ranches, sunflowers, corn, sugar beets and cactus fences lined the road. Near Cadiz were extensive salt flats. Around Jerez (source of sherry wine) cotton, corn, grapes, cordas, wheat and olives grew. This and the Ronda area, was part of the Hemingway country (*For Whom the Bell Tolls*).

"Fair is proud Seville; let her country boast her strength, her wealth, her site of ancient days" (Byron, *Childe Harolds' Pilgrimage*). Come to Seville with a prepared list of superlatives for you will need them to convey your impressions of that fabulous city. Seville, situated on the muddy Guadalquiver River, is a bustling city of 700,000 and may be Spain's oldest. It has a proud literary and artistic association. The Murillo tradition is still much alive; both he and Velasquez were born there; Cervantes was in prison there; Columbus is entombed there and El Cid has a monument. As we will see, architecture reached great heights in the olden days. Indeed, Seville is a veritable Paris of Spain.

We put up at the Cristina Hotel. Bob and I then walked many hours during the two days and nights. We saw the cathedral (third largest in the world); the Giralda and the Alcazar. We paused in the Patio de los Naranjos, the Parque de Maria Luisa, the Plaza de España and let the doves rest on our arms in the Plaza de Los Reyes. We threaded the labyrinth of the narrow streets, one called the "kissing street" because one could lean across and kiss a girl. Cafes afforded al fresco drinks. Gardens of bougainvillea, plumbago, hoya, roses and geraniums lent color, as well as the many buildings constructed of *albero*, which is an unique sand found nowhere else and which produces a golden ochre when mixed with paint.

As Harry Franck said in 1910, "All Spain mixes freely." We found it so among the Sevilliaños. Like a child, they "live now." Families gather early in the plazas and amuse themselves, eating, drinking, children playing, guitars playing. "Every Spaniard is a musician," in general if not universal. In Seville the flamenco reigns along, of course, with the popular disco music. Here the *Malaguena* reaches perfection in the Andalusian city, a popular act of music, song and dance, seen on the stage only in Madrid.

The second afternoon we walked across the river to the Barrio Triana district, once the haunt of the gypsy, but all gone now to Granada. It is now a burgeoning area, modern. Down river from the bridge is the 13th century, 12-sided, Moorish Torre del Oro (Tower of Gold). We saw it in the glowing sunset.

That night I sat alone in the little triangular park near the Puerta de Jerez, near our hotel and as I watched the street life flow past I fell to musing. I think I felt as Borrow did in 1842 when he exclaimed, perhaps in a similarly mood, "Oh, how pleasant it is, especially in spring-

"An atmosphere instead of lawns", Serville

time, to stray along the shores of the Guadalquiver! Not far from the city, down the river, lies a grove called Las Delicias or The Delights ... trees, long, shady walks. This grove is the favorite promenade of the Sevillians and there one occasionally sees assembled whatever the town produces of beauty or gallantry." It did not seem real that I was in Seville imbibing its history and life. I thought, "All these glorious days are being lavished upon the people. Yet the charms are being wantonly wasted in so far as most of the world is concerned."

Next day we rode into the Sierra Morena highlands and got into good farm land shortly after, especially around Zafra (rest stop). We entered the Extremadura area of Spain, a brutal, wild, isolated, though romantic region. It has two of Spain's less developed provinces with poor soil and poor people. In Zafra I talked with some boys, the eldest naming himself Jacinto Sala Cortes. I photographed them and gave them coins, which they had not expected. Zafra is a lively, attractive town where Hernan Cortez stayed before going to Mexico.

We passed through the city of Badajoz, a "nothing-city of the west," as Michener says. He gives an inordinate space to Badajoz (76 pages) but he has his reasons. George Borrow lived in Badajoz a while selling his Bibles. Here we crossed the border into Portugal and a few miles out ate lunch at a poosada in Elvas. The town is on a hill with two old forts separated by a valley. Borrow doubted the need for a fort for there was not much to protect. We observed workmen laying small, white, quartz rocks on the sidewalks by hand which made a pretty mosaic. Elvas has one of the best preserved aqueducts in all Portugal.

Rich, level plains spread out as we approached Lisbon. Irrigated rice, sugar beets, wheat and corn grew. Pines, olives, eucalyptus and cork trees were frequent and we passed two trucks loaded with cork strips. We entered Lisbon from the north, along the right bank of the Tagus.

Bob and I took a final walk along Avenida do Libertad and packed our luggage, stuffed with souvenirs. That night we boarded a 707 plane for home.

The long flight gave us time to think, with mixed regret and pleasure. Had it all been real or a dream? But I doubted not that we had seen "Castles in Spain," lack of psychological terms not withstanding. "Oh, lovely Spain! Renow'd, romantic land" (Bryon). Despite its faults, Michener sums it up in one evocative word Duenda, meaning "mysterious and ineffable charm."

"Which city, scene or experience sticks in our minds - Granada, Seville or what?" I asked the nodding Bob.

"What about that quiet, lazy day in Malaga?" he returned.

"Hard to beat," I said. "Almost edges the others out. But if I am pinned down to one it must be Seville."

I looked at Bob. He was asleep.

Of our 15 days, I say with Homer (*Odyssey*), "Of many men the states and learned their ways."

New York! And a bus tour of the Big Apple.
                                                            –Written February 2000.

Mexico Revisited

Mexico! Land of paradox, of contrasts, of varied topography, exotic beaches, towering mountains, plateaus and steaming tropical jungles - a history as tortuous as the Balkans. It is a land I came to love, to become *simpático*. The history of its people - the Spanish, the Indians, the mestizos - and its relations with the United States is worthy of a lifetime of study and travel. I have crossed its borders eight times.

In 1932, as a healthy, active youth of 22, I took my first vagabond trip to Mexico. I stopped in Monterrey, Saltillo, Quertaro, San Luis Potosi, Mexico City, Puebla, Cuernavaca, Acapulco, Morelia, Uruapan, Patzcuaro, Chapala, Guadalajara and went by rail along the west coast to Nogales, 18 states. Home again, I wrote the book *Mexico for Me!* in spirit if not in the manner of Charles Flandrau's *Viva Mexico!* The book was never published but it ran serially in the Golconda, IL *Herald Enterprise* in 1933.

I contend the adage "familiarity breeds contempt" is equivocal; too dogmatic to serve as a safe guide to conduct, either of mind or body. Familiarity should deepen friendship; it should increase our enjoyment of a good book, one re-read many times. Contact with nature should further inspire us. Good habits become more firmly entrenched. Then why should not more visits to a country once thrilled over not be revisited? That first feeling will not, of course, be repeated quite the same. Like a changing floating cloud - mayhap in the form of a Grecian God - the evanescent first emotional response will not be experienced. But the first acquaintance will not dull our second or succeeding returns. I am speaking of Mexico as a personal example. I might well exclaim *un pais grande*! (A great country).

True, now I have not the fire, the curiosity, the youthful and romantic spirit as I had during the epochal 1932 trip. Most of the cities I have not revisited but I have added Tampico and Chihuahua, as the succeeding lines will relate.

This is a travelogue interspersed with observations on changes that have occurred in Mexico, which include the economic, political and social aspects. I should not hope to encompass many other changes such as that of mining, electric power, labor, social conduct, art, music, literature or the entertainment world in this short paper, for which I express my regret. Candidly, much of this has been gleaned from my readings of books and news clippings since 1932.

Twenty-eight years later in 1960 - a whole generation - wife Hazel, son Bob and I in a new Studebaker Lark drove to Chihuahua. We crossed over to Villa Acuña first on a bus and strolled over its rough, narrow sidewalks awhile. It was not a pretty town. We crossed back and drove to El Paso and there crossed into Ciudad Juarez. We then drove the 232 miles to Chihuahua over dry, semi-mountainous country and put up at Palacio Hilton Hotel.

We strolled, reveling in the Mexican atmosphere of this city of 150,000. The next day, Sunday, we attended a Methodist church. More sight-seeing. Alone, I walked far out on Cuahuatemoc Avenue, saw its statue and the Sanctuary of Our Lady of Guadeloupe and rode a bus back. We, of course, saw the cathedral and other principal buildings. We saw evidence of the "semi-illiterate peon turned bandit, turned general" Pancho Villa (real name Doroteo Villa). He was a "Sanguinary beast and yet a champion of the poor." His widow still lived in Chihuahua in a rundown mansion. Though her beauty is faded, Señora Villa's memory, age 73, lingers. We did not meet her.

A somewhat related story is that of the satirist American writer Ambrose Bierce who disappeared into Chihuahua and when last heard of

A view of Chihuahua

was en route to visit Pancho Villa's troops. Tired of life, the 71 year-old Bierce sent a letter to a friend in which he said, "If you should hear of my being stood up against a Mexican stonewall and shot, please know that I think it is a pretty good way to depart this life...To be a gringo in Mexico - ah, that's euthanasia."

After spending three days in Chihuahua we explored Tijuana a couple of hours. It is one of several border towns that has experienced a sort of boom; in fact, throughout Mexico in general. Capital flowed in at a rapid pace. New industries were remaking the land. Mexico's bid to United States firms was cheap labor. In the Mexican border towns a system of twin plants arose, an "export processing" in which United States companies supplied the parts and were assembled in Mexico to be sent back north finished at low duties. These assembly plants or *malquiladoras*, used women for cheap labor. Prominent among industries was that of auto assembly. Many other familiar brand names were represented: Goodyear, Kellogg, General Electric, Dairy Queen and so on. Supermarkets USA style were now common. Many were located in the interior provincial cities; for instance, Chihuahua with a nylon factory; Queretaro with Ralston Feeds, DuPont and others; San Luis Potosi with Lockheed Aircraft; Monterey, the "Chicago of Mexico," has many United States companies. Other firms operate in Mexico City, Guadalajara and elsewhere. In 1965 Mexico's developing plants employed 30,000 workers. It was the "paycheck revolution" in which many aspired to middle class status and many achieved it.

Under the 1917 Mexican constitution the government began expropriation of excess acreage of *haciendas* and gave it to the peons in small acreage's, thus establishing the *ejido* system of land distribution which still operates. Much of the land was poor and the tracts small, so a communal system developed much like the Russian collectives. Under irrigation and modern methods, the *ejido* reclaimed over 400,000 acres of the fertile desert land, a shining example being that of Ciudad Obregon in Sonora state. Despite defects - really an economic failure - it has been a psychological and political success. However, the *ejidos* continue to produce at a lower rate than do the numerous private enterprise farms and ranches. Although the farm problem is perhaps Mexico's toughest problem, the life of the worker has been made far better. Cars, machinery, schools, health care, etc. show progress. Another problem, the *bracero* or migrant, ended in the early 1970s. But the illegal migrant is still a problem.

Near disaster hit in 1982 with the devaluation of the peso. It really hit border towns, sales off 50 percent; unemployment and underemployment; high prices; uncertainty; inflation almost 100 percent. It sent more US plants to Mexico. President De La Madrid called for an austerity program of internal economic and moral reform.

On June 12, 1963 our party of four crossed over the Rio Grande into Matamoros, Mexico, where a problem at once arose. Customs were adamant that Sheila, our granddaughter, could not enter Mexico without written consent of her parents back in Arkansas. Was our trip to be thwarted so soon? Finally, the officer made the ill-famed *morbida* touch: for $20 he would let the girl enter with our *oral* permission! We paid.

Mountains appeared after 100 miles of driving over dry, flat land. Four miles short of Ciudad Victoria a tire went flat, caused by running over a cactus shoulder. At Hotel Sierra Gorda (85 pesos, about $7) an English-speaking hotel hand got the tire repaired and became quite friendly, with the usual *propina* (tip). We had a good balcony view of the main plaza, the cathedral and the blue mountains looming to the south. We strolled and I bought a 12-string guitar in the market.

The following morning we headed for Tampico over the older Pan-American Highway. This inter-American road was completed in the 1930s and increased the flow of tourist into Mexico. Main roads all over Mexico have been continually improved. Now, instead of the Ciudad Victoria route, the Pan-Am has been re-routed through Saltillo to join the old road at San Luis Potosi. Also, one can now drive from Mexico City to Guadalajara and up the

The market, Tampico

west coast to Nogales and another new highway joins it from Durango. The road to Acapulco is now good and a new road to Yucatan is fair.

We crossed the Tropic of Cancer and paused at Ciudad Mantes awhile where we saw its First Baptist Church. We used our weak Spanish on several occasions. Near Tampico we swam in the gulf waters at Miramar Beach; then quickly motored into Tampico. What thick traffic along the narrow streets! We found the city about the size of Peoria, 122,000. We engaged a very fine room at the Hotel Imperial for 50 pesos. After dark we strolled over to the Constitution Plaza, across from the cathedral and City Hall. A band played well and we enjoyed the Mexican scene around us as we sat on benches. Young people promenaded - boys going one way, girls the opposite - in the romantic, old-fashioned way.

"How do you like that way of courting?" I asked son Bob.

"It is not the way we do it at home," he laughed.

"It might be better if it were done this way in the States," opined wife Hazel.

While the lively evening stretches on, I will insert some further remarks, not related to the plaza scene.

Mexico rode out the Great Depression perhaps better than the U.S.; only one-half of one percent unemployed as against our five to 10 percent, which showed the difference between a handicraft system and a mechanized one. The Industrial Revolution of 1750 began in Mexico in 1950. By 1952 USA capital was flowing into Mexico at a great rate and many of our countrymen where moving into Mexico because of lower living costs, disgust with conditions under the Truman administration or fear of an atomic war. In the last 10 years steel production went up 3-1/2 times. Cement, chemicals and electric power doubled. New highways, airports, hotels, housing projects, free schools sprang. However, there was a setback last year (economic growth rate plunged 3-1/2 percent and there was pump priming). But with help of over $260 million from the Alliance for Progress, a crash program eased the situation.

However, on the whole, Mexico has experienced a fundamental revolution. It has solved its problem of militarism. An active battle against poverty; illiteracy and diseases are on-going. Indeed, a social revolution is being wrought. Mexico knows what it wants and if one regime fails of goals the country goes on with enthusiasm and hope. The sad thing is that Yankee invasion has diluted and debased a vigorous and colorful culture.

Despite a light rain and a night of stomach upsets ("Montezuma's Revenge"), we strolled awhile the next morning and with regret took out Avenida Hidalog for the return to Ciudad Victoria, where we again put up at the same hotel. That night we went to an open-air movie (in Spanish, of course). Next day we bid Raymond Rodriguez and Victor Montanos *adios* and left for Monterrey.

In Monterrey we lodged at the Hotel Continental across from the cathedral and Zaragoza Plaza. From our second story balcony we had a fine view of blue Saddle Mountain. I was not overly amazed at the, to me, minor changes in the city, although the city had grown to about 600,000 from 100,000 in 1932.

Next day, Sunday, we attended the Primera Iglesia Bautistat Church, the first Baptist church established in Mexico in 1864. We met the pastor, Sr. H. Salinas and Bob and Sheila sat in Sunday School (all in Spanish). It was a novel experience. That night the band played in Zaragoza Plaza but a light rain soon dispersed all of us.

We left early for Saltillo, paralleling the dry Santa Catarina River and stopped briefly at Haustica Canyon, passing over a rocky, mud-puddle rural road to the cave site. Here Sheila rode a burro led by a boy (two pesos). We drove the 50 miles over the saw-toothed mountains and reached Saltillo and the Hotel de Avalia at four o'clock. We strolled over the quaint provincial city, as ever browsing the market and the shops. Memories of my visit there in 1932 recurred; of that hike from Monterrey, of that friendship with Maurois Gonzalez who trudged the road with me and helped procure breakfast at a roadside hut.

A day later we retraced the way to Monterrey; north over the famous Mamulique Pass with its long, hairpin curves (but since eliminated by a fine by-pass) and we entered Laredo.

******

It all started in Peoria in 1972. I was teaching seventh grade social studies at Pleasant Hill School when one morning two Mexican girls enrolled. They were visiting their Aunt Nido, a semi-pro singer, for the purpose of cultivating their English language. Thus, I had Sara and Diana Jaíme for several months. Retiring the next year and moving to Metropolis, I often corresponded with the Jaíme family of Monterrey. I was often urged to visit with them. But it was 1976 before wife and I accepted the invitation. I had always wanted to spend a Christmas in Mexico. Here was my chance.

The Cathedral, Monterrey

We stayed at the Rio Hotel the first night, December 22. From our seventh floor room we had a superb view of the city, Saddle Mountain and the Chipinque range. The night view was as good, with thousands of lights on the Chipinque slopes. Next morning we quite easily found our friend's home in Garza García suburb and were warmly greeted.

The family of Señor Don Carlos Jaíme and Señora Doña Diana Zamudio Jaíme (James) included the children: Sara, Diana, Carlos, Marcelia and Adrian, ages in descending order. It was a middle class family - whether Spanish or mestizo I did not learn - religious (Catholic), talented, cultured, educated, much traveled and mother Diana especially politically active.

Although in Mexico the male occupies the dominant role, it seemed that mother Diana took the lead and was the dominant one in the family economy. She worked as teacher (bi-lingual), secretary, translator and performed other work. She, in particular, became the far-traveler (Russia, Chili, France (to study awhile) and the United States). We found that the Jaímes had just moved into a new house which they had built among the hills of this suburb. They had a very genial young woman as day *criada* (servant) whose name was Mina.

We ate dinner at grandma Zamudio's house. We then made a shopping tour downtown where I bought a large piñata, a serape and a fancy walking cane in the busy *mercado* (market).

We ate again at the Jaímes. A big item was the papayas. The table cleared, we sat back and conversed - Spanish, some English. I lit a cigar; Señor Jaíme a cigarette. He took up his guitar and sang and picked, expert as he was. I played some on his guitar; young Carlos recorded. I received letter a few years later in which daughter Diana said Carlos often re-played that tape. In intervals Adrian and Marcelia prepared their *naciomento* creche while Carlos cavorted and went through the motions of a bullfight with his red cloth cape.

Christmas Eve. Mother Diana leading, we trailed behind in our car again to the large market. The handicrafts, the flowers, the people, the very air itself have always been the essence of my enjoyment. We next stopped at the Los Jocates Club at the foot of Saddle Mountain.

As we ate Mexicana style a six-string band played. Downtown I bought gifts for the Jaímes and grandma Zamudio. A stop at the Bishop's Palace on a high hill overlooking Monterrey ended the tour. A sort of fort, it was once seized by Pancho Villa.

Monterrey is a city of surprises in several ways. It has had a phenomenal growth (in 1992 some 2,700,000) and is Mexico's third largest. I was amazed this time at the changes. Garza García and other suburbs had grown up. The former market stalls along the banks of the river had been officially evicted and moved to Constitution Avenue and named Colon market, well-roofed and locked against night theft. A giant brewery (Mexico's oldest), a glass factory, steel, affiliate American firms and other factories make the city the largest industrial center of the country. Elegant and cosmopolitan - fascinating. All strange too, because by all reason a city should not be here because of its proximity to the USA, a history of floods and on a barren plain. One reason for its advance is sound technique, contented and conservative workers and strong initiative.

However, Monterrey shared the country's economical problems in 1976 and subsequent years. For 22 years the peso stood at 12-1/2 cents to the dollar. But in 1976 it was devaluated to 24; in 1984 to 204; in 1996 the peso was still in trouble despite a succession of presidents who promised relief. Un and under employment plagued the country. Migration to the large cities continued with most rural people not improving themselves.

One of the Jaíme girls wrote us in September 1976, "Devaluation will cost me more now to visit the States. President Eschevierra is as dumb and crazy as Woody Woodpecker." In 1979 mother Diana wrote, "Can't do anything else but work harder. Prices are shooting up like rockets." In 1980 a letter said, "They say this year will be a worse one, but Monterrey is pretty well off compared to other cities." January 1983, "Gas has increased from $6 a liter to $20. Inflation is rampant." And as late as 1996, from daughter Diana (now married), "It is a year of not knowing what is going to happen. Fewer clients can afford our car wash, though we charge the same price. Inflation 50 percent; supermarket items 100 percent."

Christmas Eve night some 20 kinspeople partook of a sumptuous dinner at the home of Lic. Angel Lopez Siller, an old gentleman lawyer and Notary Public. A Christmas tree and gifts, an abridged *posada* enacted, general conversation and song and guitar by Señor Jaíme (one song raised eyebrows among the women) were features of the evening. It is an understatement to merely say Hazel and I enjoyed it all. The

The extended Jaime family, Monterrey

girls left for midnight mass at the cathedral as we left for the Jaíme home to spend our second and last night.

The Jaímes led us out to the Saltillo highway next morning and bid us *adios*. How fortunate to have this family as friends! And still as corespondents. It recalled my one week's stay in Puebla in 1932 with another Mexican family, the guest of city school superintendent Señor Hernandez, his wife, daughter Otilla and three teenage sons.

In Saltillo we took a room in the unprepossessing Hotel Primier. We walked awhile, seeing the interesting people, shops and life. Next morning I was awakened by the bray of a donkey down the street.

We wound through the 6,560 feet pass south of Saltillo on Route 57, one of the finest roads in Mexico. Clouds enveloped us. Then the road fell and straightened. We snapped pictures of the yucca and organ cactus. We passed several *ejidos*. We spent an hour in Matehuela, an old mining town of 50,000 with three factories. Although it was Sunday, outdoor and indoor markets were open. Again we rose into heavy cloud mists. Sixty miles on we passed through Huizache Junction. We did not dare stop for aggressive Indian vendors and beggars lined the road for miles and would have pestered us no end, maybe plundering our car or assaulting us. Farther along we saw two-wheel oxcarts, cow and goat herders and burros ("Mexican jeeps") loaded with corn fodder. From Huizache many big transport trucks passed us and traffic grew as we neared San Luis Potosi.

We reached the quaint colonial, but new ultra-modern, city of nearly half a million people about five o'clock and put up for two days and nights at the Hotel Concordia. Here in this city I first met the older Hernandez youth in 1932 who was a traveling thread salesman.

We reveled in downtown San Luis Potosi; walking; throngs of people; seeing the shops and sidewalk *puestos*; seeing a wedding in the Cathedral Carmen; browsing in the huge market place of Mercado Hidalgo and becoming tired, sat on a bench in Plaza Armas and watched the night life pass by. On impulse we ate as we felt during our stay. Perhaps it was our activity or the high altitude (6,200 feet).

December 28, found us on the road back to Huizache where again was the army roadside vendors. We took Route 80 some miles, then branched off onto the secondary Route 101. Soon began a climb - some in second gear - with breath-taking mountain views of the Sierra Madre. We spent the night in Ciudad Victoria, in the same hotel as 14 years before. After a pleasant drive the tired out wife and I crossed the Rio Grande at Matamoros at 3 p.m.

So we left our friends and dear old Mexico.

******

I shall take the remainder of my allotted space to tie up some loose ends of the confusing Mexican political and economic arena.

The Revolution Institution Party (PRI) has ruled Mexico for the past 70 years and never lost a national election, although a few gubernatorial and mayoral posts have been lost. Congress is a puppet of the PRI and the whims of the president. Bureaucracy and corruption have been rampant. However undemocratic the system, it has insured a measure of stability and created continuity. Mexico, plagued with problems of a diverse people, weak economy, soaring population, revolution and lack of a national consciousness, is unique in history. Many think that political unrest will be cured only by raising the standard of living. The Mexican people are increasingly demanding both. It has been forced to industrialization and to becoming a real world partner.

I list Mexico's presidents from 1932. The presidential election is held every six years in December and he may not succeed himself. Rubio 1932, but served only briefly. Why? Cardenas 1934. He became on of Mexico's best-loved leaders. Men who followed him gave maturity to his programs. Comache 1940. Aleman 1946, a spendthrift, wasted government money; he and the big men salted money away (in

Swiss banks?). Cortines 1952. He cleaned house; a severe, hard-working, concerned man. Under him there was internal peace, quiet growth and a move toward democracy. Mateos 1958. Ordaz 1964. Social Security was introduced but not to all 29 sates. Eschevierra 1970. He was severely criticized for some of his measures. During these years there was an open Communist Party. Portillo 1976. Madrid 1982. Gotori 1988. He said the paranoid, super-nationalistic Mexico must change and emerge from the historic cocoon. He pushed the National Solidarity Program, an amalgam of all welfare programs. The National Democratic Party emerged second in the election. Zedillo 1994. He was opposed in the election by Cevallos (National Action Party) and by Cardenos (Democratic Revolution Party). Zedillo's majority was heavy. He recognized the move toward pluralism. Mexico joined the NAFTA. Ten billion dollars of foreign capital left the country. He clandestinely devaluated the peso.

Zedillo said he voted for all three candidates, knowing, of course, that his vote would be lost! He wanted to show his neutrality in the hopeful end of one-party rule.

Update: Vicente Fox was elected president on Sunday, July 2, 2000 of the National Action Party (PAN), He broke the 71 year rule of the PRI Party, a revolutionary event, which reflects a changing and maturing nation. He promises "responsibility" and a resolution to the US-Mexico immigration problem.

Shall we just skim the news headlines for a picture of the economic scene through the years? It will further my design to note the changes in Mexico since my first visit in 1932. In 1938 Mexico could see only the rosy side of expropriation of oil, etc. The 1960s saw a solid and steady growth. Industrial output climbed; 25 percent of the budget was for education; over one million North American tourists visited; the United States made great direct investments and farm income increased along with better transportation and communication. Bank loans began. Installment buying began. Sears even issued credit cards! The cattle business grew with improved breed. USA books, records, cosmetics, etc. became common. Supermarkets appeared. Advertising increased. In the 1970s increasing population posed problems. Feeding and educating the young (one-half of Mexican born were under age 15) seemed impossible. The country's worse economic crisis since the 1940s hit. Half of the workers were out of work. Yet the '70s were times of relative splendor, counting its natural resources and substantial revenue from foreign investors and tourists. In the 1980s Mexico suffered financial crisis. The foreign debt was $81 billion. Factories closed. Oil, coffee and silver prices dropped. In early 1990 the economy all but collapsed. Peso devaluation's were made. NAFTA bid well to help Mexico, along with even more presence of US corporations. The outlook is optimistic what with rising consumer buying power, a more democratic system and better international trade policies.

I had intended some comments on Mexico's cities but space is running out. A few sentences must suffice. Change, growth, characterizes most of the provincial cities. Residential and industrial sprawl continues.

No more are Queretaro, Puebla, Morelia compact. At mid-century Guadalajara's population had doubled in 10 years. Playgrounds like Puerta Vallarata arose along with Cancun and Cozumel, unspoiled places heretofore. Lake Chapala, Acapulco and other places continued to be popular with American visitors and residents. Despoilment was already occurring, the "blight of bourgeoisie Mexican taste at its most garish." The most startling and the most alarming change has been in Mexico City and the Federal District with such a rapidly growing population and suburban spread. Long the biggest city in Mexico, it grew from 2 million in 1960 to 20 million in 1992 (Metro), the world's third largest city. In 1932 all of Mexico had 16 million inhabitants. By 1960 it had doubled. Estimates now are at over 95 million.

In 1962 Samuel Ramos, a native of Michoacan state, probed the mind of Mexico in his *Profile of Man and Culture in Mexico* and came up with an analysis of what he called the "National Conscience." Said he, "...the national conscience has steadfastly sought for true natural introspection," but "the examination has not been undertaken with rigor, depth and an objectivity..." Mexico suffers depressive complexes, one, that of painful feelings of inferiority. A love of knowledge will foster their erasure and come to terms with the white man, who (the Yankee) could be of great help financially and technologically. These notions of inferiority have become habitual since Mexico's independence in 1821. Some Mexicans have attained a desirable sense of superiority and are less susceptible to deceit and distortion. They have been turned to man's basic nature.

The entire issue of the *Journal of American History* for September 1999 (an organ of the Organization of American Historians) is devoted to Mexico. I recommend this work to all Mexaphiles. Students of Mexico doubtless have already read Madame Calderon de la Barca's classic work (1843), Prescott's *Conquest of Mexico*, Flandrau's *Viva Mexico!*, Beale's *Mexican Maze*, Chase's *Mexico*, James Mischener's

Mexico and a host of other books. The OAH report comes from 16 scholars, all Mexican but one and is an in-depth analysis of the present state of Mexico's political, economic and cultural situation with some earlier history thrown in. I encapsulate the content of the report.

Along the American-Mexican border are common problems that require collaboration: trade, immigration, intermarriage, crime and the police, the American corporation in Mexico, the untraumatic diaspora's of Mexicans to the United States and so on, all of which involves international economic, political and cultural crises. They are trans-national matters (a major burden of the essays). Fused interests beget similarities. The Mexican National state has lost control over basic features of its life. The transition to democracy has begun. National interests are not based on principles but on interest. Mexico has been forced to accept plurality. De facto economic and cultural integration grow. People are becoming trans-nationalized; the sense of Mexican nationalism has blurred. The trend toward a more global liberal model is exemplified in NAFTA. Mexico has been forced by the outside to change. The key word is "modernization." That and "democracy." The first battles (1821-48) was for a national identity along a shifting border. Now, although still only semi-democratic, Mexico seeks true identity through the process of trans-nationalism.

Viva Mexico! *Un pais grande*!
                                                        –Written March 2000

Adventures
Afoot
❧

In no other activity do I so indulge and cherish those memories associated with plain walking and hiking. I am told that at the unremembered age of around 3, I ran away from our hired girl and was found a quarter mile down the road. At age 12, as narrated elsewhere in this book, I hiked to New Columbia. Aged 15, I made a two-day hike to Dixon Springs and Golconda in Pope County in July 1925, trudging 44 miles and taking the train for 22 miles. I slept upon a hill on an old couch overlooking the park. I thoroughly explored the scenic area and drank (to my later discomfort) of the strong mineral water.

Were these early jaunts indicative of a propensity, a "get away" call to future wanderlust? While my father was in the army in France during WWI, I was left liberally to my own devices and with a cousin we rambled over the community, fishing, hunting and trapping and roaming the river hills and the cypress swamps. Of course, there were other necessitous walks, to school, store, neighbor visits and parties - when cars were scarce. Later, farm work required much walking and seldom really pleasurable. Then "our weary limbs did penance enough for a multitude of sins." My early reading of all the *Carpenter's Geographical Readers* and other travel adventures also fed my vagrant leanings.

What is there about walking (or hiking, tramping) that makes a boy and many adults want to get out on the open road, or over fields and woods? Is it an inborn, unconscious desire? Is it a throw back to our pre-history ancestors? Is there some alchemy of body fluids that impels one to hit the road? Is the urge taught or caught on a special fine spring day when all nature calls?

I have little hope that I can add anything new since so much has been written about walking in its various aspects, but I propose merely to tell of some of my highlight hikes; a momento of my own experiences. My second purpose is to make some general remarks on this mode of travel.

However, limitations must be set. Exclusion of certain kinds of walking is made necessary by the space allotted to walking of a special kind and by the very nature of the subject. The distinction resides in the reason or purpose for the different modes. For instance, when we walk we walk; when we go on a hitchhike trek we walk and ride and mostly the latter. As adventurous and broadening as it is, it is herein excluded, although I have done my share of it over much of our country and Canada. I recall the day I walked the Tamiami Trail all day for 20 miles without a ride until near sunset, with mosquitoes, frogs and maybe alligators lurking in the saw grass water alongside the road. Where was I to sleep? But hiker's luck gave me a ride to Tampa just at sunset.

Since walking is a universal activity - barring infants, the sick and crippled - there are many modes and purposes. Jef-

Dixon Springs, Pope County

frey Farnol's beckoning *Broad Highway* eliminates jogging, running, athletics and competitive sports, mountaineering, necessitous walks and walk-a-thons as forms of Sussman's 'psychological magic walking.' Riding the rails asks for much waiting and walking. Here, again, I have done my hobo share of several thousand miles. Out! And there are kinds of walking that are questionable although sometimes proper to an occasion: stroll, ramble, amble, stride, poke, meander, march, plod, trudge, hobble, stumble, mosey and so on. What is best is to strike a rhythm at a reasonable speed, say three or four mph. Eliminated also are those amazing feats of speed, length and endurance. All honor to those pedestrians who circle the globe: Harry Franck (*Working My Way Around the World*), Steven Newman (*World Walk*), Robert Meredith (*Around the World on $60*) and Augusto Flores (*My Hike*) from Buenos Aires to New York. Colin Fletcher hiked the length of the Grand Canyon deep down. And grandmother Doris Haddock, age 90, who recently walked from the West Coast to Washington, DC. Edward Payson Weston was our champion American speed-distance walker. Beyond my scope also are the various famous trails like the Appalachian, the Chesapeake and Ohio Canal Trace and trips by canoe or boat, cycles, carts and horseback. Backpacking perhaps qualifies; after all, even the classical walkers often carried a knapsack for food, books, note pad and pen. Shall we designate all this as "vagabonding?" Anyway, I am speaking primarily about a different kind of walking, in the old tradition.

Again, I ask, why other than walks of necessity? The real reasons are various and based upon the benefits expected. In the present day many walk for mere exercise, health, which is a laudable purpose and voiced by most doctors and writers. Dr. Chang Sen says, "There are many different methods of achieving absolute relaxation, but walking and running above all others." Donald Peatie says, "So a man who walks and lives and sees and thinks as he walks, has lengthened his life." So we walk not only for physical health but also for mental health in the days of so much stress. As Thoreau said, "We live lives of quiet desperation." Dr. Karl Menninger's beliefs are no mere theories; psychosomatic effects are real when it comes to walking; "walk your cares away."

As of the radiance of a sunny morning, so the walker goes out for the very joy of it, often spontaneously, with exhilaration, with a sense of freedom and adventure, to commune with nature and to feel its tranquillity and solitude, drawn by its subtle magnetism. Justice William O. Douglas was one of our great walkers "dedicated to enjoyment."

Some go walking to gain knowledge or experience; to see nature's wonders; to view the scenery; to discover nature's secrets; to explore historical spots and buildings; to meet people and note their different life styles. Jack Kerouac was one of those.

Walks are mind expanders. Unconsciously or innocently, they often lead to introspection, self-discovery and acuteness of thought. They improve the self-image; they give a feeling of self-fulfillment; they help to satisfy one's dream and help to reconcile fantasy and reality. My hikes have effected in me a partial "cure" for a youthful inferiority complex. All of the experiences add up to spiritual benefits.

In a word, we walk for aesthetic and esoteric reasons and that is why we call it a different kind of walking; walking in the tradition of the earliest great walkers - Stevenson, Hazlitt, Wordsworth, Lamb, Carlyle, Thoreau and in a later day Graham, Lindsay, Burroughs and Whitman. I must inject also to say that the masters usually took along a book: a walk essay by an earlier writer, essays by such ones as Marcus Aurelious, Montaigne, Emerson or a copy of *Palgrave's Golden Treasury*. These were read under a tree, while resting around the campfire or at an inn at day's close. No novels admitted!

A metaphysics of walking and camping is thus involved in this kind of tramping, a blending of fact and fancy, a pleasurable effort to know and love reality. There is a mystique in the true walking of the old times, not the mystique of today's America walking for health alone. Joseph Wood Krutch asks, "Is walking the new status symbol?" A relatively small coterie of walkers bemoan the present low esteem the general public has toward the plodding walker seeking solitude and peace of mind.

And over all - whatever the kind of foot travel - there is that thing of serendipity, a sort of euphoric pleasure we experience when we discover something along the open road that we had not expected.

"Ever just over the top of the next brown rise I expect some wonderful thing to flatter my eyes."—Charles G.D. Roberts.

"Trudge on, trudge on, 'twill all be well the way will guide one back."—A.E. Housman.

"Today I have grown taller from walking with the trees."—Karie Wilson.

"A hat is on my head, a bundle on my back, and my staff, the refreshing breeze and the full moon."—Godart, quoted by Jack Kerouac.

"Give to me the life I love, Let the lave go by me, Give the jolly heaven above and the byway nigh me."—Robert Louis Stevenson.

"I go anywhere a man can go; I see all that a man can see; and as I am quite independent of anybody, I can enjoy all the freedom man can enjoy."—Rousseau in *Èmile*.

But enough of Whitman's *Song of the Road* and sundry advice on the why, when, where and how of the noble art.

Texas Walks

After the war our family drifted down to Harris County in Texas, Huffman, to be exact. During the four years we took many a pleasant walk to the San Jacinto River through the pine land interspersed with palmetto and muscat grapevines. I spent one voluptuous night alone camping in the forest next to a brook. I served as camp counselor three of those summers (one summer in Wisconsin) and frequently led hikes. One morning I hiked several miles over the Texas prairie which bordered our home on the north to the village of Eastgate. I met nobody to break my thoughts.

San Jacinto River in Texas

City walking can be rewarding

City Walking

I have trod the streets of more than a score of major American cities and an equal number of foreign cities and I must say that such walks have rewards, but of a different kind than those in sequestered nature where solitude reigns. I have "circumnavigated" or walked completely around the borderlines of Buffalo and Peoria, taking two or three separate walks in doing so. Many cities have a personality all their own. Many are very fascinating: San Francisco, New Orleans, Boston. Here walking rhythm reduces to strolling and there are varieties of city walking. Stephen Graham took zigzag walks: to the left turn, to the right turn and thus on and on over the city. Baudelaire took pleasure in walking in city crowds and Bayard Taylor exclaimed; "one day's walk through Rome - how shall I describe it?" Gawking and shop haunting are in order. Mall walking is popular now. But the joys of city walking are not limited to the big cities; small provincial cities and towns often have their unique charm, like Provincetown, Galena or Bardstown. Much of the charm can only be experienced afoot.

Night Walking

Night walking is another species, not without its psychic charm. Despite the darkness - a full moon helps - often there is great joy: the stars, night insects, the owls, passing cheerful, lighted houses and a decided tendency to drift into thought. Dickens walked the London streets many a night, partly to cure insomnia. Any night walk may be a blend of various pleasures.

On July 3, 1927, I rode the train to Marion, rode back on another line which only went as far as West Vienna, where at 10 o'clock of the night I began the 20 miles hike home. I trudged steadily at a four mile pace over the rail track. In the Heroan Pond area, deep forest and swamp land, I momentarily got quite a scare. Hoot owls and frogs I loved but suddenly a wild, shrill scream broke the silence and made me quicken my pace. Bobcat or bird, my good sense told me I was safe. Dawn had broken when I reached home and fell into an exquisite bed.

It was not long before I hopped a freight train one late Sunday afternoon at Choat, near home and hopped off at Herrin Junction, 50 miles from home. I was absolutely due to help dad paint the house the next day and although I had really broken a parental law in hoboing, my moral sense told me I must show up.

That hike was perhaps the least enjoyable one I have ever made. I lay down on the grassy rail bank awhile, but could not sleep, what with the heat and mosquitoes, I began walking the rails about midnight. Mid-morning I took to the Vienna highway. It was 108 degrees there about one o'clock. Those were the days before hitchhiking became common; in fact, I don't believe the word was in my vocabulary. So I plodded on. I used a branch of a tree as a shield from the glaring sun. Late in the afternoon I got one ride for several miles, but the last four were afoot. I reached home at sunset having about reached the limit of endurance and partially disenchanted of hiking. But never a word to dad next day as I painfully mounted the ladder to paint.

It goes without saying that I have walked dozens of nights at all hours the five miles from Metropolis back home. Upon particularly fine nights, with stars aglow, I have had elevated thoughts and rather enjoyed many of those necessitous walks.

My most grueling hike was a comparatively short eight or so miles but required several hours.

Leaving my grandparent's home after a visit, I proposed to walk back to my home just north of Samoth on the Massac-Johnson County line. Unfortunately, it had snowed that night with a light drizzle which froze hard. Shod lightly, the day was beautiful and fairly mild, but I soon saw what I was up against. The icy sheet would not bear my full weight but was just hard enough to prevent one foot from readily breaking through; each step had to be individually maneuvered and calculated. There I was, up-down, slogging painfully on. The long and steep

New Columbia hill was even more difficult. At the New Columbia store I rested and Mr. Cagle gave me an old pair of overshoes. The remaining three miles was much easier. Home at last, fatigued, I partook of a generous bowl of soup and although still early, hit the bed. There were no ill effects as I went to work next morning.

Mountain Walking

One can scarcely equate climbing or mountaineering with walking; scaling rock walls is not our task but we can do considerable pure walking among low mountains along their slopes. Thoreau said "There is something in the mountain air that feeds the spirit and inspires." Hamilton Wright Mabie said, "There is something liberating in the mere physical range of a great view." Said Goethe, "On every height lies repose." And Wordsworth, "...Early had he learned to reverence the volume that displays the mystery, the life which cannot die; but in the mountains did he feel his faith."

I have walked (and climbed) to 15,000 odd feet on Mt. Popocatepetl; walked the easy first half of Mt. Katahdin; to the summits of Mt. Wilson and Gregory Bald and ranged over the Porcupine Mountains. I scrambled rather than walked the mountain overlooking Jack London's Valley of the Moon. In prospect, the ascension of Mt. Washington afoot seems a foolhardy and reckless act to attempt by a 10 year old boy, a girl not much older and a not-too-agile wife, but our family did just that. However, up the rock wall the wife hesitated, stopped, sat down, unable, she later averred, to climb a step farther. We left her there to rest and went ahead out of sight and paused. In a few moments there came the wife! She said she had prayed for strength and courage to go on. The rest of the way was easy.

Mountain hiking

What a wonderful feeling one has on a high mountain top! Breathing is easier, delicious, almost euphoric, or of getting that "second wind." Some years later I felt that same glorious release from atop Mr. Fairview by Lake Louise. That hour I was alone with my thoughts and views of the magnificent panorama.

A Tramp to Saltillo*

Going along Hidalgo Street in Monterrey, I had little difficulty in finding the Saltillo highway. the distance was about 55 kilometers to Saltillo and I planned to walk it in two days.

The morning was ideal, although rather too warm for comfort as the day advanced. At my back lay Saddle Mountain and Monterrey; on both sides of the road the precipitous Sierras and in front the bone-dry road with Sierras ahead.

A few miles out of the city I fell in with a young Mexican going my way. I was resting under a shade tree when we greeted one another. After a short conversation we walked along together but the almost running pace he set was more than I cared to keep. When our ways parted I slowed down to my three or four miles per hour.

Eleven o'clock found me in a *pasejero* where I got a good bread-like cake and a glass of water for four centavos or a little more than one cent American. Conversation with the shopkeepers, man and wife, was easy for both spoke clearer and understood my collegiate Spanish better than anyone I had met with yet. Perhaps my mind had been sharpened after the three hour walk or that I felt more at ease among Mexicans as time passed.

I met several people along the road. Some rode burros so small that I would have felt ashamed to mount. However small, they can carry and endure much. I almost took the ditch when several of those cumbersome, creaking, two-wheeled carts came along, each drawn by two oxen. I was going incognito and as if I had no money so I did not disclose by borrowed camera. To have revealed my camera I felt would have excited more curiosity than I would have desired in these lonely stretches. I took pictures only when no one was around. But those I met were invariably courteous. For hours not an automobile passed although the highway was good enough for motor travel. A courteous *buenos*

---

*Condensed from Chapter 2 of my book *Mexico for Me!* (typescript), *dias* or *holas* I gave for a greeting and was greeted in like manner, with an *adios* at parting. Some of the men looked wild and fierce but I had no fear in daytime. Moreover, they could see I had little wealth for I had no pack. I wore two pairs of pants and two shirts but with a three-days growth of beard and dirty, unkept shoes, I presented not a very attractive appearance.

Nevertheless, one is not safe among the poverty stricken natives after night. Without food, shelter or the ordinary pleasures of life as we know them, it is not surprising that they should harbor ill intentions toward well-to-do well-dressed persons coming by their way. It is caused to a great extent by the government system and unequal distribution of wealth and opportunity.

I rested in the plaza of the little town of Santa Catarina from 12 until after two o'clock. The sun beamed down from a cloudless sky with un-abated heat, nor did the imitation of a plaza do much to ward off the sun's rays. I dozed on a bench. Very little occurred to relieve the monotony of the scene. A policeman was talking to a citizen. At 12 o'clock (I guessed, I had no watch) the church bell rang at intervals. The two men talking walked slowly away for lunch and the daily siesta. Shop doors closed tight. For a long while I was left to myself, frequently dozing and feeling as if I would never get back home if that languor did not go away. At two o'clock the bell rang again at most annoying intervals. I expected a shop across the street to open but it did not.

A temporary break in the silence occurred when two burros got into the plaza and proceeded to crop the scant grass. Someone emerged from a building and drove out the invading burros with a stick. I thought they entered the door of the town hall and I was inwardly laughing until I discovered that the animals had entered a court instead of the town office. Later, at a *panderia* or bread shop, I bought three flat cakes of a sweet, brittle sort, but good.

Along the Saltillo Road

Then followed several hours of walking during which I became quite tired and hot. The road was almost all up-grade, the elevation of Monterrey being 1,500 feet while that of Saltillo is more than 5,000.

Twenty-two kilometers from Monterrey a road branched off to Villa Garcia, where the railroad runs. At one miserable looking adobe hut I stopped for a drink of water. It was what is known as a *posado* or place where one may stop for food and rest. Greeting the woman through the open door, I asked her "*hay agua?*" "*Si, Señor,*" she replied, where-upon calling another woman, she gave me a brimming glassful. As I was very thirsty, the "*muchas gracias*" I gave her had no more appreciative tone that I felt.

The open doorway gave me good opportunity for observing the interior of a Mexican peon's home. The hut, made of dried mud bricks, consisted of two rooms almost bare of furnishings. Three women were doing some work. The water had been given me out of a typical stone jar. A couple of dogs skulked near the door.

In the course of the afternoon I fell in with a young man who spoke English. He once had been a taxi driver in Texas. From then on I depended upon Mauro Gonzles for inquiries along the way.

[The question arises among walkers as to whether or not a companion is desirable. Cid Traeger (1964) who followed in the footsteps of Stevenson's *Travels with a Donkey*, says the best way is to travel alone in the outdoors. Hazlitt said he liked to go by himself, "The soul of a journey is to get rid of others." Thoreau preferred aloneness. Other walkers of old wanted a companion. Graham tramped the Rockies with Vachel Lindsay. But the majority preferred going alone. Solitude and silence are golden.]

The road continued up and down but mostly up. The road itself was uninteresting in the extreme. The only redeeming feature were the sharp, fantastical-shaped peaks of the Sierra Madre, which were grand but bare of vegetation. It was indeed a desert at this time of year. Cacti and mesquite grew and rocks were numerous. Dwellings were few and far between. A few cows and goats now and then were the only means of livelihood visible.

Mauro and I saw we were up against it for a sleeping place. We reached a goat herder's house with a little store and gasoline station in connection. He had no room for us inside, the sun had set and there was no alternative but to sleep, or rather lie down, back of the store. Rinconada was too far away to reach before night, although visible in the far valley below. Moreover, we were too tired and footsore to go farther. To sleep out in the wasteland would have been almost too cold and have left us at the pleasure of prying animals, snakes and scorpions. But to stay at the man's store also lay us open to robbery or abuse. Mauro thought it best to stay where we were for the night. Somewhere in his travels he had perhaps found it best to be off Mexican roads alone at night.

After some oranges and bad water to drink, we resigned ourselves to fate, lay down on the dusty ground and tried to sleep. Looking up at Venus shining so brightly, I felt that this was one redeeming feature of this night in Mexico in the open. Then there were my old friends Jupiter, Orion and a little later in the night, Mars.

The mountains grew black against the western sky. How comfortable the old Mexican no

The Cathedral, Saltillo

doubt felt in mind looking upon his little mud-dried shack, his store and his heard of goats and his imperishable company, the mountains. Truly, home is the place to feel thoroughly at ease, where is no fear, no uncertainty.

The wind blew strongly and whistled about the one lone stump of a tree. Around the corner of the store it sounded very mournful. I recalled windy nights at home or a rainy night. It was as if the wind came from another sphere of life and was telling a strange and melancholy story.

The night passed although it was cold toward morning due to the altitude. It was a task to brush the dust from our clothing. My sheepskin coat caught the most of my dust. It was not quite sunrise, when looking up near us, we saw clouds about the mountain sides.

Mauro and I left without a drop of water to quench a thirst (the store had not yet opened). Prospects were slim of getting any for some time. As Rinconada was several kilometers off the main road, we skipped it and walked more kilometers. At last, at a little adobe village, we stopped at a hut and got a cup of water. I was afraid of typhoid or dysentery but being so thirsty we drank it. The old hag inside gave us a corn cake (*tortilla*) between us. This was my first taste of that national food. A short way farther we bought two pounds of poor bananas for 12 centavos. Another big drink followed. A rough and villainous looking number of tall men were within the shop but I had gotten to the point where I did not care how many Mexican people were around!

Mauro thought that the railroad that now paralleled the highway would be better walking. A short walk on it proved worse. After crossing the Nuevo Leon-Coahuila State Line we returned to the highway.

The concluding way into Saltillo was not as I had expected; it was across a monotonous plain and the scenery slacked off. I had also expected on this hike to have had readier access to food, water and a decent sleeping place. I was not too much chagrined over all this. Although I like to tramp and saunter for pleasure, to run it into work is a different matter. Nor did I have to walk, considering I had more than 300 Mexican pesos to spend.

A big parade was in progress as we entered Saltillo. At first it gave me cause for alarm. The parade was of working men who carried banners to the effect that the American and foreign exploitation of Mexican labor should cease. Evidently, it was only hot air and I, since a disguised Americano and dared not speak freely, was not molested.

A Second Pope County Hike

It was August 1939 and the work in my truck garden was caught up. Thus, one day an urge came upon me to take a hike. I packed a light rucksack with food, a United States geological map and reading matter and hopped into the '28 Chevy and drove several miles to near the Pope County line. I left the car, with permission, at a farmer's house and headed for the picturesque hills of that venerable county, alert and eager to be afoot. My purposes in going were to learn first-hand about that previously unvisited area, to enjoy leisurely walking and to recapture some of the charm of the classical walkers.

Along the shady lanes I *walked* with birds twittering around me and wild grapevines drooping over the way, not yet ripe. I observe how many an old hill has been saved by lespedeza seeding! From a point 490 feet above sea level, near Mr. Pleasant Church, I see eight miles to Paducah where the bridge shines brightly. Smoke rolls in the hazy blue atmosphere. An amphitheater of hills clad with forest lies before me. I hear a tinkling cowbell. What more musical sound! Fire Station Road No. 320 appears. All this country lies within the Shawnee National Forest. What an enticing view from the churchyard!

There are still creeks to ford. Near County Line School much of the road is impassable for vehicles. Should those roads ever have been built? Shouldn't much of this county have been left for the wild folks of the forest? The National Forest is perhaps the answer. I note an overgrown concrete bridge. This area had more inhabitants formerly.

I lose my way in Barren Creek. The road follows the bed of the stream. I see plants I have never seen before. I get thirsty. I get still more lost along the banks of a larger stream. I consult my map. I must retrace my way to find a crossing place. I think of venomous snakes in this thick cane growth. I come to a ford and climb up a long, rocky hill along the semblance of a road. How refreshing to walk in the shade, hat in hand, with a breeze fanning my brow.

A better road and a refreshing drink follow. I climb a steep, red hill and stroll down an arbored way. Suddenly, topping an eminence, I gaze north through an opening and enjoy a sight of the broad, blue Ohio River. I take a shortcut to little Friendship School which I wish to visit. Near the school I get a still more magnificent view, that of the upper, graceful curve of the river with a little island all framed with the blue, wooded hills.

Upstream from Friendship School

I arrive at Friendship School just at recess. I visit until the noon hour with Miss Virginia Welch who has been teacher here for six years. We talk school teaching, as I am a rural school teacher, too. What an inspiring view the pupils have of the hills, forest and river-unique in winter-sufficient and conducive to noble thoughts and great studies.

I trek across the fields along a private path to the main road. I eat lunch in a lady's yard near Azotus Church. I rest two hours underneath a giant oak. I read, I write, I nap. I pull off my shoes, light my pipe and send scarves of smoke. Then I slog on. A light shower doesn't deter me. The Azotus store is gone long ago.

I am struck with the number of abandoned and tumbled-down houses. Has the county seen better times? Has the Shawnee National Forest evicted the people? Today, maybe it is the heat, I find I must speak vociferously to arouse anyone for a drink.

In Dog Creek I bathe my feet. I seek a drink; no one home but a big, brown police dog bounds out; I am glad to get away sound in flesh. Rain overtakes me at Neely School which had not opened yet. I sit out the heavy shower in the boy's toilet. What a lowly place for philosophical, pedestrian meditations! But it is only for a short while and I am on my way.

I am now at the foot of a long hill on a new, wide government constructed highway. My watch says 5:30 and I am hungry and tired, with a slight pain in my side. I see not many yards off the road a farmstead that seems to beckon me to try for food and a bed. I am successful in both.

An old gentleman Billy Weeks (and wife) immediately make me welcome once I tell my mission. Mr. Weeks talks a steady stream that informs me that he has been a trader, farmer, businessman, a jack-leg lawyer, a speculator ("plunger") and knows every nook and corner of Pope County. I get few words in edgewise. From him I first learn of Queensbury's Rules and a lot more. The wife feeds me supper and breakfast-no charge-and I bed down in the loft of the old log house. So I am fed physically and mentally; this a good case of serendipity?

Next morning, following Mr. Week's directions, I take a "blind" road which runs over the hills west for several miles. I have some hard walking through bushes and briars. Then a pleasant walk along a cow path in the old road bed, heavily bordered by honeysuckle. I run almost headlong on to two friendly red cows. I chew the aromatic sassafras to keep my thirst down. More walking, more views, through a woods, lost again, on to the known road and to my car.

I cannot get the old man off my mind. A conversationalist on every subject, of firm convictions, narrow in some views - an adventure I will scarcely ever equal. (In fact, Billy Weeks became the "villain" of my future novel *Walter West's Probation*).

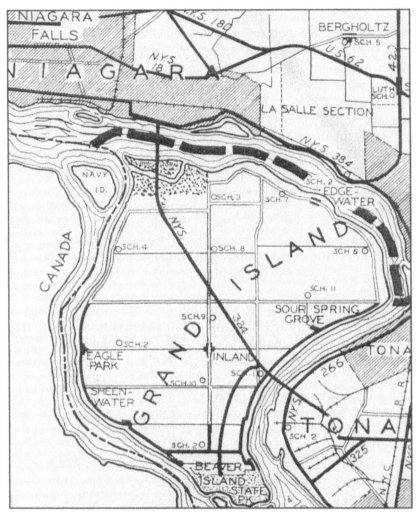

Map of Grand Island

Grand Island Winter Hikes

Pear-shaped, Grand Island lies near the middle reaches of the Niagara River between Buffalo and Niagara Falls, some miles above the mighty falls "flowing on forever in its glorious robe." It is a large island, embracing a whole township.

Working in wartime Buffalo, I often felt cooped up; in fact, fed up on the monotony of factory work. I needed a hike! A map drew me toward this unique island.

By city bus to Tonnawanda, I walked the bridge to the island and turned south along a rural road to Beaver Island State Park. Nearby was rural school No. 20.

It was a morning late in winter, the skies were clear and a four inch snow clothed the countryside in the 32 degree temperature. I would revel in a world of snow. Roads, ground and trees look different in winter. Gone is the green of summer. Bare, brown, stark tree limbs predominate, relieved only by an occasional pine or cedar, contrasting with the rays of sun scintillating over the snow cover. It was just such a day as I, a college student, had joyfully tramped on a similarly morning from Peoria five miles cross-county to Pottstown village.

Keeping to the road, I turned north, passed Sheen Water and halfway to Eagle Park turned east. I passed school No. 10. (There are a dozen rural schools on Grand Island). I crossed Baseline Road. Two jogs and I was back to the river bridge. Thus ended by several miles of pleasant winter walking with some of the spleen out of my system. It had been a happy and compensating jaunt and I had proved that I still possessed the buoyancy of youth and the ardor of life.

Some weeks later, snow gone and the bloom of spring apparent, I re-hiked Grand Island along the east part, past Sideway School, north past schools No. 8 and No. 3; then south following the riverside from the settlement of Sandy Beach, past two more schools and through Sour Springs Grove settlement. A short distance farther and I had completed my circle tour, made tirelessly over flat land. On neither hike had I met anyone. Truly, I had experienced that poetic "bliss of solitude."

A Hike over Scenic Jo Daviess County

I had toughened up somewhat that July by a float-paddle trip down the upper Rock River. It involved some walking and hitchhiking to shuttle to my car, side walks for supplies, etc. and I must have walked several miles.* I had made numerous short Peoria County rural walks also over some period of time. But the fact remains that the most difficult thing about taking an extended tramp is the "break away" from the normal routine. Happily, most hikes are not ones of that syndrome.

I purposed a week's tramp over scenic Jo Daviess County, IL to "learn more of the meaning of those hills" and to experience again the

---

* Down Illinois Rivers is my account of float-paddle adventures down eighteen little Illinois Riverm

vagrant ways of the open road and I hoped to meet and talk with people: "By homestead old with wide flung barns" (Whittier).

Galena! A unique town (4,400) with curving, tiered streets upon the hillsides. Lead ore mining in the early days swelled a boisterous population. In those days steamboats plied the lower Galena River. Still standing is the home of Gen. Ulysses Grant.

Late of an afternoon I parked my car at a Mr. Giles and with 23 pound pack took to the road north toward Council Hill. Fine panoramic views. I crossed the Galena River and got permission from a lady to camp in her woodland along the bank. I bathed nude in the clear, cool water; then pork and beans over a small fire. I fell asleep to the music of the babbling stream.

Next morning I followed a gravel road. A man said he had just cleared out some rattlesnakes at a bridge and that deer abounded in this area. I took the hilly Scales Mound road and reached that village at high noon where I ate at a cafe and rested a long while enjoying the deeply-etched view. In 1830 Samuel Scales put up an inn and the town grew in this land of pleasant views and today of woods and cultured farm fields.

I hiked up to the top of Charles Mound some miles north. It is the highest point in Illinois (1,241 feet). The view from the summit is very fine, unfolding to the Mississippi to the west and to the nearby Wisconsin on the north. I gazed rapt and silent.

It was after five o'clock when I began to look for a camp. I found the farmers suspicious of pedestrians carrying a pack; what I thought was an unreasoning distrust, even after I had explained my mission and identified my status. I stopped at a walnut grove which was

All set for the open road, August 1969

also an old cemetery and had baled hay stacked in one part. I walked half a mile to fill my folding water bag but almost before I had back-tracked to the cemetery the farmer had informed the landowner by telephone and three men gave me a third degree and read my ID. I could stay overnight if no fire was lighted. I made do with cold foods. Early on, abed, a police car drove in and got my name and address. How news travels! I was surprised and angry but clamed down as I returned to my tent.

I arose with the sun, shaved in cold water and hit the road. As I approached Sumner Mound (second highest point in Illinois) I became hot and weak in the stomach. Sucking on raisins helped relieve. At noon I stopped at a farmhouse occupied by a young farmer, his wife and two children. With explanation, I sat down with them and ate a fine dinner. No charge. Now why did that young farmer decide to feed me? Was his work hard and drab? Did he hope to find in me some diversion? Was it mere curiosity? He well could have refused me. Possibly an act of noble help-fulness or compassion. Down the short lane I rested, read and wrote.

About a mile from Apple River I became aware of a crease-like feeling underneath a big toe. Handily, there was a bridge over a brook and I bathed my feet. A blister was developing. A little gopher came for a drink. A compress eased my foot and soon along a blacktop road I reached the scenic Apple River State Park along the Apple River. Here I camped early. Only a late camper with loud babies, loud adults and two dogs disturbed my sleep.

The road now went south toward Stockton. Tanked up with park concession food, ice cream and a packed ham sandwich, I began hik-ing. As the days before the skies were cloudless and the air hot. On I plodded, paralleled the good-flowing Rush Creek, over hill and dale. Near day's close I found a sequestered wooded area beyond a cornfield and padded down, safe, I figured, from any ill-natured farmer. With some tram-pling of weeds I set up the tent but made no fire. The day had been a good one, rolling hills, quilt-patch farms, woodlands and wide prospects. While eating the next morning a pronged deer approached within 30 feet, looked at me a few moments and leisurely walked away.

A stop for water next day resulted in a cheese sandwich from a lady. Across Rush Creek a foot bathing. Two long, steep hills put me into Darinda Center, nearly a ghost town now. A man sold me a Pepsi Cola from his home. From a long, winding hill I stopped under a shade tree and looked down upon an enclosed valley with a farmstead far below, one of those nooks and corners of Jo Daviess. But even children's voices carried up to me.

Galena, Illinois

It was three more miles to Hanover (pop. 1,300) on the swift, rock-bedded Apple River with a dam 10 feet high. It was Sunday with no stores open but I put up at the only motel and made out. The bath, shave and sleep were good.

Next day I climbed several exhausting hills. Sucking an orange under a tree, I rested and finished reading Henty's *Young Coloniste*, throwing away the last pages as I had done so all along, to reduce my pack weight. I passed the road leading to the year-round ski resort (Chestnut Hill) where once I ate at a banquet held by the state historical society. Down a very long hill and I was at the Mississippi River. I found a cleared area along the foul lily pad slough and made camp. I backtracked to a cottage for water and cooked supper among host of mosquitoes. All night an apple would fall now and then from a nearby tree and I could hear opossum eating on them. Frogs and night water birds made an orchestra. The stars and planet shone brilliantly these nights in the clear air. Although one sleeps lightly, one arises fresh in the pure air. No city air here!

Along with the last of my bacon, oatmeal and preserves I fried some of the apples for breakfast. I was now only seven miles from Galena. With a lightened pack, I strode over some hills and with only one brief, pipeful smoke-rest, reached Galena just before high noon. In a restaurant I drew curious eyes. I sort of enjoyed it; children love it. I visited the *Galena Gazette* newspaper office and it wanted an account of my seven-day, near 100 mile tramp.

A rewarding jaunt, but friends and relatives will never quite understand your motives and often, least of all, one's wife.

Final advisory: The night before a hike bathe the feet in alcohol and salt water; it toughens the feet and it works!

Hiking Calhoun County's Apple Land

In retrospect the Jo Daviess hike seemed so soul-satisfying that, came the next August 1970, I decided to take a similar hike over the storied apple country of Calhoun County, IL. It is a relatively isolated area of the state and has had no other railroad than a short, one-fourth mile private one that served a coal mine and brickyard many years ago near Golden Eagle. It was at defunct Wineberg. Shaped like a string bean, the county is surrounded on three sides by the lordly Mississippi as it flows parallel to the lady Illinois River with only a narrow strip between. Consequently, all the creeks are short. The area is small and houses a small population. Edna Ferber in her short story "Farmer in the Dell" tells about a Westerveld family that settled early in the county, "then almost a wilderness but magnificent with its hills, majestic rivers and gold-and-purple distance." My prospects for a good hike looked bright.

I took the road No. 100 north from Hardin, the county seat, at 3 p.m. My pack felt five pounds too heavy. I made camp opposite Diamond Island in a Wild Life Conservation area, with facilities. I fished with no luck but a neighbor camper gave me a carp which I baked in some foil I found lying around. The sun set behind a high limestone bluff. The moon arose a pretty rose; abed for a fitful, mosquito-laden night.

Vehicles kept crowding me onto the weedy shoulders as I tramped to Kampsville, a town of 400 souls. I talked with several

Bank of Calhoun County

people and smoked. From here I headed west for Baytown or Mozier Post Office, the road paralleling a rocky, gurgling brook for some miles. Weakened by the heat, I paused at an elderly man's house and rested and talked with him.

He proved to be almost as interesting as my Billy Weeks of years before. He told of steamboat days. An unidentified Negro roustabout fell overboard from a boat and drowned and was buried in a field. He said black people now (1970) are not allowed to live or work in Calhoun County but may come and fish daytime. How does the area get by with this in these days of Negro militancy?

Not far away was the babbling brook now swelled into quite a stream (Fox Creek) and the land owned by my recent friend who gave his okay to camp there. I camped on the sandy creek bed but did not set up my tent. Rain clouds soon threatened as the yellow-billed cuckoo or raincrow bird had spoken last night. Only a few sprinkles fell. My pedometer registered 18 miles; I say 15 - set too high.

A light rain began the next morning and I donned my slicker and soon reached Hamburg where the ferry plied from the high bluff over to Missouri's low shore. The village church was in session and the hymns vied with the birds singing in the trees: mockers, cardinals, a bob white - more like spring than hot August. An illusive association made me think of Nova Scotia and Virginia. I spoke with three old men. Later, I bathed my feet in a small creek and lunched from my pack. I read Emerson's "*Self Reliance.*" Although the heat grew, I was a happy hiker that day.

Off the road a mile west along a slough of the Mississippi I made camp at Titus Hollow Boat Launch. The lily-padded slough or creek had a boat dock and tables but no drinking water. I was so exhausted that I did no cooking. I alleviated thirst from my canteen and an orange "saved" my life, in effect. Mosquito repellent made sleep tolerable. I was told later and I thought that this spot was rattlesnake habitat. Frogs kept up a joyous chorus and I had a strong sense of isolation.

I reached Batchtown at 9 a.m. Many years past, on a visit to a dear aunt in Winfield, MO across the river, I had helped load a truck with apples in Batchtown for shipment. It was renowned for apples even then, 70 years ago.

I misread the map and took the long way to Beechville; thus, I changed route which put me in Miffin Village. Here I got a surprise. I stopped at a tavern, ate a ham sandwich with a small Budweiser and rested. The place was run by twin midgets who couldn't see over the bar! We talked. They often played guitar and sang at Batchtown.

Again I took a wrong road, the last mile over an abandoned road but seemingly still used by tractors or jeeps; some mud and water. But whichever new road one takes, for the hiker, it is adventure, e.g., the midgets.

I reached ghost town Beechville with its few houses. I kept seeing apples and peaches peeking out from fruit trees, which was a better sight than the revolting pig pens I sometimes passed. Once I rested in a lane near a farmer's mailbox. The man

Near Batchtown

and wife finally saw me, even from the distance and kept looking toward me. Soon they began to walk down the lane toward me, each with a mowing blade! I was not frightened just wondered why the notice. I departed upon their pausing at the foot of their hill.

A long, steep hill led into Brussels. It was a small town but with a large hotel in the old tradition, a fine Catholic church and another fine large building, besides a water tower. The town is well visited by tourists who seek the unique. I put up at the Whitmont Hotel for $7.85, meals and tax included, something quite unexpected. I gathered local history and geography from a table sharer. The hotel also ran a grocery, souvenir shop, tavern, post office and odds and ends of other merchandise.

I awoke with symptoms of a cold. Strange that I've never had a cold from sleeping out in my entire life. I left the hotel minus pack but with canteen, rain gear and pipe and tobacco. I made a 10 mile circle hike to Golden Eagle with no retrace. The circle of high hills gave me a panoramic view most of the morning, with its quiet, dreamy atmosphere. Golden Eagle is another host town. It is still three miles from the toll ferry to Missouri. Peach and apple orchards were numerous. I saw the largest osage orange tree I ever saw. Lunch at the Whitmont.

On the school ground under a tree I lingered. Two school girls talked with me and gave me chewing gum. Some boys came over and joined the conversation. On the road an hour later I stopped at a 66 gas station and drank a Pepsi and some chocolate milk. The attendant was a teacher in Bushnell, IL, but a Calhoun native. We talked education. So one meets his likes at various places at times when on the magic road.

The Hadley Camp Wild Life Area lies on the Illinois River and as I had tramped nearly 20 miles, I set up tent. It was a nice place with facilities and easy to wash up and get water for utensil washing from the river. I was the lone camper. A barge passed at midnight. Two cars once drove in, perhaps either drinking people, or "breeding," as the old Fox Creek gentleman had termed it. The moon was full and was reflected upon the water.

Next morning the *Virginia and Poling* barge passed down. An hour later the *Calloy* went up. Two fishing parties drew up, one a Negro group. The river had risen a foot overnight, but probably by dam handling.

At high noon I reached Hardin about on schedule. I kept meeting boys and men who had seen me either in Brussels or on the road (I recognized some) and even the police whom I had met as I started the hike. Good natured banter. Most were surprised that I had gotten over the road so fast. I had lagged into Hardin hot and quite exhausted but after eating I was refreshed and felt quite jaunty. I visited the *Calhoun News* office and spoke about my 75 mile hike. They took my picture and a write-up followed on August 17. Some of the classical hikers thought it out of place to proclaim such personal exploit.

My winding pilgrimage completed, I counted it a very compensating experience. Treading those hot miles I had sometimes pictured myself in a cool room or under a tree with beverage and ice cream. So anticipation under duress has its ultimate rewards.

I drove through Brussels and crossed the ferry to Grafton and camped the night at Pere Marquette State Park.

Sadly (June 2000), I have had to cease hiking and I ask, with Francois Villon, "But where are the snows of yester-year?" Old age (90) has caught up with me. With a bad back and hip, I deplore my inability, I only walk limping. I must find other compensations for the loss of the joys of the open road.

–Written June 2000

In camp south of Hardin, August 1970

History

The Significance of Gettysburg*

Introduction

Among the many catch-words which have been used to character-ize the Battle of Gettysburg, the most common are: "pivotal," "most significant," "turning point," "crisis of the confederacy," "epic," "greater than Waterloo," "high water mark of the rebellion," "climax of a 50 year struggle," and "immortal." "Decisive" is the one most used. The clichés have been conned by schoolboys until they have become mere verbalisms. Only a closer study will reveal the reasons for these claims and more than likely such an analysis will result in a qualified verdict. It shall be the purpose of this paper to enlarge upon some of these names and to try to arrive at the true significance of the great conflict.

The Setting

Today, in the popular mind, Gettysburg, PA is associated with be-ing the home of President Eisenhower. It is a county seat town of 7,000 people, but in 1863 it contained only about 4,000. It lies 35 miles south-west of Harrisburg and about a dozen miles from the Maryland state line. The town lies near to the west bank of Rock Creek and rather between two ranges of steep ridges and hills, some 500 feet or more in elevation. The gently sloping depression which is the valley of Gettysburg was, in July 1863, a quiet scene of orchards, meadows and fields of waving grain, with fine oak trees standing upon the slopes of Oak Ridge, Seminary Ridge, Cemetery Hill, Cemetery Ridge, Culp's Hill and Round Top and Little Round Top hills. For the purpose of a battle Gettysburg was strategically located: 10 or 12 roads converged there and the rocky eminencies provided a natural defense.

The Action

As the two natures of man are in continual warfare - the good and the evil - and some unforeseen circumstance forces a quick decision

---

*Footnotes in this paper have been deleted for easier reading

Gettysburg National Military Park

for better or worse, so it seemed that some unseen hand was directing the Confederate and Union armies to a showdown point at Gettysburg on July 1. Neither army had planned on fighting there. Hill's Rebel Advance Corps under Heath stumbled or blundered into action with a Union Cavalry Force under Buford. Like a true soldier under inspiration Buford selected the battleground. His superior, Gen. Reynolds and the Iron Brigade soon came up and relayed a message to Gen. Meade stating, "Here is the place to fight." Reynolds was killed soon afterwards. Thus, it was that the newly-chosen Meade had the decision forced upon him to fight Gen. Robert E. Lee, who likewise was being led into an action at a place not of his choosing.

The Union success in the morning of July 1 changed for the worse in the afternoon. The Union forces were split in two by Gen. Ewell and driven to Cemetery Ridge. Ewell did not pursue his advantage as he had no orders. Nothing but miracle could have saved the Union Army if not for the "providential inaction" of the Rebel Army. The Confederate Army itself was across the valley on Seminary Ridge.

Like the Greeks and Persians neither side was anxious to renew the fight on July 2. This was to be a soldier's battle where the plans of generals were upset. The enraged victims of Lee's countryside raids muttered angrily in the vernacular: "By gravy, if he (Lee) does come we'll just lick the poop out of him." They had clashed and each side was taking careful measure of the other. Gen. Meade had arrived during the night and by morning Cemetery Ridge was strongly fortified. Gen. Sickles threw out a salient far out into the Peach Orchard, apparently against orders. Blunder or saving maneuver, it developed the battle. Longstreet's tardy attack failed to dent the Union line. By day's end the army of the Potomac had been "hammered into a good position."

Ewell had tried the right wing on July 1; Longstreet had failed July 2 on the left. Both were invulnerable. The Union center, Cemetery Ridge, was Lee's objective July 3, Meade's council of war had decided to fight again only if Lee moved offensively. Pickett's Spartan charge was repulsed by the Federals, but only after a critical five minutes in which the result hung by a thread.

As Lee began his retreat the Union soldiers saw it as "the harbinger of victory and peace." It was a glorious trilogy - July 4. Vicksburg fell, the first Union troops entered Chattanooga and now Gettysburg was won. Meade did not pursue the retreating army and for this was censored by many people.

Contemporary Significance

Lee had several logical motives for invasion. The military situation in Virginia demanded some such operation. Not only was Richmond threatened but supplies were low. Hooker's Army enlistment terms were up and there was draft resistance in the North. The Emancipation Proclamation was unpopular and the "peace party" was apparently strong. Pennsylvania could supply Lee. Invasion might draw Union troops from Vicksburg. Possession of several border states might result in the fall of Washington. Strong opposition was not expected, for the Federal Army record had not been good. Among Lee's problems was to do the bidding of Jefferson Davis, which often interfered with planning. Gettysburg was Lee's last chance at executing his own policy for Davis wanted a defensive war. Neither did Lee have a well-defined objective nor sufficient sinews of war. Perhaps the truest motive was for food. For the North the prime motive was defense of their property. These were sufficient motives for collision.

Lee's army was characterized by high enthusiasm, boundless confidence and a supreme contempt for the Federal Army, "as proud and puissant an army as was ever marshalled." The Union Army management was halting, irresolute and wanting in firm direction. As the three-day battle progressed there was a reversal of these moods of elation in the two armies.

Lee was a military gentleman of the old school. Perhaps he was not stern enough. Time has called him not only a great general, but also a great man. Gettysburg was his worst-fought battle. As soon as he began the retreat, his errors ceased and his every move was one of foxy normalcy. Meade's handicap was not of his doing; Lincoln had chosen him to replace Hooker on unexpectedly short notice. He had to face the possibility of lowered morale, to unify seven Army Corps, to seek out the enemy, beat him and do all this with speed. Meade's vacillation may have been due to lack of moral courage, or it may have been the enormous problem to be solved so quickly. Despite Lincoln's lament, "Is that all?" when Meade did not pursue Lee, the choice was good and Gettysburg brought out some of Meade's good qualities.

The Union strength has been estimated variously at from 82,000 to 100,000 but according to Meade's testimony it was 94,699. The Confederate forces were numbered between 69,000 and 75,000. Almost 6,000 killed; 26,000 wounded and 10,000 missing or captured for a grand total of 43,000 killed or wounded.

The terrors of Gettysburg defy the brush of the artist or the words of oratory, though many have tried to do so. The cannonade was most terrific, unparalleled and the most concentrated on an equal space, anywhere in history. The Confederates had 125 to 150 guns as against 80 or 90 for the Union forces.

Planned tactics and strategy in this battle were nullified on short notice by the errors of Meade, Lee and their leaders and the quick-changing circumstances. The campaign went on without conforming at all to the plans but "as a result of the real relations of the armies in motion." Terrain was the most important factor. It counted for little what Meade's war council decided. The men were by then defiant and anxious to fight; the army itself, the mass, had settled the question. Meade might choose to play a waiting game, but Lee could not afford it. Lee's first day's success and the belief that the attacking army had the moral advantage may have influenced him to an offensive action. The grand military theory of the South had been defensive and at times offensive at the opportune times. This combination tactics had met with success at Yorktown, Fredericksburg and Chancellorsville. This defensive policy was disregarded in the perilous undertaking of invasion into hostile country. The larger defense and local offensive policy was disregarded. Promising not a tactical offensive yet, Lee lost equipoise and did just that. He turned toward Gettysburg from Cashtown and attacked. The two decisive points in the battle, the Peach Orchard and Bloody Angle, were won by the simple incident of securing the defensive. It gained the victory for the Union Army.

As has been intimated, theory and strategy were intermixed with errors of leadership on both sides. Military men have spotted many, but only a few will be mentioned here. Though logical in some respects, many have admitted that Lee's invasion was an error in inception because it overstepped the Southern theory, committed Lee to perils and lacked sharp objectives. Once in battle, the cause of Confederate failure may be reduced to one: the lack of coordination. This was true from troops on down to whole brigades and regiments. All great men make mistakes and Napoleon and Lee were no exception. Lee might easily have maneuvered Meade out of his strong position on the heights. He should have used his 40,000 to attack the Union 20,000 on July 1. It was his high tide of victory. Inaction on the morning of July 2, due to Longstreet's reluctance and slowness, allowed Meade to concentrate his forces. When Longstreet finally attacked Sickles there was further lack of cooperation. Lee should have occupied Culp's Hill during the night. Lee gave too excessive a development to his line and tried to attack by his two wings, which, coupled with vague orders and lack of coordination, resulted in failure to break the Union lines. The absence of Stuart's cavalry was also a handicap. Meade also missed his cavalry. In an offensive campaign by defensive fighting both sides needed the cavalry for rapid, decisive measures.

For the salvation of his army, in action and in retreat, Lee owed all to Meade's hesitation. It actually helped the South for months because Meade was psychologically conditioned to want Lee to take the offensive. Meade made other errors: he should have gone to Gettysburg himself July 1; the orders to Sickles were too vague; he did not know or prepare for Picket's charge; he failed to launch three brigades against Longstreet. But it is the consensus of the world that Meade's worst error was not in vigorously pursuing the Confederates soon after Pickett's charge; certainly on July 4. Meade gave Lee a "bridge of gold" instead of a "wall of steel." Meade was the center of criticism from those in high places to the lowest soldiers. Lincoln deplored the idea that the enemy had been driven from our soil, saying, "Will our generals never get that idea out of their heads? The whole country is our soil." Meade rode out the charges of the Joint Committee. Despite Sickles' insinuations, Meade was kept on by Lincoln and emerged bowed and bloody but the victor of the second battle of Gettysburg.

Only one of Lee's objectives had in any way been accomplished: he had procured rations and other supplies. His other hopes were squashed. In Lincoln's view nothing had been "repossessed." Though chagrined by Meade's failure to pursue and annihilate Lee's weakened army, Lincoln looked upon his three-day Gethsemane as the "shadows of coming events." *Harper's* magazine commented: "The Battle of Gettysburg was less decisive than had been hoped." The "American soldier's battle," a battle of great magnitude, a struggle of prowess and courage and unparalleled tenacity and unselfish devotion, it was decisive to the field but not to the larger struggle. The rebellion up to Gettysburg had reached its zenith. Neither Lee nor Meade at this time realized its significance.

Of the motives for Lee's invasion two more may now be considered, with the results following defeat. They were in the nature of political and economic hopes. The confederacy had long looked to England and France for help. Lee hoped by a victory on Northern soil to gain recognition. From the various actions up to this time it was not a forlorn hope. Until Gettysburg, the United States was looked upon by most European nations as in the last throes of national dissolution. This was despite the prophetic statement of De Tocqueville in 1835 that the Union might be retarded but not dismembered. Gladstone and other Englishmen invested in Southern bonds. Lord Macauley prophesied a speedy smashup for the Republic. Carlyle scoffed at the North. Only Russia favored the Northern cause and this more from motives of antagonism to England and France. Defeat killed all hopes for foreign recognition. It was no longer a case of sentiment; it was a hard fact of political economy. Rebel money became worthless and the blockade shut off resources, while Northern manufactures and finances remained strong. At news of Gettysburg, the English textile workers were joyful and a revulsion of pro-southern sentiment became general over England. Mexico, a revolutionary government itself, refused to recognize the Confederacy in December 1863.

The economic effect on the South was severe. Wall Street gold went up; Confederate money went down. Confederate shipbuilding stopped in England. The cotton loan collapsed to 36. Confederate equity was gone. Realizing that the war would be a long one, cotton prices rose. It was a shock to the whole internal economy of the South. Victory made the drafting of 300,000 new men easier, though the draft riots in New York made it appear untrue. The riot itself perhaps had occurred because many home guards had rushed to the Gettysburg emergency and left the city short-handed. California silver, which was badly needed, reached the Sanitary Commission at this time and the Commission thought this reaffirmed "the united efforts of the Nation."

Another motive of Lee's was to enlist from the border states those disaffected people who through dissensions, hopelessness and war weariness had in many cases allied themselves to subversive organizations, such as the Sons of Liberty, or joined the "peace party." These and outright "seceshs," of which many were suspected around Gettysburg, failed to give Lee any perceptible help. His defeat ended his chance to win the war by long attrition and Fifth Column means. Last ditch attempts to free Northern prisoners in Chicago and Rock Island and to set up a Northwest Confederacy failed. The raids of Morgan, Forrest, and Early were too feeble.

It is difficult if not impossible to divide minutely the intangibles of morale and emotion (feeling), though both are highly important to an individual and to an army or nation as a whole. It is not inconsistent with Napoleon's axiom: "In war men are nothing, a man is everything." It is questionable that the rebellion was the expression of the common people in the South. Nevertheless, the myth of Southern military invincibility had been built up and morale was high. Psychological warfare was not known by that name then, but something analogous to it was a factor for the first two years and had infected officers on both sides. It was shattered in three days. the Confederates suffered as heavily in morale as in material. Invasion was not again possible. Such temporary depression counts for little with the American solider, we suffered defeat two years in the Pacific in WWII and Pollard, a Southern writer and others, maintain that Southern military morale soon rose again.

On the eve of Gettysburg, morale was lower in the Union Army than in the Confederate Army. Union morale was fair despite the bungling generalship of two years and the low pay of the soldiers. With 100,000 men, the army should have been more confident. Hooker's replacement by Meade seemed not to have lowered morale. Rather, in the view of one, "I now felt we had a clear-headed, honest soldier - that there would be no repetition of Chancelorsville." Meade's decision not to retreat after July 1 probably did much to build up morale.

One of Lee's great errors was his contempt for the Federal army. Nearly all his generals underwent the contagion and the illusion of invincibility was common among the ranks. The rebels grew bold and incautious because of this spirit of contempt. But the Union army felt it only needed a good commander. The army felt cheated when Lee slipped away and confidence ebbed. The chagrin of the Northern people burst out in anger the more so because they thought that Lee was to renew at Williamsport the capitulation's effected previously and again somehow, they connected the New York City draft riots with his withdrawal. Tactical and strategic considerations hinged upon the contempt for the estimate of the Union Army. Lee's equipoise was threatened by this over-confidence.

Invasion awakened the North to the possibility of defeat. The war had come into its midst and it had the salutary effect of alarming the country into vigorous preparation in Pennsylvania and in the sister states. Commented a citizen of Chambersburg to a Confederate officer, "(We shall fight) as long as you Southern people are able to fight... the people here have scarcely awakened yet to the fact that there is a war upon their hands; but this invasion will open their eyes to the fact..." shouted the Pennsylvania "Bucktails" in their enthusiasm which laughed at death, "We've come to stay." Fighting on one's own soil and for one's home has a magical effect. Like a stream of water forced up by a pump, Lee found increasing resistance, the moral effect of which was to unite all men to run back the stream at any cost.

Historians have usually brushed away Edward Everett's two-hour long address at the Gettysburg dedication ceremonies, Nov. 19, 1863 and it has been overshadowed by Lincoln's more epic and significant "Address." However, it is well to remember that Everett echoed some of the sentiments and ideals of a nation at war. The great orator outlined the action at Gettysburg, stated the Southern motives for rebellion and orated upon what he thought was the significance of the great battle. He laid the blame largely upon Davis and the slaveholding aristocracy. They were wrong constitutionally; it was not analogous to the American protest against George III; it was not a rebellion against tyranny. This was a battle for a righteous cause, a fight for homes in a spirit of "exalted patriotism." From the histories of civil wars in European countries, Everett saw a great ray of hope for eventual reconciliation. Many in the South were already yearn-ing, as this battle showed, to greet the old National flag. One of the great lessons of the war was that "it is impossible for a people without military organization to withstand the inroad of a veteran army." Gettysburg, spoke Everett, was as decisive as the Grecian wars against the Asiatic despots. It was one of those all-important days upon which the fate of the republican union depended. The battle settled the question once and for all of which was supreme, the Federal government or the States. Gettysburg, at last, seemed to articulate this great question, to bring the war to a focus, to clarify the Northern ideology. There is "no brighter page than that which relates the Battle of Gettysburg."

Harper's Weekly took note of Lincoln's speech. It and the Springfield (MA) *Republican* were the two outstanding journals which recognized at once the greatness of the "Address." "Thus far," said the former, "was thundered to the rebellion." It "marked the highest tide of the war." The periodicals described Lincoln's words as "simple, earnest, felicitous, from the heart to the heart." The *New York Times* praised its manner of delivery. On the other hand there were critics. The total view, however, seems to be that Lincoln made a good impression. "What makes Gettysburg immortal," said Barton, "is less the military victory than the speech of Lincoln." "It was an interpretation," said Lord Curzon, "of the spirit of the occasion. It was a declaration of America's fundamental principles." Miers and Brown declare that Lincoln created an epic in American history. Lincoln made clear the issues involved and epitomized to the world for all time the concepts of democracy. Pennsylvania State Historian, S.K. Stevens, wrote recently that with each passing year the document not only remains one of the very greatest of our heritage, but also takes on fresh meaning as our nation participates more and more in world affairs. The document is good English, concise, clear and sets forth the very essence of our national spirit. It reaches "to the world frontiers of liberty and freedom, where many of the people are so benighted." For its close relation to the battle, for its even transcending it, the writer of this paper makes no apology for discussing the Gettysburg address.

Present Day Significance

An attempt will be made now to articulate between the way Gettysburg looked to contemporaries and how it looks to those living today. The attempt will necessarily result in some overlapping, because much of the way Gettysburg was regarded then is so regarded today. However, there have been some revisions of fact and opinion in particulars which perhaps do not differ radically from the contemporary view.

In the first flush of success the Northern people of 1863, on the whole, thought Gettysburg was decisive. Enmity against the South was strong. "It took 20 years for men to begin to reason." Time is not only a great vindicator, but it is also a great pacificator. Those who fought then, met to the number of over 50,000 as friends 50 years later at a great reunion.

There has not been a great revision of facts, since the particulars of the action were fairly well learned when articulate veterans began to write their histories and memoirs. Many of the causes for particular tactics, the tactics themselves, logistics, the psychological intangibles and the verdict of historians, however, have been subject to various differing and changing opinions.

No other battleground was so memorialized during the Civil War as at Gettysburg; perhaps none other since. Tens of thousands visit it annually. It is the opinion of the general public today that something significant happened there. Opinions vary from the belief that the rebels were "within a stone's throw of peace," to the belief that Confederate victory would not have affected the final result much; it would have been only a temporary Northern setback. It remained for future generations to more maturely evaluate Gettysburg. From a dogmatic "turning point," "a second Waterloo," "climacteric" view, qualified opinions are now given by historians. Coupled with Lincoln's address, it was a re-affirmation of democratic principles. It was practical because wrought in the fiery crucible of war. Beitler thought the greatest thing about the battle was that it made possible the speech of Lincoln.

While John Richard Green thought that Gettysburg was the most momentous battle in history, a number of historians, especially since 1900, have called it a drawn battle and considerably less than decisive. Formby called it "tactically indecisive." It was not a decisive battle but "a repetition of Antietam, with this difference only...the Confederacy was one year nearer its end," and "it was decisive in what was prevented." A Confederate veteran, Rev. James P. Smith, called it a drawn battle. Meade never claimed it as a victory and Stackpole calls it a draw. Meade's failure to pursue Lee seems to be the crux of the controversy and has a direct bearing on whether to characterize

Gettysburg as decisive or a draw. Miers and Brown in 1948 seem to defend Meade; Stackpole in 1956 censors Meade. Pratt, another modern writer, says that Gettysburg was not decisive; only Lincoln's address was decisive.

"The war was not won at Gettysburg; it was won in the West." Increasingly, modern historians are taking this view. In 1951 Pratt thought Chickamauga was the decisive battle; but in his latest book, Vicksburg seems to be given the decision. Lee's defeat was due to the "peculiar American type of combination" which existed in the North. It was, and is, a complex spirit of voluntary cooperation. Lee's personality, his resources, his cause, his tactics did not measure up against this Northern monarchical singleness of control.

One new facet of the battle has been called to note recently. The effect of the breech-loading rifle and the worth of these guns in the hands of sharpshooters has been noted by three writers. Buckeridge's thesis is that Gettysburg was won in great part by the use of the Spencer repeating rifle. Gen. Custer and others gave favorable reports. The 3,500 rifles gave Meade the equivalent of 20 extra cavalry regiments. Buford, in that first day, had only a few, yet they "were the first strands of psychological and material destruction." Wrote Lincoln's third secretary, Stoddard, "His (Lincoln's) choice is a kind of Spencer."

Dr. Benson J. Lossing, in a speech at Gettysburg in 1889, first coined the phrase "16th decisive battle," in the manner of Creasy. He called it the most momentous, decisive and pivotal battle ever fought in human history. This panegyric has been soft-pedaled by time. It has often been compared with Waterloo. There are many similarities: the topography was similar, the tactics, the season, the forces engaged (French 80,000 vs. Allies 72,000 and Union 82,000 vs. Confederate 70,000); the losses, the waves of attack, like Pickett's charge and the failure of the British to pursue. By employing contrast it becomes apparent that the results of Gettysburg have been exaggerated. There is little or no analogy between Waterloo and Gettysburg. The former ended a war, turned a dynasty and settled the European map for a generation. The great Northern cities were never in serious danger. This comparison with Waterloo is a lot of rhetoric. It was not decisive in the same sense as Waterloo and Tours. It was a turning point and in that sense, decisive. Federal success must be measured by the boldness of the confederate plans.

The Battle of Marathon has been brought up as another parallel. True, the Greeks were on the heights. At Waterloo neither side seemed anxious to fight; both sides were anxious to fight at Gettysburg. For that matter, the Battle of Hastings might be analogous. It was a case of one society trying violently to place its society over another. And as the Norman conquest had a long-term good effect, so the South has derived an ultimate benefit from its defeat. As William made possible Magna Carta 150 years later, so Lincoln (the North) made possible the epoch of universal freedom. Victory brought a *status quo ante bellum*, a renewal, of that early national harmony.

Pickett's charge, "a monumental act of heroic desperation," has been compared with the charge of the 600 at Balaklava. Pickett's charge was repeated seven years later by the German guards on the field of Gravelotte and failed even more disastrously. The lesson was learned that massed infantry cannot charge across a wide stretch of fire-swept ground in the day of modern weapons.

Gettysburg is a textbook for military students. Perhaps no other battlefield has been so carefully studied, marked and described. It offers a magnificent study to soldiers and historians and to the mass it affords an object of supreme interest. Lee's defeat was due to many factors, the imponderables, *ad infinitum*. That may be the "principal reason why Gettysburg offers such a fascinating subject for study, for conversation, for far-ranging speculation and for delightful, friendly argument." Military students of foreign armies have come to Gettysburg to study it. The tactical movements will always furnish a fruitful theme for speculation, as possibilities and probabilities will suggest themselves.

No other 'passage of arms' in the Civil War has been so extensively written about. The literature divides itself into three parts: "the historical, the oratorical and that which is synchronal with the events themselves." Poems, plays and novels have been written about Gettysburg, represented by such dramatists as Edgar Lee Masters (*Gettysburg*) and Percy MacKaye (*Gettysburg*) and the novelist MacKinlay Kantor (*Long Remember*). At least 50 different historians have written at least one book each centering largely on Gettysburg.

The writer confesses, as man is ever prone to do, an inclination to derive spiritual lessons from great events of history. It is very true of Gettysburg. The event determined in part that the authority of the Union was to be supreme on American soil and that Liberty as incorporated in the National Constitution was destined to survive war and to endure. Free popular government ceased to be an experiment. The Constitution would remain the organic law of the people and that government would be "of the people, by the people and for the people." No longer could the old aristocracies of Europe hope and gloat. Gettysburg taught that the United States were not dead. And in an individual sense every man has his Gettysburg. Let him fight and win it. The battle provides lessons and has an indirect influence upon the free institutions of other lands. It will provide an incentive whenever in the future peoples are called upon to take up arms. Gettysburg symbolizes "the struggles and the sacrifices and the terrible hopes of people in a great moment of crisis." Lincoln stood at Gettysburg as the world's foremost spokesman of democratic government. He hinted that popular government could and might perish and that Jefferson's proposition that "all men are created equal" was being tested.

Some have seen lessons applicable to the present. Beitler saw that it meant a nation must fight to live; that it is wisdom to buy freedom, safety and sweet honor with blood. He saw in Gettysburg lessons in the duties of citizenship: the value of patience, forbearance, charity and higher ideals. Woodrow Wilson said on July 3, 1913, at the Gettysburg reunion: "The day of our country's life has but broadened into morning. Do not put uniforms by. Put the harness of the present on." How well did we need both kinds of raiment on April 6, 1917! There is need, as in 1863, for continual struggle to hold inviolate our most cherished national and international rights. It will require good statesmanship. Nor must good everyday citizenship be ignored. Then patriots "Will point to thee as consecrated ground, Nor Marathon nor Bunker Hill is holier name."

Synthesis

From a military view Gettysburg was a drawn battle and from the failure to destroy Lee's army it must be considered indecisive. Coupled with the victory at Vicksburg and with the fact that it was an invasion of Northern soil, the battle derived a significance based largely upon sentiment.

It is generally agreed that Meade should have risked a more immediate pursuit, but with Gettysburg, Vicksburg and Chickamauga in memory Northern morale would never sink as low as it was after Chancellersville.

The true evaluation of Gettysburg lies in its spiritual symbolism. In that aspect it was highly decisive. Lincoln's address has evoked a significance far above the intrinsic worth of the battle. For the first time Lincoln expressed for the people the aims and meaning of the war and reaffirmed those ideals which continue to lend direction to the nation. The address must be included as a true part of Gettysburg, the bone and sinew of that symbol of the fight for Liberty and Union.

Random Thoughts of an Amateur Historian

Dr. Yates and members of Phi Alpha Theta: I welcome the opportunity to talk with you tonight on local history, its study, research, writing, publishing and promotion, a subject in which I believe many of you might be interested. Although talking is second nature for me in my school classroom, yet the situation is a little different tonight. In both instances I have a captive audience but I cannot scold you or keep you after school! Also, I face a more sophisticated group.

I confess to be guilty of inflicting upon the American public another one of the 30,000 (now 60,000) annual book titles - *A History of Peoria County.*

The glorious story of Peoria is a challenging one and one that needed to be done, for the last Peoria history book was published 55 years ago. Some of the topics are a challenge even to the professional historian. Among them are the Fort Creve Coeur controversy, the French Claims and Peoria politics.

For those many Peorians thus far who have bought copies I express many thanks and also for the many accolades received. I would be less than human if my heart was not thus warmed.

I think I can guarantee that I will not shock you the way Eartha Kitt did the ladies group at the White House back in January of this year (1968). However, I am at the age and stage of my teaching career (near retirement) that I can afford to speak about as I please. I have nothing to lose and I am not looking for financial gain nor seeking added status.

Who was it, Walter Duranty, back in the 1930s, who wrote the book *I Write As I Please*? My living is made, I seek no honors, I have no mentor, I have no axes to grind. You know, I used to liken myself to Jesse Stuart, that old Kentucky mountain boy who came up the hard way. But, of course now, he is circulating in a little higher company and is withal a world traveler.

Some weeks before my Peoria book came out I was asked about another edition or printing. A second printing! I was surprised, shocked almost. Is there anyone so naive or optimistic to believe that a local history book could sell out even the first printing? Few do so because of their localized nature. I recall my own disillusionment with my *History of Massac County* (1955). There was no knocking down of people to get to the scene of sales on opening, autographing day. Nor later, either. It is an experience common to most local or regional history books. A few hundreds, yes, but not thousands. Like Thoreau's first book *A Week on the Concord and Merrimac Rivers* of which he said: "I have a thousand books in my library, over 900 of which I wrote myself."

Why isn't every native an eager buyer of a local history book about his own county, city or area? Last summer, down at Fort Chartres, I was discussing this matter with the park ranger. "You know why local histories don't sell?" he asked. I gave some possible reasons. "No," he said, "the reason is that everybody thinks he already knows about the history of his own town or county." Not a bad answer. In fact, on autograph day, an elderly gentleman said to me, "I know all about what's in that book." A prophet is not without honor save in his own country." (Matthew 13:57).

Why did I come to write three local histories? It seems I was born with almost a congenital interest in local history, dating even from grade school and continuing through high school. Let me quote the opening paragraph of the Massac book Preface:

"As a little boy 4 years old, the author remembers his parents taking him to old Fort Massac one Fourth of July. At the age of 7 he was taken to live with his grandparents for one year. The home was in an area which commanded a sweeping view of most of the county and part of Kentucky. Those were impressionable days. At night the grandparents told many tales of yore about the region. A love for the home county was thus early engendered in the child. As time went on he became curious to know more."

I went into these projects with no expectation of great gain; in fact, with the realization that it would be quite possible to lose money. It was a labor of love. Yes, sales have been slow. It took 12 years to break even on the first Massac County book. I hope to dispose of all 1,000 Peoria County books by June the first. Fond hope!

I trust you will pardon these rambling remarks, part reminiscent, part philosophical, part expository and part advisory. Like

Duranty, I speak and write as I please! Of one thing I feel sure, that I shall not write another local history - one that spans the time between the mound builders and the current year. My experience on my Bradley University thesis was that I was led far away from the local history and that I had to delve into national politics, slavery, economics and so on - background material. The task is formidable. The experience has enforced my resolution never to write another county history; I shall turn to biography or something else. Perhaps the major responsibility of local history is to keep the record. That I have tried to do, making valid generalization, syntheses and interpretation.

A combination of inspiration, perspiration, trial and error gets the job done. Quotation permits must be secured and copyright arranged for. Then a re-write with agonizing attempts at condensing. Only a writer knows how sweet his words seem to him and he regrets to cut out cute phrases, daring ideas and romantic turns. One soon learns that it is easier to write a long book than a short book. Next, the typing, which itself often constitutes a partial re-write, for numerous changes will now seem wise. Next, there is the choice of a printer and the various technical points concerning type, style, pictures, binding, etc. Finally, come the galley proofs and the binding proof. Then follows the anxious wait. To hold your first book in your hands is an almost indescribable feeling. If we have our agony in the writing, so we now have our ecstasy!

But what is the value of all this localized history, after all, especially so much of it which we have read and seen in an earlier year? The garrulous reminiscer, a "stream of consciousness" volubility which tells much anecdotal detail but gets nowhere? What is the meaning? So what? This raw material needs interpretation and a relating to broader principles of economics, social life, politics and so on. I don't think I have to convince you of the values of and the joys of learning about Peoria history. You would not be here tonight if you did not already realize that. Rather, I would like to indicate a few historians who speak about the matter.

Philip Jordan says that local history has altered with the times. It is becoming less localized, more regional and inter-regional. With that I agree. Our own historical society masthead is "dedicated to the preservation of the history of the Central Illinois Valley." That takes in more than one county. Really, there is no such thing as local history, divorced from its neighbors and free from outside factors of a state, nation or world factor. A world war affects the local; so might a new law of Congress, or an act of the state legislature. Local history is simply bringing detail to the foreground. Local historians, in keeping the record, should not be equated with antiquarians. They should be something more than mere chroniclers; they should fix some criteria and goals in their record-keeping and in their writing.

At this point we might note Cellini's remark, "It is a duty incumbent on upright and credible men of all ranks, who have performed anything noble or praise-worthy, to record, in their own writing, the events of their lives." I know not if I approach such status, but I have written my autobiography in two slim volumes. As I have said before in various talks, John Richard Green, Lord Macauley, Woodrow Wilson and other historians have attested to the values in local history study and writing.

We turn to the kinds of local histories. Like cakes, there are two kinds, good and bad. On example of the bad kind is the so-called "mug book," pictures and laudatory sketches of prominent local people. At the 26th annual meeting of the American Association for State and Local History (Atlanta, Oct. 6, 1966) the president in his message severely criticized this type of history. He called them simply vestigial remains of the pioneer society impulse. No wonder young professors fresh from the German universities and later in American, viewed with contempt the perversion of their craft.

Since the 1930's local societies and local history writing have grown up. We have come to realize, with Woodrow Wilson, that local history is "the ultimate substance of National history" and is important. But the local history field still awaits full utilizing. In most universities it lacks parity with other historical fields.

Many intelligent people are ignorant of the heritage of the locality where they presently reside. Many are newcomers. The local historical society and the writer cannot presume background knowledge. The presentation must be basic and fundamental. It must be interpretive with simplicity, without being simple.

As Carl Becker said 35 years ago in his book, *Every Man His Own Historian*, local history still offers an exciting field. For writer and non-writer it provides a means for identification with the experience or history in a discernible form or area.

The new-type local histories try to use all the social sciences - sociology, economics, political science, geography and psychology. From psychology we may use the principles of social control. Statistics take on meaning. Moreover, the new-type tend to be regional, although we have recent attempts at urban local history and company histories. Tarbell's *History of the Standard Oil Company* is the early and classic one. The titles of others follow; *Pittsburgh, the Story of an American City*, 1964; *The Waterfall that Built a City* (highly praised), 1966; *With Pride in Heritage*; *History of Jefferson County, Oregon*, 1966; *The Story of Lenoir County* (North Carolina); *Chattanooga Country* (a model for those who aspire to write with professional skill), 1963; *A History of Lubbock* (Texas), 1966 and *Kansas City and the Railroads*, 1962. There is also a recent history of Milwaukee. It is also well to study Lynd's *Middletown* which is of a sociological nature.

A new tool is the computer, as reported in the *Journal of American History* for December 1967. Increasing numbers of students have come to recognize the value of such electronic data processing equipment. It does not necessarily imply that the researcher or writer himself deal with the equipment; he simply applies to the proper storage center (archives) and the materials are quickly received in readily usable form. Examples: combining sets of data, preparing special tabulations, performing complex analyses. The first project of the Inter-University consortium was the collection and processing of basic county election returns from 1824 to the present. Other projects involve county-level demographic, social and economic data. An innovation in historical studies, it will likely lead to shifts in emphasis of goals and methods, a reorientation. It will also remove much of the drudgery and I might add, also, save eyesight!

Many county histories are being issued during this Illinois Sesquicentennial year (1968). Not a few are team efforts: Henry County (four people), Mason County (six people plus a high school class), Grundy County (seven) and Winnebago and others. My fear is that, unless the editor does a good job, the book will lack unity and that viewpoints will conflict (See the *History of Lubbock*); that too many people working on a single book may impair a possible central theme; that discontinuity may result.

And so, says Edgar Johnson in his *One Mighty Torrent*, "In huge heaps of the most incongruous things, rubbish and jewels, delusions and blinding flashes of truth, lyric poems and advertising folders, the historian delves for the significant."

******

According to O. Henry, the two saddest phrases in the publishing world are "please remit payment" and "the editor regrets." The story is told of one hard-pressed writer who, enclosing his poem, had written on the cover letter:

"Please, gentle soul, if you are able,

Accept my poem - yes, please do.

If you refuse, I'll blow a fuse,

For my apartment rent is due."

The editor wrote back: "Which poem are you submitting? The piece about your rent being due is by far the better."

The period of waiting - often for months - is almost always one filled with trepidation for the author, before acceptance and often after publication. Just after Lés Misérables came out, Victor Hugo sent a letter to his publisher consisting of simply a ? mark. He was overjoyed when his publisher replied simply with an ! mark. However, the writer of a local history has little fear of not being accepted. His book is privately printed by a strictly commercial printer and financed by him alone. The only question is, will the printer produce a good book.

This renews the question of getting your book trade published or privately printed. There is a peculiar economics in publishing. That and the technology of the media affect what is widely available to the public. Of course, it is true that anyone with a trace of merit can get into print in some way, even if he has to have his book printed at his own expense. It only takes a few thousand dollars. Recall my own purpose was to supply a need for a Massac and Peoria history which no one else had seen fit to essay; to write as I darned pleased - let the chips fall where they might and not to venture the effort for the purpose of making money.

There are only three major networks and two major press services in America; only one newspaper in most cities and two or three TV stations; but there are literally hundreds of publishers and printers. As I see it, the chief difficulty for an amateur is press and advertising coverage to insure distribution. Certainly, a printer can print a book as cheaply as a legitimate trade publisher, but then you will have to be your own promoter. You will also lack the prestige of the trade publisher.

With some 60,000 new titles in the United States annually, your book faces tough competition for mere attention. In addition, only about one percent of the adult population is a regular patron of a bookstore. That means only 1,000 or so for all Peoria County. Moreover, your local history will have a limited local readership, not national. There is no way to learn bookselling except by doing it and no one to help you but yourself. Yet there is a point reached of resistance to the pressure of publicity which one must consider; it can be counter-productive. Moreover, there are only about 4,000 real retail book outlets in this country and less than 500 serious ones. And Americans devote 12 times as many hours to merely thumbing through magazine, watching TV and seeing movies as they do reading books. So a book - especially a local history or novel - has a poor chance of selling well. A *How to Stop Snoring* book might pay, or a *Decorating Cakes for Fun and Profit*.

There are at least one million writers in America but comparatively few are successful. Most members of the Writer's Guild earn less than $3,000 per year. Many people are one-book writers. It is an unsure way to earn a living. The cost to accumulate the equipment (to prepare for a writing life) is enormous. Hear what Upton Sinclair said about his book *The Jungle*: "I have been 15 years in getting the education to write it. During 12 of those years, I have actually been practicing at writing and during that time I have written not less than five million words. During the same time I have read certainly four or five thousand books, including all the worthwhile novels in the five languages which I succeeded in acquiring. To enable me to write the first chapter (a musical scene), I had to spend nearly three years studying the violin and attend many hundreds of concerts. I had to get married and become a father to write other portions of the book. The cost of the whole equipment would certainly not have been less than $20,000."

Assuming again now, that the only way to get your local history in print is to pay for it yourself, you are a likely customer for some printer or for some so-called subsidy or vanity publisher, such as Pageant Press, Vantage Press or Exposition Press. In modern trade publishing there is no break-even or profit for the publisher under 10,000 copies sales. You would never want that many. And so the lady in Pekin writes me recently asking how she can get her family history published. She had received quotations ranging from $7,000 to $10,000. Too much. She, like me, will have to work with printers from who she has had competitive bids. Really, there is nothing wrong or illegal about a reliable subsidy publisher. Through the ages many writers have had their early works privately printed. Upton Sinclair did so for 25 years, for no trade publisher would accept his radical or muck-raking books. Some subsidy books have almost made the best-seller lists. But a warning as to the terms of the contract is in order. You pay for the books but get only a dozen or so of them "free;" the rest of the books you will have to buy (at a discount). Meanwhile, the company loses nothing if sales lag (they usually do) because it has already been paid. Nor is there a certainty that the company will even print more than a few hundred copies, or even less.

Concluding, I think that any labor connected with local history is laudable whether it be its study, writing or publishing. I would like to see more of it done. It is a challenge to young or old.

I has been good to be with you tonight.

(From three versions of a lecture given in 1968 to the Peoria Historical Society, Phi Alpha Theta, the Sertoma Club and the Pleasant Hill School faculty. Rewritten June 2000.)

Sermonettes

Indian Missions

We have been astonished in times past in our own locality at the response to appeals for help when someone has lost his home by fire or such like misfortune.

We are conscious of the needs of our local people; also, as Baptists, in particular, we are mission-minded as regards the foreign field. It is our answer to the question "Am I my brother's keeper?"

There is, however, a segment of our national population which we are apt to forget and neglect. I refer to our own American Indians. An appeal for help has come from the Rainbow Baptist Mission at Keams Canyon, AZ.

But first I want to survey the Indian missions briefly and give a few statistics as to the extent of the Indian mission work and a few other general facts. My basic source has been this book *Within Two Worlds*, which is in our own church library.

Originally, the US Indian population was about 850,000 when America was first discovered. This is twice as high as most history textbooks give. In 1940 the census gave 396,000.

At least one-third of the nearly 400,000 Indians in the US have been reached by the Christian churches. Many more have been exposed. In Canada 97 percent are attached to Christian churches. Beginning after the Revolutionary War treaties were made with the Indians at different times and they were put upon Reservations. By the Dawes Act, 1887, the Indians were given individual ownership of the land.

The Indian problem had already been a serious one for the government. Unfortunately, much of the land given to the Indians was unproductive. Of course, oil has made many Oklahoma Indians very wealthy, but most of the Indians elsewhere eked out a meager living. The Reservation system has not always been well administrated either.

Although the Indian has largely carried on his own local self-government, it was not until 1924 that they were made US citizens and they did not vote until about 1947.

The plight of the Navaho has been particularly bad the past 10 or 15 years. Our own Gene Autry, in a photoplay a few years ago, vividly and truthfully showed the destitution of the Navaho and some of the things that could be done to alleviate the situation. Much has since been done, but not enough. Magazine articles have also been numerous. Only last autumn *Look* magazine contained an article on the Sioux Indians. These conditions all constitute an indictment of as to how the American people have sometimes treated some of their people.

Many Protestant denominations have been and are now active in the mission field. Schools and churches have been established by Methodists, Presbyterians, Episcopalians, Mennonites, the Society of Friends, the Reformed Church and the Lutherans. The Catholics are also in the field. Mission work has been carried on among all Indian tribes, as well as with resettled Indians in such urban centers as Brooklyn, NY.

In the early 1800s, Baptists worked with the Miamis, Kickapoos and Cherokees. Many Baptists since then have heard the Macedonian call and gone to work with the Indians.

The Baptists early evangelized a large part of the Florida Seminoles. The Spring Baptist Church, for example, first pastored by Chief John Jumper, is now 100 years old. There is also Baptist activity among the Oklahoma Seminoles. In Oklahoma City there is a Baptist Interdenominational Center. One-tenth of the leadership of the Pima Indian Presbyterian church in Phoenix, AZ is Baptist. Within two generations they have become model Christian Americans.

Baptists began work with the Crows of Montana in 1903 and assumed full responsibility in 1921. Tribal leadership is largely Baptist.

Educationally, there are government schools, elementary and high school. There are 33 high schools operated by the government or the Indians. They are strongly vocational. The National Council of Churches sponsors religious programs in the larger of these schools.

Bacone College, Muskogee, OK is the only four year college for Indians in the nation. It was founded by Almon C. Bacone. In its second year the American Baptist Home Mission Society sponsored it and has continued to do so ever since. (See the November 1955 *Baptist News* which comes to your homes). Since it serves other denominations also, it is seeking aid from other denominations. The inscription on the cornerstone of Bacone Chapel reads, "A Christian school planted in the midst of a people becomes one of the most powerful agencies in the work of civilization."

Recently, especially since 1947, after the post-war exodus back to home, the government and the churches have established relocation centers, community centers and recreation centers in many cities and communities to meet the needs of the Indians, many of whom had gone into war work or in the military service. Those programs sponsored by various agencies did much to meet the Indian's needs. I might say also that there are several hospitals in the West to serve the Indian specifically.

The Northern Baptists have been especially active among the Navaho and Hopi in New Mexico, Arizona and Nevada. Work began in Arizona in 1910; in Nevada in 1920. The Northern and Southern Baptists have cooperated in several of these endeavors.

The Navaho total 75,000 scattered over 16 million acres, mostly dry and bare land. It is the largest tribe today in America. In WWII 3,600 men served, the most famous Ira Hayes, the hero of Surabachi who died recently of alcoholism.

Most of the Navahos either have not heard the Gospel or have not been won to Christ. The task of contacting is great in this large and sparsely settled area.

The Indian is naturally deeply spiritual. He makes a good Christian when he is given a good chance. The Indian mission work is part of the total Christian World Mission, of which it may be said that "Christ came that they might have life and have it more abundantly."

Yes, the churches have a particular responsibility. As Mr. Phillip Frazier, Dakota Indian, says: "We need Christian leaders who will put on the whole armor of God and get into the hot spots of society."

Our own local church today has an opportunity to help in this Indian mission work.

Our appeal comes from the Rev. Weber of the Rainbow Baptist Mission, Keams Canyon, AZ. Located in north central Arizona at Keams Canyon, some 80 miles southeast of Tuba City, it is within the Hopi Indian Reservation. There is a good deal of rivalry, jealousy and ill-feeling between the Hopi and the much larger Navaho Reservation.

Our pastor Rev. Daniels is personally acquainted with Bro. Weber, who once pastored in Farmington, IL and I believe Rev. Daniels had some contact with him in Southern Illinois also. The need is there and it is a worthy cause. I think we should give this appeal our hearty support and do what we can.

It was three decades later that the wife and I were first able to drive out to Keams Canyon to get a closer look at that mission field. The Rev. Gerald Lawton was the pastor of the white-Indian integrated church at the time of our visit and he further informed us of the work and the financial needs. Since then he has moved in to the Cherokee (North Carolina) Baptist Church.

–Second Baptist Church, Peoria, IL,
1957 talk.

A Prayer

Father, we come thanking thee again for the opportunity of meeting together once more. We thank thee for this series of little prayer meetings and we trust that much has been said and prayed about which meets with Thy approval. We have tried to present our petitions in all earnestness and meekness. Father, we thank thee for the dawning of this new day. Almighty God, we know that without Thy ruling hand we would not have been permitted to see this day.

We thank thee for this revival. We feel that much has been accomplished for Thy glory, but all too little in Thy sight. Father, help us to overcome the barrier of timidity so that we may utter just the desires and prayers that are needful.

We pray further the richest blessing upon this revival, to end within a few more hours. May someone be led to Christ, even this last night. If there are any doubting persons in this community who ask "Can any good come out of Huffman Church?", let the answer be "come and see."

And now go with us through the rest of the service, through this week and the next and through all future time, so that we may say at life's end with the apostle Paul, "I have fought a good fight."

We beg thee things in the name of the Lord Jesus. Amen.

—1947

Miracles in the Bible

The Holy Book tells us that Jesus performed many miracles. Who does not know the half dozen or so that are common knowledge even to a child? Jesus' first miracle was the turning of water into wine at the wedding feast in Cana. Later, He healed the ruler's son and the man of 38 years impotence. He fed the 5,000 from a little bread and two small fish. He walked over the Sea of Galilee. A blind man was restored to sight. Yeah, He even raised Lazarus from the dead, great still, Himself in the Resurrection.

Just what is a miracle? In every day life we often remark of an unusual happening - like coming out of a car wreck unscathed - that one escaped injury "by a miracle." However, in scriptural terms a miracle is an historic event or natural phenomenon which seems to violate natural laws but is attributed to Providence or the intervention of the God and causes wonder, awe, even terror, in us.

Moses himself performed 42 miracles and through the Bible runs the continuity through Jesus and His Apostles. Often Jesus worked

His goodwill on the Sabbath to the consternation of the conventional Jew of the times. In the face of the unfavorable view Jesus sought to reveal His divinity and to present Himself as one equal to God, His only begotten Son.

There was much disease then, blindness, leprosy and other ailments, but of a rather different kind from those afflicting people today, such as heart disease, cancer, polio, flu and the disorders attributed to "fast living" of which mental problems make up a large number. Where would we find a ministering Jesus in a modern city? We might expect to find His presence in our hospitals.

What were Jesus' motives in healing people, of raising Lazarus? Certainly, it proved His power over death and the grave. One motive, surely, was His concern for people. It is agreed that sin often causes sickness. Mankind disregards proper health habits; he indulges in alcohol and drugs; he worries too much; he schemes for money and possessions. Fallen Adam remains fallen and is so often a discredit to his maker and to his vast possibilities.

The Mosaic miracles were not so much a proof of God's existence as a revelation to the faithful of God's covenant love. Miracles were expressions of God's saving love as well as His Holy Justice. They were for salvation but also for historical judgment. The various Egyptian plagues, the daily manna, demonstrated His love for His people.

The New Testament miracles were rather of a different kind and purpose although the thread of the Lord's purposes cannot be entirely broken. Here He declared that His miracles were the fulfillment of the promises of the Messiah's Kingdom as foretold by Isaiah (24:18-19). They were signs of the presence of the Kingdom of God. The miracles pointed to deep spiritual truth, demanding obedient faith. Every such story was a sign that God's salvation was present. Death was overcome and Satan bound. These miracles wrought so often upon most unlikely people, were not of a theatrical nature. He offered salvation and demanded decision. Also, the gifts of the spirit was a way by which believers ministered to others, beginning with the early Apostles.

Are there miracles today? Some would say so. We have medical care for the unfortunate; we have a legion of doctors, nurses, medicines, operative skills. We have offered prayers in proportion. Wonderful cures are effected in our world today. Do we dare say that these things are not miracles? Ships in storm, prayer for rain, World Wars I and II "miracles," faith healing (many stories here!), the prayer circles for sick folks, a mother's prayer for her children out in life and prayers for salvation answered. Is there not proof?

Two views are current on miracles: that they are truly acts of Providence or actual God interventions, or that these modern "miracles" only follow primal natural laws, coincidence or chance, with no spirit intervention. But, like one of my old Texas Baptist preachers always said, "If this thing happened by coincidence or chance, I give God credit anyway."

Christ performed miracles to convince people who thereby became His redeemed followers. He gave us life first; then Liberty (John 8:31-36). John teaches that Christ is Life. "I am come - this is Life eternal. Even so I send you." Faith in Jesus means life - physical and spiritual. He has such actual power today, though difficult for some to realize. One appreciates His message to those in sorrow, in times of death, cynicism, stoicism, despair. The deadly moral and spiritual malaise of the modern world can be likened to a deadly gaseous mine, its poisons made ineffective by oxygen machines and masks. Mood, tone, health are bound closely with peace of mind and freedom from fear. It means that we should commit ourselves to walk in the spirit of Jesus in the presence of human needs today (World Relief efforts). Christ is compassionate, responsive, convincing. Why will not everyone accept? He is available ("Behold, I stand at the door and knock").

In conclusion, we may know that Life, Salvation, Liberty are responses to the vicarious death of Jesus. In the second miracle we see how faith was born in the noble (John 4:46-54). Jesus gave health in response to personal faith (John 5:1-14). Jesus gave life in response to a wavering faith. Jesus Himself is the source of unending life.

In His miracles and in His brief life span we see the various purposes - His mission worked through. One of our church denominations believes the grandest purpose of His mission here on earth was to vindicate His name and that of His Father, God.

Jesus *is* the Resurrection and the Life.

–A Sunday lesson February 1947.

Faith

What is Faith? We exercise it every day, consciously or unknowingly. We trust. We have faith that our old jalopy will get us to town and back because didn't the mechanic in the shop yesterday tells us the car's trouble had been righted? Don't we trust our bank? Do we not trust our grocer, our friends, our wife? Obviously, in the context of our Sunday School lesson today, we have a different meaning attached to the word faith - a concept upon a higher, spiritual plane. I am assuming this morning that personal experience is nearly always of more interest to auditors than mere talking of precepts and discussion of the topics and possibly of more real value in trying to get points across. In this view please pardon the personal references which I may advance in this session.

Hebrews 11:1 says that "Faith is the substance of things hope for, the evidence of things not seen." In Matthew 9:29 two blind men came to Jesus imploring healing. Jesus said "according to your faith be it unto you," and they went away seeing. Our faith (belief) is a measure of what one gets out of life. One must believe in himself first; faith may well follow. However, we do not inherit faith; it must be gained by some experiences. Young writers, as myself, need it; the aged need it and by virtue of their age should have a sufficiency of experience stored up to have an abiding faith in the Lord and his bounties.

Some years ago you may recall that a kind of figurine was marketed and widely circulated among Christians and others. Inside the little plastic, angel statuette was an element of phosphorescence which glowed in the dark but when brought to the light, faded. That brings up John 15:5: "He that abideth in me and I in Him, the same bringeth forth much fruit; for without me you can do nothing." Without Jesus the glow of faith begins to fade but we can turn on the light (the little angel figure) and renew our faith.

Three requisites of Christianity are faith, hope, charity. Dare I add prayer and thanksgiving? To me, faith is expressed partly by our thankfulness; it is a corollary of faith.

It seems to me that I have been somewhat of a pioneer through the years - not the American Western pioneer - but in my moving about the country, setting up housekeeping in nine different places, from New York to Texas, including Illinois and Indiana. Several moves I made on sheer trust - no job in view, no lodging. As each move succeeded I tried to express my thankfulness in my humble way; in each location I associated myself with a church. I continued to lead my life with a good deal of pure faith. An old car got me and family to Texas and back. (One good church brother said later: "I hardly thought you'd make it"). At Searcy, AR, I thoughtlessly left $100 in a motel. One hundred miles down the road I discovered I did not have my wallet. But this all worked out (wife praying silently) and I got the money back within a few hours.

I have taken jobs that I did not possibly see how I could handle them at first. Hard work, prayer, faith saw me through. My family struggled through the calamitous Great Depression, with an attendant deep indebtedness. We survived. These outcomes were not simply fortuitous or accidental. But even so we gave God the credit. Passages like I Corinthians 10:13 bolstered our faith: "God is faithful, who will not suffer you to be tempted above that ye are able but will with the temptation also make a way to escape, that ye may be able to bear it." It has meant much to me. Simple things: like when a dear old lady's Ford car died out on the road one time. She prayed while on the road bank, got up and the car started. Is this all akin to the advice the Hawaiians give to a visitor: "Hang loose?" Could be!

It is usual to remark of our missionaries; "They sacrifice to go out." But do they sacrifice by leaving the American lifestyle behind? In fact, it seems to me, they would be sacrificing *not* to go. Faith has impelled their decision; they really want to go.

We are not what we think, what we admire. We try to emulate those to whom we look up to. It is true, as Emerson said, that we should hitch our wagon to a star; not failure, but low aim is a crime. But in all this secular life we should take God into our daily life. Faith is expressed by quiet action rather than by oral declaration. Perhaps the best rule is to keep our eyes on Him, as Ernest was so transformed as he gazed upon the benign features of the Great Stone Face in the story by the same name. In the book, *In His Steps,* the people of the whole community undertook to follow Jesus in their daily life.

Many times we get discouraged when things become difficult. Who or what helps such a one to persevere? Faith, a continuous faith, is the biggest, most important help at all such times. We must have faith in the physician who is treating us. Faith is the creator, the restorer of life. Christ reminded his followers that without faith He could do nothing: "According to thy faith be it unto you" (Matthew 9:29). Practically, God is always on the side of the best prepared, the best trained, the most vigilant, the pluckiest, the most determined. There are no fortuitous results. "God helps those who help themselves" is a truism. Eschbach, the German medieval poet, has said, "If there be a faith that can move mountains it is faith in one's own powers." In Hawthorne's

The Paradise of Children, Pandora let Troubles out of the box. To assuage the pain, sorrow and fear a little bee named Hope stung Pandora and her friend Epimetheus and all was well. Asks Hawthorne, "What in the world could we do without her?" And added, "Hope spiritualizes the earth." So with faith and hope we overcome. The two transcend and conquer troubles. Read Habakuk 2:4, "the just shall live by his faith."

Orison Marden, who has inspired many youth, especially of the last generation, says, "If we had faith in God we could (1) remove all mountains of difficulty, (2) cure our wills, (3) work miracles, (4) travel Godward infinitely faster than we do." We are aware of the cult of self-help; that we use God and His infinite powers to advance our own self-confidence and fortunes. We include Mary Baker Eddy, Dr. Vincent Peale, Bishop Sheen, Branden, Dyer and a host of other so-called inspirational writers and speakers. Yes, even our television characters. We even include some of our charismatic preachers. Once popular reading was *Making Mountains of Molehills*. All seemingly currying to the God of Success. Certain phrases have become clichés, "Confess it, possess it," "name it, claim it" and others.

All that inspiring us to higher self-esteem, greater self-confidence? God forbid that we have not both in a measure, for our own sanity. But a deep, sincere and abiding faith in God transcends all this striving for earthly power because it is more powerful and secure. Yes, I, we, our church, with such a faith, can move forward.

–March 1999, from old notes.

Freedom Under Christ's Authority

Authority is of many kinds and degrees. It is a cliché to say that parents, teachers and the laws of our land should be obeyed. The other side of the coin is embodied in such matters as "freedom under law." We cite Magna Carta, the Bill of Rights, the Declaration of Independence, the four freedoms of Franklin D. Roosevelt and other guides to our personal and corporate freedoms. All are opposed to a totalitarian regime. A Communist country could never erect a Statue of Liberty that would be real and meaningful.

However, this morning we are speaking on a higher plane. Authority and freedom are intrinsically related; the first limits the other and *vice versa*. The authority of Christ is analogous to the relationship between a parent and a child. John 8:32 says, "And you shall know the truth and the truth shall make you free." Galatians 5:1 states, "Stand fast therefore in the liberty where with Christ hath made us free and be not entangled again with the yoke of bondage." We are asked in I Peter 2:13-19 to submit ourselves to authority - for the Lord's sake - as by His example. Servants are to be subject to masters. Jesus' first parable (Luke 6:48-49) of the two builders is introduced by "Whosoever cometh to me and hearth my sayings and doeth them, I will show you to whom he is like." Then the sturdy house on the rock is contrasted by the house built on the earth (sand).

The Rev. Alfred Nevin in *The Parables of Jesus* has a very fine study of the above parable. He says, among other things, "It is intended to designate such as profess to believe Christ's words and declare their determination to obey them, but while calling Him Lord, do not the things which He has commanded. All these classes of people have this in common: that while they have the means of obtaining acquaintance with the words of Jesus, they refuse that subjection of mind and heart and conduct to them to which they are entitled and without which, from the very nature of the case, saving benefit cannot be derived from them."

And further, "The mere professor rests upon his own righteousness in opposition to the sacrifice and righteousness of Christ - His benevolence, liberality, morality - or upon the mercy of God irrespective of Christ' death..."

But the heaven-taught sinner has another foundation. He digs down deep and builds upon a strong rock-bound, Christ-founded basis - a Rock of Ages.

In Matthew 17:25-26 Jesus asks Simon Peter whom he thought the kings of the earth took tribute from: of their own children or of strangers. Peter said "of strangers." Jesus then said that the children were free. In other words, the children of kings (God) are free.

This is a provocative lesson for this Sunday. It poses questions both spiritual and practical. It probes our inner motives; it poses questions and situations with which we are confronted almost every day, nay, every hour. Can one ever over-drive himself under authority? Is the rule obsolete? Is Truth relative or absolute? Are there such things as eternal values? (I once had a chance to affirm the verities in front of three or four young and very-doubting collegians. I am afraid I made a poor impression!). Will not failure to live up to the demands create a guilt complex? I know Christians and some preachers who cracked up. Are these problems purely spiritual things, metaphysical, practical, socially oriented, or simply caused by long-term health problems? When does the heart step in? When does the mind take over? Is there any place for pure reason? Are we allowed foibles? Do you have the right (freedom) to lessen efficiency by the use of alcohol, drugs or over-indulgence in food? Or, as your lesson book asks, "Does living under the authority of Christ result in a restricted, barren life? Or a free, rich life?" All are questions to ponder on.

As we were created with free will, so each one of us must make choices. From a deep study of the Scripture and the use of reason, aye, of common sense, the choice to submit to Christ's authority is beneficial. We obtain freedom from fear, a clear conscience and a sinless life in so far as it is humanly possible and the concomitants that accompany joys, health and peace of mind and body. Thus may we sing with Longfellow:

"Let us do our work as well,
Both the unseen and the seen,
Make the house where God may dwell,
Beautiful, entire and clean."
"The Builders"—1955

Flag Day

This is Flag Day, a day to honor our flag and to show love and respect for America.

Some years ago I gave a miniature "oration" on "What America means to me" to a local organization. In it I stated my feelings about my country and my flag. I recalled that day many years ago when in Buffalo, NY, I attended that city's "I am a American Day Celebration." Alone, homesick for family, the program of that day found a ready lodgment in my heart. Patriotic emotions swept over me. Again, some years later, our plane returning from Europe, circled the Statue of Liberty, that symbol of freedom and welcome. I felt even more deeply what America meant to me.

I don't believe any of us worship our flag but we pay it tribute, we salute it and pledge allegiance, unlike our friends the Jehovah Witnesses. We are reminded of Sir Walter Scott's words:

"Breathes there a man with soul so dead,
Who never to himself has said 'This is my own, my native land?'"
But do we have the moral right and Biblical authority and ap-

proval for so saluting our flag as representing our nationality and patriotism?

I do not find the word flag in the Bible. However, I do find banner and standard. The word ensign most nearly corresponds with our notion of flag. Webster says an ensign is "a flag (or badge) flown as a symbol of nationality." The ensign is found in numerous places in the Bible and I quote a few references in whole.

Among seven is Isaiah 11:12 "and he (the Lord) shall set up an ensign for the nations and shall assemble the outcasts of Israel and gather together the dispersed of Judah from the four corners of the earth."

Isaiah 31:9 "and he (the Assyrian) shall pass over to his stronghold for fear and his princes shall be afraid of the ensign, saith the Lord..."

Number 2:1,2 (1) "and the Lord spoke unto Moses and unto Aaron, saying "Every man of the children of Israel shall pitch by his own standard, with the ensign of their father's house..."

And among three: Psalm 60:4 "Thou hast given a banner to them that fear thee, that it my be displayed because of the truth. Selah."

Solomon (three times), Zechariah and Ezekiel all mention ensign. I find no references in the New Testament.

Then we must be doing right in flying "Old Glory."

–Church Talk June 14, 1987

Why Puzzle Over Star of the East

Dear Sir:

I was much interested in the article "That Christmas Star - Its Wondrous Mystery" appearing in last Sunday's *Peoria Journal Star*. I am not even an amateur of things astronomical but do have more than a casual interest in the subject. Two scientific theories are brought out in Mr. Triff's article: one, that the Star of Bethlehem was an occultation or conjunction of two or more planets; the other theory is of an exploding star or super-novae. These theories appear perennially.

For some words of refutation from a scientific standpoint I would like to refer those who are interested to an article in the December *Moody Monthly*, a religious magazine procurable locally. One point, among others, is that the planets are never seen closer than within eight degrees of the zenith. They keep to the plane of the ecliptic. That would never place Bethlehem in a position to have the planets over-head.

It seems strange that those who accept the modern scientific miracles of things unseen and those who otherwise believe the miracle of Christ's birth, should still argue and seek an explanation for that one special star of all time, the Star of Bethlehem!

–Letter to the Editor, Dec. 26, 1958

Miscellany

Gloom Chaser

I learned to strum the guitar when I was about 11 years old. For years I found times when nothing seemed to cheer me up except my old guitar. I also sing with my guitar from a collection of old, sentimental hillbilly and religious songs. The gloom that comes from much mental work is one of the hardest to chase away. Believe me, my music is then the best and sometimes the last resort. It has been known to stop a headache, too.

–Sold to the *Journal of Living*, February 1954 for $5

My Neighbor or I Knew a Man or To W.O.W.

I

I had a friend, a neighbor good
Who farmed his farm the best he could.
Many's the time we talked quite dense,
Of various things across the fence.

II

My friend was versatile, 'tis truth to tell;
His carpentry skill was known as well.
An artist he was in drawing lines,
Was able, if need, to paint some signs.

III

His interest varied, and widely read;
A Voltaire addict, so 'twas said.
But yet a pessimist, a cynic, sour;
Eccentric, people said, and often dour.

IV

He used big words in common talk:
'apprehensive', 'paradox', 'circumvent' - we'd balk.
At church he'd quote from Micah four -
An obscure passage - and hold the floor.

V

He loved music, and, fiddle in hand,
Would rosin up to beat the band.
The more he bowed the faster gut;
'Twas all could do to follow - tut!

VI

He'd start a waltz but end two-step;
'Twas not because he played inept.
He sawed like a whirling deverish;
Oh, but his fiddle sounded quite devilish.

VII

Friend neighbor's sister a better tread;
Her goggle eyes looked straight ahead.
She'd fiddle the strings on "The Fall of Napoleon,"
Who'd said: "History is a fable agreed upon."

VIII

The blackberry plot was tended well.
He said; "We pick and can and work like hell.
Then come winter with berry fare.
We eat it up to leave us bare."

IX

He met his match with a Ford twenty-five,
Result of the Lizzie's sudden dive.
His first car and he not taught;
In unskilled hands with danger fraught.

X

He left the yard with sudden dive;
Wife Belle just missed in a wild drive.
"No way to stop her now," he cried. "Consarn!"
Felled a gate and smashed the barn.

XI

So ran the course of neighbor man.
Trials, trails, joys, he all did mann.
My gifted cynic, skeptic now is dead;
I feel a loss from now ahead.

XII

God, house him not with godless Voltaire.
We'll never know, for Life's a game of solitaire;
A game like cards is our reward;
Only hope and faith to look toward.

–Jan. 28, 1994 by George W. May

Charles Tiers-Gutarman[*]

The day following our visit to Kincaid Mounds we entered the office of one of the county officers and inquired the way to the young man whom the librarian had referred to a few weeks previously, one Mr. Gutarman.

We followed the direction given us by the gentleman which, to our surprise, led to the residence of young Charles Tiers. We were still further surprised and perplexed to learn that Tiers and Gutarman were one and the same.

We shook hands warmly and then asked, "Explain this, sir. We were directed to Mr. Gutarman but find Mr. Tiers. The librarian and the officer stated the name Gutarman."

Charles laughed and then said, "You are excused to be confused. The truth is I have a double surname which probably should be written Tiers-Gutarman. I am known intimately as Tiers but more formally the latter name takes precedence."

Our friend appeared so open-hearted and congenial that we could not help asking, "How did you acquire the compound name?"

"My parents came from Florida, of Cuban lineage. The Andulasian custom is to add the mother's maiden name to the husband's, by inserting the Spanish equivalent of 'and'. However, the 'and' is usually dropped. Therefore, I have the compound surname.

"We are told," said Mr. Dale, "that you have a fund of information on the local history."

---

[*]This is a deleted chapter from my book *Massac Pilgrimage* (1964). At the time of publication I had reasons for not including it with the other 19 chapters. In this book, Professor Robert Dale and his aide, Wib Yam visit Massac County, IL and do research on the local history. The story is narrated by Dale's alter ego Wib Yam. This unpublished chapter opens with a visit to a local historian.

"Well, yes. I have a little," said our friend modestly. As he said this, he seemed to withdraw within himself. Pensive expressions alternated with stern, hard lines. The eyes seemed to grow darker beneath dark brows. He became reticent and Dale was taken aback by the quick change of mien, who at first had so greeted him and Yam. Had we over estimated the man this early in the interview.

Tiers noticed the surprise his demeanor had caused. "I have tried to school myself to this momentary state of mind," he said. "Several enterprises in which I was highly enthusiastic and confident have failed. I have said to myself 'I won't brag hereafter until I know of the certainty of success.' You will pardon me, gentlemen, if I seem a little loquacious and taciturn in turn."

He smiled cordially. "I understand your interest, I believe and I want to help you out all I can. I want you to like this county and I shall be glad to help you like it."

It was a hot July morning and we had been sitting on the porch. Tiers now asked us indoors where we could more easily refer to his notes, clippings and manuscripts. We met his young wife and two delightful children, a girl and a boy.

"We should have brought Constance, my little girl," said Mr. Dale to the girl.

"Yes, next time bring Mrs. Dale and Constance," said Mrs. Tiers. "We should very much like to meet them."

The historians soon immersed themselves deeply into the subject. I perused various volumes in the fairly adequate library. From the titles it seemed that Tiers was interested in everything. "This indicates," said I to myself, "what any humble home might attain to in the way of a small, ever increasing library of useful and informative books. Pure literature is also represented. Nor have the children been forgotten, for I see a number of good juvenile classics."

At last the two scholars arose and we took a turn around the yard. We returned to the porch.

"Mr. Tiers has been very kind to me, Wib, in furnishing me with a very completed bibliography of material pertaining to his home county. He has also has given me some points of personal contact, besides a wealth of information which will make clear many points we may come across. In truth, he has given us enough starters to keep us going all summer, if we were mind to do so. I thank you very, very much, sir."

"You are more than welcome to the little I have helped you," replied Tiers earnestly.

"How long have you been working on this mass of material?" I asked.

"About 15 years, off and on," returned Tiers. "The whole mass represents untold hours of copying, writing, planning and original research. I have pestered the librarians of a dozen cities, besides many people in this county. But it has been fun."

"Give us some of your early background," I said. "We are not idly curious and I am sure it would interest us extremely."

"I recognize seriousness, sirs. Men of your caliber are true scholars and for that reasons I shall tell you some of my very personal experiences. I hope, however," he said smiling, "that you will not betray my confidence too much in any work you may hereafter produce."

"We promise not to," I said. It is for this reasons that the identify of the person and scenes in this relation are not readily recognizable. The story was given in trust.

"In the life of everyone," began Tiers, "there is some outstanding characteristic of mind or of character. The greater part of our individual traits is known to our fellowmen and it is through these personal traits that one man comes to know and recognize the other during everyday life. Underneath these external traits of action, however, there is always another self, the real soul of the man which he alone is aware of and acknowledges. It may be a love for something which is the dominant trait of this inner self; it may be a desire to attain to certain heights; or it may be a mental conflict. Whatever the case may be, it is one which he seldom if ever confides to his friends but retains it within himself. The essential of any true and complete autobiography is the statement of this inner story, at least if not the actual explanation and history of it."

Knowledge versus Use

Tiers continued. "Mine is the story of the development of my love of knowledge and the conquest of my inferiority complex, a struggle which, until quite recently, was in full swing.

"I early evinced a love for all kinds of book knowledge. Even before I was old enough actually to read, I would run my eyes down the margins of the pages, looking at the first word of each line. I would go through half a book in this manner and would call it reading. I can recall those days as vividly now as if it were yesterday. The psychologist says such early scenes as these are so impressed in our youthful minds that the details of even recent occurrences are not remembered nearly as well as events occurring remotely.

"This struggle was continually one of relating the acquired knowledge to human nature and to practical use. They were problems which should not have concerned me then. I was too young and immature to so relate and classify what I had read and I formed many incorrect conceptions. Such a situation paved the way for a very curious kind of feeling of inferior complex, the nature of which I am yet attempting to analyze. I am not so sure whether a psychologist, with his knowledge of mental complexities, could give me any consolation.

"In my early school work I evinced virtuosity of mind far above the average of my schoolmates in the small rural school which I attended. I say I was interested in a great many things. That, I think, was my trouble. I attempted to be as practical as the other pupils, in work as in play and at the same time to continue with my interest on the side. It was a task I could do without difficulty. While the other children got their lessons and spent the rest of the time in play, I read.

"I was extremely interested in all divisions of geography - world, continental, national, state and local as well as physical geography. I carried out map-making projects of my own initiative. After I had sketched the map of each country of Europe I turned to the Asiatic countries, to Africa and had proceeded to Australia when some other interest overpowered me - stamp collecting, I think.

"While I was making maps I would make imaginary journeys to all parts of the world. This love of faraway places was first begun through a foolish, small-boy conversation with a young cousin of mine one day in the woods. We had just been reading Castlemon's *Frank in the Mountains* and were discussing bears and wild beasts of the jungles. The (to us) visionary Rocky Mountains loomed in our minds. I suddenly asked where I could secure a pet monkey. My cousin, who was 5 years older, but as ignorant as I was, said, 'In the Rocky Mountains, of course.' Both of us, then and there, vowed we would go to those mountains when we grew up. That vow, the purpose somewhat modified, remained with us until consummated some years later.

"Short hikes were an outlet for this latent ambition to really travel. My cousin and I after much earnest persuasion with our parents, hiked to the village of New Columbia, eight miles away. It was my first experience in sleeping out under the starry sky and away from home. I yet recall with a smile how I felt about an hour after lying down for the night I suddenly awakened and discovered the moon coming up 'in the north.' When I was a little older I went on fishing expeditions with my father and uncles to the group of pretty little lakes above Brookport. It was an ideal experience to me.

"I was more interested and able in history than in an other subject. I often pondered over books far above my intellectual capacity and vocabulary but I did acquire a point now and then of lasting value. I desired to know how man began, how long this world had been as it is and to know the answers to other pertinacious questions not commonly asked by a growing and inquisitive child. I received a prize for being the best pupil in a class in ancient history in the fifth grade and this further stimulated me to more reading and study.

"By the end of the grade school course I had several fundamental precepts clearly in mind but the inferiority complex had quite a running start."

Omnivorous

Tiers seemed inclined to go on.

"At the age of 12 I became intensely interested in music. The opportunity to learn music was of necessity denied me. This furthered my case of inferiority, although I learned to play some 'music by ear'. But I had a strong desire to learn, I had a musical ear and an excellent sense of harmony. I was unable to take music lessons and my musical aspirations were nipped in the bud. I was inferior in performance, yet felt inwardly superior in many ways to my fellowman.

"We often run across in our reading 'What's in a name?' Sometimes there is justification in asking such a question, for often there is something of significance in a name. As often there is not. At a certain stage in my life, which I cannot now recall exactly, words did take on a significance. Euphonious words and words which sounded mysterious, such as astronomy, geology, zoology and botany, caught my ear and eye. I dug into several books upon such subjects and soon was able to identify many stars and to acquire many facts and principles upon such subjects as I have mentioned. I gradually became capable of appreciating the beauties of nature, which is, indeed, true knowledge."

Renaissance

Still Tiers spoke.

"It is truly said of high school that it is a new world. The boy or girl enters an entirely new realm and finds new experiences. High school proved to be my renaissance. This statement is a reiteration of the thoughts of many others in regard to this new experience. My interest in all former subjects continued but upon a higher level of intelligence.

"The desire to travel was still present and seemed to be an instinct. My cousin and I made a train trip to Parker City, where we fished and slept out. This was practically the first time I had been out of my native county. Several motor trips followed in succession. During the four years of my high school career I made several overnight hikes to points as far as 50 miles away, alone. I considered a sort of accomplishment to have hiked through a new county or town. These little trips and hikes, snatched in intervals when work was not so heavy on the farm, were of more benefit and influence than was outwardly apparent.

"My struggle with Mr. Inferiority Complex yet continued during those four years. He became very personal to me and I was painfully aware of his presence."

Virtuoso

"Now I had one strong weapon by which I believed I could give Mr. I.C. a distinct and telling blow. I had not failed completely in my music. I had learned to play the harmonica pretty well in addition to performing to some extent upon the piano, guitar, ukulele, banjo and mandolin. I had an apparatus whereby I could play two instruments simultaneously. My attempts with the violin and cello were almost nil. The opportunity came to perform and I did so. I became more confident. Numerous chances came to perform before audiences, in conjunction with opening assemblies at school, play interludes and at rural gatherings and dances. I had scored a distinct victory over my enemy.

"During my last two years in high school I awoke to other beauties which heretofore had been hidden. I became intensely interested in American and English literature. As formerly, I began an outside reading program of my own. I read poetry and for the first time began to appreciate it.

"I had been keeping a diary ever since I was 12 years old but it was somewhat desultory. Now, for the first time, I really concentrated to see what kind of a daily record I could produce. Systematically and conscientiously, for more than a year, I made my entries each day. Henry David Thoreau was my foremost model and I tried to think that I had secured as great an inspiration from nature as he had. I recorded events in his vein of thought. If I did not produce a literary diary I at least learned something about summarizing daily thoughts. Nor am I so sure but that it gave me a little lesson in being conscientious.

"Aside from diary writing, which is perhaps natural for everyone to some degree, a latent desire to really write reappeared. I became first associate editor of the high school paper and tried my hand at writing editorials. Since then I have written much."

Who says a School Ma'am Can't Correct an Errant Boy?

Tiers ran on.

"We often hear men and women state reminiscently the influence their former teachers had upon them. It is not often they arrive at an estimate of the value until years later.

"I had no intention and did not decide to attend a college, until the latter half of my senior year. My instructor in musical theory, through a commonplace question fired pointblank at me one day after class, started me to thinking. The result today answers the question - I am a college man.

"My success and conflicts with old orders are still going on but I suppose they are inevitable circumstances of any person's life."

Thus concluded Charles Tiers-Gutarman.

"Yours is a very interesting and expert analysis of your younger years," said Mr. Dale. "Suppose you proceed with the last 10 years, which I have no doubt are just as full."

"I would rather not," he said. "for personal reasons I would rather not. In fact, the last 10 years on the contrary have not been nearly as important as the 10 I have talked about. I sometimes feel that nothing much has occurred since my college days but, of course, that is not true."

It was now high noon and as we had promised Mrs. Dale to return by noon, we left the shade of the "L" porch and bade farewell to Charles Tiers-Gutarman.

–Written 1939

Not by Bread Alone

What would you say to a man if he told you that you weren't worth much? Plenty, I have a notion. And it would be couched in no mild language, if you are a man of my temper.

Yet I have had, in the past several years, just such opinions expressed of me. Did I answer them according to my temper?

I should say not!

Why not?

They didn't say it to me directly. See? Just implied as much, or a lot more. You can't hurt a man for unevidenced damage. You can't assault and batter a man and get by with it, unless there's a good cause. Indeed! Some of them are ladies, so what can you do?

Listen. Here's some of it and you can see that I have dabbled into several things and no doubt bungled some of the jobs:

Said my teacher (no, she didn't speak it out, but I could read it in her eyes), "Sir, you'll never make a speaker, I'm sure. I doubt if you'll ever be able to address your classroom, if you are ever so lucky as to land a job."

Well, I got the job and have held it 10 years in spite of her. But I suppose she is still throwing cold water in the faces of other timorous college freshmen.

I had a harsh county superintendent once. What he said would happen to my career was plenty, if I didn't start cutting some sassafras sprouts and use them on the boys. I felt bad for days; I thought I was holding a good school. I started in as per instructions at the first breach of discipline. It took me the rest of the year to get the boys back in humor. Next year was election and he was up for reelection. The superintendent came again. He was all smiles, no criticism, which saved some hot reflections on my part.

I traveled a little. I say a little. Close relatives (and I must not leave out a parent) thought it was out of reason for a poor boy in debt to travel 3,000 miles through a country like Mexico. I've never been able to discuss the trip like I wanted to since. They probably wouldn't appreciate it either.

I got married. Eyebrow raisings were as common as trips to the Chicago Fair. I was terribly in debt, I must admit, but why did they wish to cloud our matrimonial horizon? The heartiest congratulations we got was from the town's most popular bum. Encouragement? Yes. Some. But it was meat of a kind and we didn't know how often we would have bread alone.

Teaching only eight months, I had the summers free. Immediately after marrying, I started out to sell the books of a well-known publishing house. Headquarters were in Nashville, but after receiving two weeks training there, I took up the work in North Carolina. Climbing over mountains and penetrating out-of-the-way places, I managed to eke out a bare subsistence and to send a little back home to my wife, whom I had left behind. It was rumored back home, in one of our circle of acquaintances, that I had left my wife. She didn't tell me about it until later, after the book-selling season had ended for me.

The following summer, we both tried night work in a glove factory. We had to start at midnight. It went hard with me at first, cutting into a routine which I practiced rigorously for eight months out of the year. Relatives advised us not to try it. "The lint from the gloves and night hours will hurt your health," they admonished. So we quit.

Next, wife started a route for household products of a well-established concern. Before she started, we heard it said that it was a "poor job." I taught my wife how to drive the car and after running up two or three telephone poles, she learned to drive it very well. She made some money, but would have made more if the habit of asking credit had not been so firmly ingrained in some of the prospects. She quit and used the carrying case for baby's wardrobe when he arrived some months later.

I then proposed my most fantastic plan. That was to go on a lecture tour. Sometimes I smile about it yet; but at that time and for the duration of the idea, I was serious. I had some sanguine hopes that I could succeed, if only in a small way at first. I had traveled about in four countries of North American, had visited most of the states and large cities of the nation, had rubbed elbows with many types of people and had a way of observing life intelligently where I saw it. I had given two such talks or lectures to good-sized audiences and had received acclaim. I planned to give these talks in public halls and in the schools of small towns.

Even my wife, this time, listened to my plans dubiously. In the face of her lack of confidence, I gave it up. I still believe I would have succeeded in giving the lectures. As to whether it would have earned me any money, I am still doubtful myself.

In opposition to the silent negations of my close relatives, I enrolled in a Civil Service correspondence course one winter. I mastered it and then waited for an examination. I am still waiting. I followed it up with correspondence courses with my Alma Mater. At least I received credit.

I was never a man of strong build. A 120 would catch me now. As a boy, I was bookish. However, I could hold my own in most sports and I was never sickly. Only one doctor knew me; he was the one who brought me as a baby. I was troubled by nose-bleed a good deal. I followed the plow for hours with a bloody, dripping face. Unlike many of those nose-bleeding, puny, farm youths who worked long and hard under a stern father, I had good health and a kind, indulgent father. Perhaps, If I had been more like those unhappy boys, I would not now be flaunting my discouragers. How many of those noble boys have borne their lot and risen to great heights, when more fortunate youths are still in mediocre stations? Perhaps I haven't had enough punishment yet. Well, I'm still getting it. Listen awhile:

Wife and I proposed to move on to a small truck farm and truck patch during the summers. We did. We had a wonderful experience. Made some money, too, but not enough commensurate with our labor. My father, yes, my father, the same as told me I was making a miserable failure. Well, we had lost a little. The market on some things went bad just as our crop came in. We had to invest some capital to get ready to raise chickens. Then those prices fell to the lowest point in 10 years and we barely broke even. My father knew we loved the work, knew we worked hard; but small encouragement he gave us upon a change of crops which we were contemplating. Uncle Dan gave us the sour look.

I had dabbled in writing since a mere child. I began again, more in earnest this time. That debt hadn't been erased yet. It stood before us like a great, black, insurmountable Gibraltar. I flattered myself that I was not without talent; it only needed exercise. I had won a few prizes and filled 50 columns in the local paper on various things. I began by writing a bunch of stories. Crude stuff, mostly, but it cleared my mind up. I bought a typewriter (on credit) and started in.

Mother-in-law (yes, they pop up yet occasionally in reality) happened to be visiting us. (I must not forget at this point, to state that I thought it advisable to use a *non de plume* on account of the personal references I might wish to make. Someone, you know, purely by chance, might see my real name; then, I would become liable to more abuse. As I said, I couldn't fight a lady. I know some I'd like to cuff).

Mother-in-law (I prolong her treasonable speech) belittled my endeavors. Usually we were very liberal towards each other. She said, "You might not sell the stories even after you get them written."

Well, that went all over me. All these years I had stood the gaff.

What I retorted to my wife's mother will not appear in print. Sufficient to say, that after 30 years, I have learned some sense.

What is the best way to meet silent criticism, eyebrow raising, cold-water throwers? Shall we tell the authors that it is none of their business? What will you gain? Nothing, except unfriendliness. They will seldom admit to you that they said anything or if they did and it is proven, they will express sorrow that you took it in earnest, they didn't mean it. It is this lack of seldom being able to pin the authors down to what they really think about you and your projects, that is so exasperating.

There is one thing you can do. It is the *only* thing you can do. Pay no attention to it. You know better than anyone else what you can or cannot do, given certain conditions. Follow Elbert Hubbard's motto: "They Will Talk Anyway." Lay your plans, pursue them, hew to the line and you will get somewhere.

More and more, since I arrived at this conclusion about the matter (and I reached it rather later than I should have), am I positive that complete disregard is the only course to take. Never before did I feel so free as when I threw off the inhibitions of rumor, gossip, criticism and self-consciousness, (which some would call an inferiority-complex) and lurched out self-willed, free, confident. I feel as if I were going somewhere and that I will not arrive at my destination too late to enjoy some of its fruits before I am too old to do so.

I am going on. I'm teaching my way and taking no orders; I'm going where I darn please on my vacation (you bet I'm going to take one); I'm writing as if the whole world was begging for my work and say, if you happen to come along my way about the middle of May, I can show you the finest strawberries you ever saw. Raised them myself, the first of the kind ever raised in this county.—1930s

Peoria - Land of Plenty

The Peoria Indians, a tribe of the Illinwek, called Peoria "the fat lands" or Pimiteoui." Joliet and Marquette came in 1673 and said, "We have seen nothing like this for the fertility of its land." LaSalle came in 1680 to build Fort Creve Coeur and for the next 100 years various settlements were made by the French. In cultivation of the land, the area was recognized, but the French were easy-going and they could not envision the Peoria of today, the real "land of plenty."

The Americans built Fort Clark in 1813. The first permanent American settlement was made in 1819 and in 1825 Peoria was made into a county. A Peoria orator once said, "The history of the pioneer constitutes the heroic era of Peoria County." The first seven settlers in 1819 fenced 15 acres and planted corn and potatoes. A great flood of immigrants poured into the county in the 1830s. Peoria village grew rapidly and in 1835 was incorporated. Peoria became a city in 1845. Farm related manufacturing also began at this time.

Life was hard - "A panorama of rugged experience, trouble, waiting, triumph" - but Peoria's early pioneers were resourceful people. Why did they come and stay? The pioneer saw the prospect; they had a vision. they were attracted by the cheap, productive land, the good climate, the adequate rainfall and the mixed timber and prairie. The location was strategic and there were unlimited resources of fuel and water. There was a charm in the lure of the West. Perhaps they consciously wanted to found a new civilization. In 1856 citizen O.E. Root prophesied: "Peoria has just begun to prosper." Others looked far ahead to the 20th century and saw the fair prospect.

Now we in our turn can look back. Area people have lived up to the bright hopes of their predecessor. Economic progress has been agricultural and industrial. The pioneering people "of indomitable spirit and unquestioned vision" have made the area a good provider. Area agriculture gave impetus to many types of manufacturing. Through inventions the farmer was lifted above the hand-to-hand struggle with nature. Peoria farmers long experimented with new-type crops. A great livestock industry developed. Truly, Peorians have more than met the challenge of their ancestors.

There where many periods of hard times for area farmers. Inadequate return from labor and investment, debt, soil depletion and other problems plagued them. The 20th century became for the farmer a time of intellectual awakening. Farming grew into a science. The old dream of organizing became a reality for Peoria farmers when a Farm Bureau was organized here in 1912. Henry Truitt, the first Peoria farm advisor, was the ninth such person in Illinois. The primary purpose has always been the same, "Better living for people of Peoria County."

Much has been accomplished in soil improvement, pest control, proper land use, farm-home development and general conservation practices, to name only a few. In April 1956 *Prairie Farmer* magazine featured the county in a long article in which was said, "Peoria County leads the state by a wide margin in use of terraces."

Farm value statistic tell the wonderful story. Many natural advantages, plus the energy and ability of the people and an informed, conservation-minded farmer, have helped shape Peoria County's destiny.

This, then, is the "Land of Plenty" - Peoria.

–Written for the Peoria County Farm Bureau, 1961

From *Springhouse* Magazine

Fiddlin' 'Round*

"I am the champion fiddler in Massac County," fiddlin' George Laird confidentially declared to my wife one day on a street in Metropolis. And truly, Laird was an excellent fiddler, but one never loath to brag about it; he was not only zealous but jealous of his art.

A news article Dec. 7, 1938 on the occasion of his being elected county commissioner, briefly outlined his life. Laird was a general farmer with a lot of livestock and a sawmill on his 165 acre farm near Midway. A wife and seven children made up the family and of the boys, two were also country musicians, one on double bass and one on guitar. The Lairds were welcome guests at any social gathering and they fiddled away many of the worries of themselves and friends. George Waters Laird, also known as Derby, was of that breed of country fiddlers who inhabited Massac County in the 1920s and 30s when I was a teenager and beyond. Laird became an area legend in his own time. During those years I accompanied with different instruments at least two dozen different fiddlers. It was my privilege and good fortune to have played with Laird many times.

All those old-timers are dead except one, 79 year old Millard Grace, now living in Michigan. It was our good fortune to get together the past summer and again to play some of the old tunes, perhaps for the last time.

What is music? Not a good question, for everyone is sure when he hears it. Yet different cultures in our world have differing notions. Are the "rough accents of Negro fiddlers" music? Is the African tom-tom music? Or the American Indian chants? Webster says music is "intelli-

---

* The following four articles are reprinted from Springhouse magazine by the kind permission of Mr. Gary DeNeal, editor-publisher.

gible combinations of tones into a composition having structure and continuity," of which "rhythm, melody or harmony" are essentials. Is flamenco, opera, a cappela, jazz, blue grass, rock n' roll and gospel music? Certainly so. They are merely different types, of which old-time fiddling is only one and any one genre may have gradations of excellence. Castiglione says that "even rude (fiddlin') music is good." Perhaps, to repeat a cliché, "Beauty is in the eyes (ears) of the beholder," a corollary being that the burden of this essay may seem to be an apology for "fiddlin' 'round." So be it. If Nero fiddled while Rome burned and got away with it, then our country fiddler may the more be pardoned for fiddling around the countryside. Let the sophisticated musician and his listeners, look down upon our rude music. Willie Nelson put it simply, "Music is anything that is pleasing to the ear." The gum-chewing, crap-shooting Ocie Smith, a good, jolly old boy, with his superb rattling bones was often an addition to our country parties and everyone enjoyed it. Music? Try as I may to avoid judgment, as one of the music genres, perforce, I must champion the old breed of fiddlers, unwilling though I am to justify them from the criterion of theme, technique and all manner of time and tempo between. We must agree as Longfellow wrote, "Music is the universal language of mankind."

Perhaps I should ask pardon for injecting some personal references but it is part of the story. I began "seconding" on the guitar with

Sunday afternoon music

Instruments of the art

my fiddler uncle, John May at age 10 or 11. Since then, as I have said, I played with two dozen different fiddlers, nearly all the music that of the old-time kind. I have used the piano, guitar, mandolin, tenor banjo (and tenor guitar, both noted the same), ukulele, harmonic and the ocarina. The tenor banjo and ukulele were the "in" stringed instruments in the 1920s, the mandolin having been in eclipse since around the turn of the century. Whole orchestras at that period were made up of mandolins, mandolas and mando-basses. Before my time Pope County had the McClanahans and my dad either played with them or heard them on mandolin. I worked with the violin and cello a little but soon gave them up as a task unequal to my poor talents and patience. One of the most difficult situations in which I chorded (with guitar) was with a Louisiana French Cajun on his harmonica. To me they were unfamiliar tunes in a strange mood.

Our music was strictly fiddle-led; not the melodies led by mandolin, guitar, etc. They were only accompaniments - "seconding" or "following," as we called it - the so-called rhythm guitars, etc. of the Nashville sound. Only major chords were used; there was seldom a minor and that maybe only accidentally. The chord pattern was 1, 2, 3 or 1, 3, 1, 2, 3 or the dominant, sub-dominate and tonic chords with variations. A four-chord pattern was rare; still rarer would be a fifth or sixth chord in the same music piece (e.g. a C, E, A, D, G sequence). The poorer rhythm guys would simply disregard these more intricate variations. My father, for instance, good as he was on the mandolin, never became acquainted with a fourth chord in any key. Naturally, we all played "by ear." There were no diminished or augmented chords, no modulations, progressions or "voicings." (The fifth chord voicings, to me I might say, are right pretty). There were some seventh chords used but not so often.

Old fiddlers, but some were young, commonly played in the key of G, C and D. No more than one or two pieces would be played in A or E during one evening's stand for the simple reason that the fiddler did not know any more in those keys. The key of F was rarely played;

never in B or the so-called flat keys. Bill Copley was the exception. By some strange quirk, he told me he picked up the fiddle and started off in F; thence, ever since. George Laird knew one or two pieces in B flat. He always insisted on tuning up to A sharp. This forced me to adapt to the so-called "black" piano keys. Most times we played in first position; consequently, the finger board stayed smooth as new down to the sound hole. I doubt that any fiddler regularly practiced at home and so it is remarkable that he or she played as well as they did.

They were no Renfrow Valley or Hee-Haw sessions. Our social gatherings and at some house square dancing, were quite informal, unprogrammed. Gurley's Park square dance was the only regular event over a three year period. We were, of course, previously invited to a home or other occasions. The usual instrumentation was one or two fiddles, one or two guitars, mandolin, tenor banjo (or tenor quitar) rarely a five-string banjo, ukulele, piano, harmonica and double bass viol (bowed, not slapped). Of course, we never had all these at any one occasion - alternates, substitutes, "doubling."

What a joy it was to me and shared by 99 percent of party goers, to see Laird or another assume the position, to tune ourselves up and to break out with "Leather Britches," "Mayfield," "Turkey in the Straw," "Wildwood Flower," "Buffalo Gals" or some waltz like "Over the Waves." The evening then became a mixture of two-steps, waltzes, polkas, a brief schottische and maybe a fox trot. If square dancing was possible (furniture shoved back against walls, etc.) or permitted, then the action began in a riot of dancing heels, laughter and the formation calls, 100 percent hoe-down! With regret, at 11 or 12 o'clock, Laird closed with "Home Sweet Home" or "Show Me the Way to Go Home." Theory, technique disregarded, we just played joyfully, unaware of our shortcomings. Only a good violinist would have cringed at that hoe-down music but it didn't bother us.

I extract entries from my diary which recorded the various musicales we attended and in this manner show the extent of our "fiddlin' 'round." The first entry seems to be on April

With tenor banjo, 1926

21, 1926 when a classmate and I presented before the high school assembly a harmonica and guitar skit, repeated at a later date. On May 22, 1926, our impromptu band played on the lawn at the Choat Village store and repeated later. My first introduction to Gurley's Park in Metropolis was Aug. 26, 1926 when I played two hours and earned $2.50, a proud moment, for I was now a paid musician! Until September 1929 I played there with George Laird during the summer dance season. Our bass viol man was elfish, jolly Seb Ragsdale and he was a good bower. Why is it that so many times the smallest man in the group plays the largest instrument, the double bass? I have observed this several times. During those years we played dozens of time over a wide county area at social gatherings, dances, house and barn "warmings," "shivarees," pie suppers and what-not. A list of homes we visited reads like a census roll: Korte, Pfrimmer, Grace, Watson, Laird, May, Stull, Barrett, Reineking, Kruger, Kennedy, Jackson, Stegman, Hille, Seilbeck, Voight, Cockrel, Wiseman, Rion, Quint, Brandon, Stoner and many others. We played three times at Henry Grothman's at which one time his guest was a Mr. Baltzman, Ohio's champion fiddler. It was a memorable night for dad and me. He was rather more violinist than mere fiddler. He had been on radio and cut records. In April 1927 George Laird fiddled at our house and reported that he had just won second place in four fiddling events in Paducah. We played with Joe Williams twice at a house square dance, although he had tendency to drift into some popular numbers, to which we could not follow well. We had a barn raising at Fritz Seilbeck's. In an empty barn (or down in a cistern!) echoes, vibrations, makes the music sound better. We followed with our own newly-built barn christening, a square dance on May 27, 1927. At Gus Voight's they danced on the porch. One night at Gurley's Park a new "modern" band tried out. It was "no go;" no one got on the floor, so that after one piece the bandmen angrily left, challenging Laird to a future fiddling contest. Jess Gurley's clientele was always strongly German and they knew what they preferred to dance by. On Aug. 15, 1927 Laird lost a fiddling contest to Joe Williams and that by Joe's tricks: playing sideways, bow held in mouth, top of head, fiddle played behind him and between knees. Laird was disappointed and angry.

Laird was a pea huller at this time and once put up with us for the night before hulling our peas next day. We made music as a matter of course, again in our new barn. The next night Laird and I alone made the square dance at Fritz Seilbeck's. On Halloween night October '27 we played at the street dance in Metropolis, followed five nights later with the same to celebrate the just completed paving of the main city streets. Three bands located separately at downtown sites provided for square dances as well as "round" or popular dances. It was a cold night down on lower Ferry Street and my fingers became numb on the piano. Leaving for college in 1928 and again in 1929 made for a shorter playing season for me at Gurley's Park.

During these years I played with a number of good fiddlers. Tom Stull was a local standby at most anytime or occasion. Smooth playing, man! Pessimist and Voltaire-reading Oscar Wood needed a metronome. As like as not, he would begin with a waltz and end it up as a two-step. Invariably, his time increased in speed within the piece being played, like a whirling deverish. His sister, Sadie Wiley, was a better fiddler, smooth, perfect. Transfixing one with those staring fish-eyes (when playing), she would saw out "The Downfall of Napoleon" and any number of other well-known tunes. Gilbert Jackson was another good player. Lawrence Laird was good but always disclaimed it. George Laird's blind brother, Frank played like a professional and could, if required, execute many intricacies of technique, but I played with him only twice, he being of a very retiring nature. My Uncle Ike Laird and Uncle Henry Laird were good fiddlers but I rarely played with them especially Uncle Henry, as he moved to Missouri.

All honor to all those fine people! They helped make my years happy ones.

As I have said, we were ready to go almost anytime we were called upon. Besides the many homes visited, we played for the Odd Fellows, the Grant Precinct Improvement Association, The Good Luck Club, Rice Brothers Joppa store-opening, the Democratic Party Headquarters and at the new First National Bank in Metropolis on April 12, 1963, two years after it opened at its new location.

A kind of hiatus occurred in my musical career when I moved to Johnson County. But in time new neighbors apprised me of those of the fraternity who also loved old-time music. But there was no dancing in this particular Benton community. Pauline (Rion) McGinnis was our best local fiddler. One special gathering I recall, my 25th birthday. Newly-married to me, my wife baked 12 pumpkin pies and called in the neighbors for a party. Music, of course, too. Other parties were held farther away at Big Bay and Round Knob. Refreshments were always served at these gatherings from 1926 on. No party was ever marred by any overt drinking. In 1935 we moved back to our original neighborhood in Massac County, where the music parties were renewed. The next year saw a reunion of my branch of the Laird family, at which time I had the pleasure of fiddling with Uncle Henry, visiting from Missouri, a really polished fiddler. During our four years in Texas I teamed up with the local McGill family group. McGill was an Ichabod Crane kind of man and he played the fiddle well. There was never any dancing for this was a strict Southern Baptist community. In fact, I hardly dared to take a Sunday afternoon stroll through the forest to the San Jacinto River, especially as I was the village schoolteacher.

At some of the musicales, incidents occurred to make them memorable. Such happened at Ed Barrett's party one night. Claude Johnson, young daredevil and trickster, had an act which he had displayed numerous times for the neighborhood boys. He would take a mouthful of gasoline and holding a lighted match at some length would expel the gasoline onto the match. A sort of explosion followed in a ball of fire. Enough to scare one, and dangerous! This night he stationed himself on Barrett's porch near to a window and did his act. Pandemonium broke out inside and in the tumult Aunt Laura, screaming, tumbled out of her chair onto the floor. Claude was finally pointed out as the culprit and got an angry scolding from the women. I recall a New Year' watch party for young people at Lillian Corson's, where we pulled taffy candy, skated on an adjacent pond, played games and made some music. One night at Gurley's Park there were no electric lights and gas lights had to be used, which inconvenienced musicians and dancers alike. Another night, at our normal eight o'clock starting time, there was no Jess Gurley. Undecided, we eventually began to play and dance anyway. Presently, Gurley appeared. He had been arrested for possession of "white mule" liquor and the delay was caused by his having to make bond. On a hot August night in 1934 we played for Lawrence Quint's shivaree, where, among other eatables, were served bologna sandwiches. By bedtime some of us were sick, my visiting cousin the worst from over gorging. It was food poisoning and it about knocked us out for a couple of days. It was memorable night but on the near-tragic side.

I have in front of me a stack of books, magazine and newspaper clippings on present-day popular music, the $60 million sound emanating from Nashville; blue grass, country western, rock n' roll, hard rock, funk, Southern rock and other regional types. This is the music borne on our radio and television waves or on records, cassettes and VCRs. I admit that some of it is meaningful to me, in tune, tone and theme. Branson now vies with Nashville and Los Vegas; Memphis is a music center. In a revolt against the hyperkinetic dance music of an earlier decade (40s and 50s), various local groups, of which West

Kentucky and Little Egypt have several, are going in for jam sessions in which a more subdued country music is played at the popularly-growing square dance. Even an occasional schottische is fiddled. (For 10 years the Quint's LQB Jamboree was held in a barn, four miles out North Avenue on the way to Round Knob. Summer sessions, two or more bands every Saturday night, no drinking, no dancing, no charge. Just good, clean country music by locals. It was a hard decision to close the Jamboree for good at the end of the 1993 season. As one writer expressed it, "Massac County is a better place because of the Quints"). A lot of fiddling is done in Appalachia, probably the closest to the kind I grew up with. There, "Fisher's Hornpipe," "Old Joe Clark" and many others of the 'oldies' are played, pure rural music, unlike the commercialized works of Elvis Presley, Johnny Cash and the like. These mountain people keep alive the sentiments of the past.

Sad is the fact that old-time fiddlers are now relatively scarce in Little Egypt. No one lives near me, which leaves me helpless, useless, in limbo; I must go it alone with mandolin and guitar.

Although Appalachia country music and much of the other music played around the nation is quite true to type, I find it difficult to describe the subtle difference between it and that played under dear George Laird and Tom Stull. First, the current fiddling, although it pretends or boasts that it does duplicate the earlier type, seems only a good imitation. It fails to capture those nuances which are all too subtle and finely wrought to describe in words; it must be an experience of feeling, impression, even of intuition. I have not been able to make this point clear to my friends. A second difference is in the almost universal use of electronics; acoustic playing is too seldom done. A microphone tends to turn me off. Perhaps no era in musical history can be exactly repeated - no era in any department of society - music, literature, speech and the unique events of history - or recalled.

No doubt fiddling and country music in general is better than in the '20s and '30s - in technique and sound - but we cannot help but yearn for a bit of the old-time "fiddlin' 'round."

As anti-climax I cannot resist taking a story from Texas writer J. Frank Dobie. A Negro fiddler was on his way to a wedding party one night and suddenly heard the howls of a wolf pack behind him. Soon the woods seemed alive with the beasts. Closer they came to him. One wolf came so close that Uncle Dick instinctively struck at it with his fiddle. The movement jarred the strings, upon which the wolf leaped back. In turn several wolves squatted down quietly. Uncle Dick took this chance to run for a deserted cabin not far away. When he quit playing the wolves renewed the chase. Thus, playing at intervals he made his way to the low cabin, darted through the door, mounted the ladder and onto the roof which was full of holes. The wolves entered the cabin and leaped up toward Uncle Dick's leg. Other howling wolves surrounded the cabin. When he played the fiddle the wolves grew still and sat on their tails grinning. When he ceased playing they howled and leapt. Thus, all night Uncle Dick was treed on the roof, running through his repertoire and repeating it many times before some uneasy wedding guest found him about dawn.

–Vol. 11 No. 2, p. 34, April 1994

Hobo Days

"Umph-ph!"

Even in the fading evening twilight I could see glares of anger in the faces of the railroad "bulls."

"Unk-ho!" Again the fat boy grunted and clutched his stomach and pleaded, "Don't hit me again, please, mister."

In the Hannibal, MO railroad yards I came out a bit better than my fat hobo partner, John Barrington, beating his way to Georgia. A "bull's" fist shot out once to my head, not too hard, but enough to stagger me against the railroad car. I carried the blue temple for a week. I never learned whether or not the Aztec Indian boy in our jungle earlier in the evening was chased out of the yards, but he was counting on catching that freight.

This was only one episode that could happen in the life of a typical hobo, even in the 1930s when hobos were somewhat more tolerated. The Great Depression was on. An estimated 250,000 young people alone were hitting the rails. Some were homeless, some looking for work and some were looking only for adventure. Most of my hoboing was of the latter and purely voluntary, for our family was weathering the hard times fairly well. I wanted a taste of Jacob Riis's "how the other half lives." Perhaps my college sociology courses whetted that desire.

The literature on the tramp and hobo is fairly extensive and such books as Jack London's *The Road*, Jim Tully's *Beggars of Life*, Josiah Flynt's *My Life*, Thomas Minehan's *Boy and Girl Tramps of America*, Nels Anderson's *The Hobo*, Kenneth Allsup's *Hard Travelin'* and A-No. 1's 11 books are classic beginning readings for one interested in the ways of the Knights of the Road.

I scarcely venture to call myself an ex-hobo after recently reading Rudy Phillips' *Hobo King - Rambling Rudy*, of our own Shawneetown. So I have been only a novice; but his book has led me to tell my story.

The life of the hobo, independence, the Open Road, has been idealized and nostalgia about it abounds today in America. But all the so-called freedom of the hobo had a cost: vagrancy laws, "bulls," hunger, injury, the weather, loss of health and the humiliation of denial. Phillips relates one horrific episode of the time when an engineer tossed an unconscious black boy, who he had first beaten, into the locomotive

Youthful trespassers

firebox where he was incinerated. I think I have read of no more cruel act anywhere in hobo literature.

As a lad I heard horror stories of train-hopping told by parents. For years there lived in Metropolis a black man who walked with wooden leg, cut off by a train. I knew the man well, Another black boy in Metropolis lost a leg up on the tracks in the '20s. Parents told the story about a local man hopping a train and who lost both legs, which were put in a tub under his bed. I forget if the man lived or not. A cousin of mine froze his ears beating his way one cold night from Chicago to Detroit. These recitals should have deterred me from any idea of hoboing or messing around the cars.

The origins of our desires and ambitions are mixed and often unconscious in our less mature youth. Early and repeated readings of Carpenter's *Geographical Readers* and Harry Franck's *Working My Way Around the World* instilled a wish to travel. An overnight hike to

New Columbia with a cousin at age 12, a two-day hike alone to Golconda at age 13 and ramblings over the hills and hollows of Massac, Pope and Johnson counties but increased that incipient wanderlust. I cut my hobo-reading eye teeth from reading Davies' *The Autobiography of a Super-Tramp*, an English hobo and writer who later lost a foot to the rails in Canada. At age 14 the same cousin and I hopped a train for Parker City (Johnson County). At age 16 I rode a boxcar to Herrin one night and walked most of the way back to Metropolis the next day in a temperature registering 100 degrees as I trudged through Vienna. By this time I had definitely developed a case of dromomania or wanderlust; I was skating psychically on thin ice. A-No. 1 strongly advised "Do not jump on moving trains, never run away but stay at home, because this might arouse the road fever, besides endangering needlessly your life and limbs." I was but fostering those ill chances to becoming a confirmed tramp.

Fortunately, I was never a tramp or hobo in the truest sense. My motives were to gain experience, as I've said, of the larger world, of a sub-culture, to satisfy my own wanderlust tendencies and for pure adventure, to sum it all up. I think it was not until the Western trip that I became interested in the sociological aspects and heightened by reading Minehan's *Boy and Girl Tramps* and *Lonesome Road*. I was also seeing some of the result of the depression and as one interested in American history, I gained more of an insight into the hard times that I could have by mere reading in the security of my home. I rode the rails not through necessity. The sociological motivation was a more conscious, mature process.

Following are some jottings from my log book taken on the road:

An old hobo at Sparks, NV suggested I catch an S.P. freight and get right over the hump (mountains) without fooling around trying to hitch-hike. To the hobo jungle I went where a bright fire and food greeted me. I listened closely for any bits of hobo wisdom although

Amateur bums on the redball

most of them seemed to think I was old at the game. Rattling over the Nevada desert I got cold and at rare stops the mosquitoes swarmed. Later, I crowded into a reefer and was comfortable. Next day mirages on the Utah desert. A dip in Great Salt

Lake at a brief stop. Thirty hours without food but a lunch and a cigar at Ogden.

Hitch-hiking no good into Evanston, WY. I caught a freight on the run. Miserable hours riding a boxcar top. Slept in a jail at Rawlins. A bowl of oatmeal from the jailer and another "rattler" eastward. Kept hidden in a reefer as the brakie didn't particularly welcome our hobo party. Twenty or 30 of us on another train were kicked off. At night we all caught a U.P. into Cheyenne. Spent the night in a mission house, bed and breakfast, but we had to work a bit after dining. Putting up at Federal transient shelters and Salvation Army missions was called "living on Sam and Sally." Next day we had a pleasant ride in a "side-door Pullman"

Nearing the yards redlight

(boxcar) to Denver on the Q line. My pick-up friend, Gene Ward and I spent 24 hours in Denver before we could catch a train east, as they were running too fast. At Limon, CO we got off the slow rattler and after several hours in the jungle caught a "hot-shot." But that night we slept on the city hall floor, where some bum stole my cap from under my head. We caught our train in the rain and held it down to Kansas City. I spent two weeks there with a cousin on a vegetable farm.

In 1933 I boarded an IC freight at Metropolis and spent two days at the Chicago Exposition. We had picked up several other riders during the trip, one a black woman dressed in overalls. I slept in a flophouse the first night and in an all-night theater the second night, to conserve my money. In Chicago's Hobohemia one could buy a good meal for 15 cents. I then hitch-hiked to Nova Scotia. Back in Illinois again, I rode the Q out of Litchfield, slept in a coal car and caught a fast Q freight out of Centralia to Metropolis.

Off to Nebraska in 1934. It grew cold near Chicago and I took a reefer. Revisited the Exposition. Got a good 10 cent breakfast (how do they do it!). Did some research in two libraries. Walked to Cicero and caught a Q train west. At Galesburg end of division. Caught another Q with a jolly bunch of young fellows. Across Iowa into Nebraska without mishap. There I saw the effects of the severe drought. I got half dead from thirst. Sick. At Lincoln I turned back toward Illinois. At Brookfield, MO a bull warned me off the yards. Never did green grass look so good nor water taste so sweet as I hit Missouri and approached Illinois. I was the lone rider as the freight drew into Hannibal, a city with a bad reputation for the brutality of its railroad bulls.

A freight out of Louisiana, MO took me to Bloomington. A number of hobos were in the jungle, washing, sewing, eating, sleeping. A thorough soaking in a coal car near Decatur at night. Then Centralia, some "stemming," and home.

Off the freight one April night just south of Chicago, on my way to Hammond, IN to seek employment, I found a hobo jungle. It was yet night. There I wrapped up the best I could on the ground and tried to doze. Next morning frost covered my person, but the sun came out and a bit of coffee served in a tin can by one of the hobos revived me.

On several trips I mixed hitch-hiking with hoboing. The problem is of keeping clean for the highway. The joys and woes of hitch-hiking is another subject unto itself.

Sometime in the '30s, I made an uneventful jaunt out of Cincinnati through Kentucky on a slow local. Later, cousin and I rode a rattler to Paris, TN to pick strawberries.

Looking back, I see two traumatic experiences of the road, or rather, since there was no physical harm, high emotional states. One was my first few train hoppings. As the noisy, steaming behemoth of a locomotive came abreast I was in a high state of stress - call it nerves. It was later that the distant whistle of a freight became sweet. Even yet a great and powerful locomotive begets in me a strange sense of awe, almost of fear.

The other experience is psychical and has to do with the practice of "stemming" or begging for food, clothing, money or what-not on the road. And herein lies the paradox: abhorrent as the idea of begging is to most people, yet a successful "touch," repeated, seems to inspire confidence in one's self. This lessens one's inferiority-complex, an affliction in my early years I needed to work on. Davies wrote in his *Autobiography of a Super-Tramp*: "I would never beg, unless forced to the last extremity, for I feared the strange fascination that arises from success, after a man has lost his shame." Just so. Around Decatur and Centralia I got hungry and my money was gone, so I hit the cafes and bakeries - with success. The sense of "shame," if that is what it is, has long gone from my psyche but I am glad in some respects to have experienced that strange feeling. Many boys have the same feelings at first as they hit the highway with thumb. A nonchalant, cocky attitude seems to take over, a feeling of confidence.

America still has the homeless problem but the old-time bona fide hobo has about disappeared. The apex was 1927. The law, diesel engines and more sophisticated equipment, public welfare, etc., has made such a life either more difficult or unnecessary. Man's seemingly natural wanderlust, economic necessity, mental abnormality and social misfits were some of the causes in the first place for the tramp, hobo and bum (there is a distinction). The dangers from a life of wandering are real and the results usually permanent: physically, morally, psychically, economically. Confirmed hoboing will destroy a stable psyche; it will be only a matter of time and conditions of the road.

As I said, my hoboing has been limited. Quite true. But I have seen, experienced and read enough about the hobo to know what can draw a youth to it and what may be the quite possible devastating effect upon him for the rest of his life. Is the first-hand knowledge gained - the learning of "how the other half lives" (or exists) - worth the risk? One who consciously tries a little of it - with eyes open to its potential dangers - may find it a toughening and valuable experience, without much danger of it causing one's self to become a confirmed Knight of the Road.

Nevertheless, a mythology has gown up around the hobo and tramp - a likeness to the pioneer spirit of our early settlers, independence, the ideology of Walt Whitman's Open Road (mostly dormant in most of us), the path to an open society, the search for Utopia. Jack Kerouac and Woody Guthrie are our modern symbols. We eye the hobo today with a mixture of envy and nostalgia. Was the hobo a loser or our last folk hero of rugged individualism? We are ambivalent.

It is this dichotomy which is so curious: realism vs. romanticism; compulsion vs. repulsion. Nels Anderson seems to reject the vagrant life in his sociological study but as the anonymous author of the satiric and humorous *The Milk and Money Route* he gladly embraces it. Glen Mullin (*Adventures of a Scholar Tramp*) declared he'd had enough of it. Rudy Philips, after being shot in the shoulder by the notorious bull Texas Slim, was led to say "This is no good." Jim Tully "both hated and loved the wastrels."

To a boy thinking about hitting the rails, I would say "Don't try it." So pleaded A-No. 1 in his 11 books early in the century; "don't risk becoming a slave to wanderlust by catching that first train." It is particularly good advice today when America has so many runaway youths - homeless, unmotivated, desperate, even violent.

This account has been forcibly made brief. Get an articulate Knight of Road talking (and many of them were well-read, experienced in every phase of the road - even writers and orators) and there is hardly any stopping him.

–Vol. 9 No. 2, p. 26, April 1992

"Dear Diary"

Edward Robb Ellis, itinerant midwest newspaper man, now living in New York, has been recognized by the *Guinness Book of Records* as keeper of the longest diary in history, 68 years and the most voluminous, 20 million words.

Began as a challenge with another boy during his high school years in Kewanee, IL to see who could keep a diary the longest, Ellis won out. And now, 68 years later, excerpts from those 20 million words have just been published in a book by the Kodansha International Press. Ellis goes far beyond the recording of daily routine. He paints detail-rich pictures of fascinating subjects, his conversations with many prominent people and observations on current American life. The whole corpus should prove a treasure trove for future historians.

But may I be so bold as to challenge Mr. Ellis at one point? Ellis began his diary in 1927; I began my diaries in 1921-22. True, they were but kid jottings - granted - but the entries became longer and more polished during the poetic, puberty years of high school.

Far from censoring the Guinness decision to recognize Ellis, I applaud it. At least he is a near-champion on wordage (after first combing the record of history on the matter) and Ellis' dairies undoubtedly surpass mine in interest and quality of writing; after all he was a professional writer.

Why would anyone want to keep a dairy?

The reasons are legion, some trivial, some serious. That it is a good idea seems to be agreed upon and furthermore that one will enjoy it. Just what are the benefits of keeping a diary? The first value is its personal nature and it follows that it should be frank, honest. It develops our sense of awareness; it lessons one's insensitivity to one's surrounding; it makes one see more. A diary trains in self-discipline and helps us to overcome sheer inertia. Make the diary writing a delight rather than a duty. A diary helps to clarify our thinking, to order our thinking and to fix things in our mind. The diary provides valuable material for the memory. It is one way to save our memories for our children and grandchildren and possibly for future historians. The diarist develops powers of appraisal - of one's self and others - and also acts as a safety valve. George Matthew Adams once said, "Literature is expression, whether good or bad; you are a part of the literature of the world to the degree in which you are able to express yourself." Not likely ever to be published; yet the royalties for you will be even greater in the ways outlined above.

Thus, the uses of dairy-keeping are many, but new twists are developing. Want to cope with stress? Keep a diary. Psychology and psychiatry are finding therapeutic values in practicing that genre of literature. Putting thoughts on paper helps the patient to discover what is troubling him and to unload his problems. The important thing is to focus on thought and emotions. Tell the bad if one will but also sweeten with the good and the beautiful. This vehicle for "catching the points in your life," says Dr. Ira Progoff, "is a natural tool for developing your inner life, without benefit of a guru or analyst." It is being used in New York and other cities as an alternative to encounter group therapy. And Dr. Stanley Krippner, director of the famous Dream Laboratory in Brooklyn, NY urges dream diary-keeping as an easy and effective way to help one lead a better life. Okay! Recording an occasional dream has never been taboo in my diary and in other people's diaries.

My diary books are of assorted formats: some are school composition books (Jay, Webster, etc.); some hard-bound and some wire-spiral bound; some loose-leaf; some "Daily Aid" or calendar books.

Diaries of various formats

Sixty-five in all. Those early jottings were short, incomplete, naive gropings toward expression. Through high school, college, married life, travels, school teaching, farming and retirement since 1973 - thus the diaries continued through the 75 years. Some of the record is embodied in separate, so-called log books; notes made on trips and sometimes transcribed into the regular diaries. From such log books have come portions of my books, like *Down Illinois Rivers* and *Mexico for Me*.

I consider my masterpiece of writing during those fervid junior and senior high school years, when my mental faculties seemed to have taken a new and increased spurt, to have been exhibited in Book No. 6, which ran from Sept. 2-Dec. 23, 1926. During those four months I covered 63 pages with close notes, with emphasis on nature, probably the first influence from Thoreau's *Walden*. One entry, November 7, was of 890 words, equaled or exceeded by others. On that day, in part, I wrote, "I was out under the open sky and had a good opportunity to observe the clouds. The clouds today were at a high altitude, streaky, filose and spray-like in character: cirrus, as the meteorologist term them," etc.

On November first I had written in a sententious vein: "Today is my birthday. I am 17 years old, which means that I have been successful in a 17 year contest against the elements and the artificial aspects with which we are surrounded in these modern times. As I make a retrospection on my past existence I cannot help but feel a certain pride, a distinct sense of accomplishment, born only with an experience with an indefinite number of childhood scenes, which are sometimes reacted in my mind's eye as a remembrance. If we had a written account of our early lives, it would be an interesting paper. Most of us, to a great extent, are subject to amnesia which makes it impossible to recall many sometimes scenes of our juvenility. I have, in my school life, read and acquired a considerable amount of general knowledge which, I hope, does me credit and as the years pass on and the future approaches, passes and is buried into oblivion, I supplicate that I may prosper in the future."

Pretty wordy, a common fault of beginning writers but, nevertheless, sincere. But no Boswell, Pepys, Franklin, Thoreau or Anne Frank.

Some entries in my diaries are short: "Colleague Buck Smith died," "Elmer King died as he was mowing," "went to a party at Corson's last night," "sawed wood all day," or longer Feb. 26 and March 26, 1949 entries: "Softball game with grade school Crosby (TX). We were beaten 24 to 4" and "About 50 children from Crosby came over and played softball. We won one game 5 to 4 and lost one 7 to 8." (I was umpire).

A log book entry on July 10, 1966 records, "Suddenly, I reached a mass of rocks and there I was on top of Mt. Fairview! The sun was out and it was warmer; my hair and hands were dry. (On the climb up it had rained and snowed lightly). I looked down upon Lake Louise, Chateau Lake Louise and upon the Victoria Glacier and around at a whole world of mountains in all four directions. I believe it was the most superb, comprehensive view I ever had...After some 15 minutes of surveying this glorious prospect, I began the descent by a more western, circuitous route...I cut straight toward the cabin below over timbered and rocky ridges. By now I was very warm."

These 65 diaries have been of practical value through the years. Dates and events are sometimes checked back upon. Countless times I have referred to them as to planting dates, yields of the garden and orchard, amount of seed used and to the annual mulching of strawberries. I have been able in a small way to help newspaper people, local amateur historians and so on by checking my diaries. For an article being done on the 1937 flood by the *Planet* newspaper, I was able to report on the weather during that disastrous time. So I could go on.

For those contemplating on starting a diary and for those already engaged in that pursuit, from desire, a sense of duty or as a practical means of daily written expression or other motives, I cite a 1995 anthology book of diaries: Miller & Miller, editors, *The Book of American Diaries*, 522 pages (Avon Books, New York). Excerpts from dozens of diarists make it a most interesting and instructive book. From the book's introduction, last paragraph, I quote the words of Stefan Kanfer, a student of the genre: "A diary is a kind of looking-glass that reflects the keeper of a diary and reveals at one and the same time the reader."

–Vol. 13, No. 1, P. 20, February 1996

A Boy of 1917-18

I was born in Massac County Nov. 1, 1909. Was I to be a witch (wizard) or a saint? The paradox, the dichotomy, of the two dates of October 31 and November 1, hanging between the unreality of Halloween spirits and Christian spiritual and ethical standards, has seemed a part of my nature, my destiny: on one side irascibility, rebellion, protest, erraticsm, iconoclasm; on the other, adherence to conventionality, the good and normal guy: religion, manners, the work ethic, etc. These threads of behavior and moods interweave like the mosaic of a tapestry.

The main idea in this article is that I was laying the ground work for subsequent action in omnivorous reading, writing, speaking, teaching, travel and a love of nature.

It was said that during my first year of school (age 4,5 - too young) I uttered scarcely a word. Certainly, I did not learn the A-B-Cs nor to read, write or talk, except the latter with family members. But, lo, by the end of my 8th year of age, I was doing all of them. Skipping the two years, I wish to focus on my 8th year, 1917-18.

I learned to read suddenly, but with little thanks to my teacher, my grand-aunt Lizzie Brandon, at the nearby Mt. Pleasant rural school. For two weeks an 8 year old girl was visiting my grand-aunt Ollie Crider nearby. The girl could read! I took it as a challenge and with the help of grandma ("Popo") Laird I began to try to read the personals and war news in the local newspaper. Within a few months I was reading Alger and other books myself.

"Each one moves to a purpose firm and the winds their sides that fill

Like faithful servants speed them all on their appointed way."— Celia Thaxter

The year 1917-18 was a tough one, what with the deep snow and ice, the ravages of the Spanish influenza and WWI raging. At age 27 dad was drafted in September and went to Camp Taylor in Louisville, KY for training. Mother, sister Bessie (age 6) and I moved the mile and a half in with my grandparents, George ("Papa") and Fannie ("Popo") Laird in Macedonia Church neighborhood. We became a sort of extended family. Grandmother May was still living; there were numerous uncles, aunts and cousins, all living within a three mile walking distance from our war home.

The house had 4-1/2 rooms, all frame except the front room which was made of logs. Later, in 1918 Papa boxed in the front porch to help accommodate his enlarged family. Inside and out the one-story house was whitewashed. Up the hill was the corncrib and barn, with an attached shed to house the buggy, or rather the hack. The Lairds had a horse, a cow and chickens. Only one male cat was allowed to catch mice. Papa never owned a dog. And I might add here that he never smoked, chewed or drank liquor. But strangely, Popo had smoked a clay pipe since age 7 (for tooth and earache - another story) and chewed twist tobacco. A shallow cistern furnished water and there was another

Playing on the strawpile

at the barn lot. During long dry spells of summer, water was hauled in barrels from the Ohio River, three miles away. The roots of a huge walnut tree growing right next the kitchen often damaged the cistern. Many's the night, sleeping under the low tin roof of one bedroom, have I been lulled (?) or awakened by the rattle of pouncing walnuts, especially on windy nights and by the noise of the roof moving up and down. Pleasant memories, come to think of it! The farm's exit was a private lane on cousin Joe's father's land, a half a quarter mile from the mail or main road. Papa's farm was 40 acres of rolling farm land, shrubs and a fine stand of yellow poplar woods. This description of the farmstead where we spent 15 months, I would say happy months, despite the flu, the weather and the war, must suffice.

Home life was typically rural. Our diet may not now be sanctioned in all respects but for us it was adequate. We had home-butchered bacon. Chickens and the cow supplied eggs and milk. Flour came from our own wheat (oats we bought). Cornbread was served often. Sorghum molasses was always at hand. Of fruits we had peaches, cherries, quince, grapes and the other small fruits. I early learned to pick strawberries for table and market. We usually went to bed early. Routine was sometimes broken by visitors and peddlers. Popo once bought from one of these a large *History of the World War* (the war hadn't ended yet) and an equally large *Daniel and the Revelation*. I have both books yet. The Watkins and Raleigh men made rather regular stops with their loads of merchandise and free chewing gum for us kids. Sometimes Popo would tell stories of her childhood and when she told of seeing the table being tipped (spiritualism) we children had an eerie feeling within us. Papa sometimes reminisced and more than once told of the giant footprints in the dusty road which he saw in his boyhood and how it caused quite a fear among the people. I will not reveal that mystery. I might interject here to say that I lived with my grandparents almost a whole school term at the age of 6. The home had a large loom for making carpets and rugs to sell. I have often awakened at 11 or 12 o'clock at night to hear that whir and boom of the loom in the room next to me as Popo and Papa worked to get out a rush order. The German people were especially frequent customers. The winter of the Spanish influenza put us all in a state of anxiety. There were many deaths. The Lauderdale youths had a double funeral. Our great-aunt Ollie died from a set-back of a case of the flu. She had gotten out and milked the cow before she had fully recovered.

The war raged on. Dad had two or three furloughs before he was shipped out, to spend some months in the trenches of France. Uncle Merritt had already been in France a good while (2nd Division and a sergeant). Rationing began, which meant more cornbread, less wheat biscuits; more brown sugar, less white and so on. Food Administrator Herbert Hoover (on slogan posters) declared "Food will win the war." Mother bought a war bond. After Armistice Day she bought a horse and a piano. All in all, the Laird home fared well.

Since my cousin's house was a quarter of a mile away over fields and thickets (longer by road) through which wound a well-beaten path, we spent a lot of time running back and forth. The Bill Graces had three or four boys and girls near my age and Uncle Isaac Laird had three boys. We did a lot of sashaying around in the woods, sometimes afar. We hunted, trapped and fished. We went nutting. We searched for ginseng, yellow pacoon and golden seal. At $20 a pound a match box of dried ginseng gave us some spending money. Rabbits were the prime game. Once a weasel. Cousin Florence Grace and I trapped rabbits on halves for a time; one could always sell a carcass in Metropolis. One

A 'soldier' with air rifle

time we dug out a large possum which had 16 babies in its pouch. Three of these cousin "Skinny" Joe raised as pets, which by spring had become pests about the house. In summer

"Sixteen little babies"

we paddled and swam in Morgan's Pond, as well as fished it. We sometimes fished the dredge ditches and even as far as the dangerous Ohio River.

Our games were always unstructured. Homemade string balls served in three or four varieties of ball games. Other games were andy-over, the dangerous Snap the Whip and shinny using tin cans. Marbles and top spinning got their share. Stink base and Red Rover were played. Even a simple thing as helping Papa at the woodpile gained my interest. In winter the box wood heater's appetite was voracious and of course, food was cooked on a wood range. One day Papa failed to cut wood at the woodpile. "Papa," I asked, "Can we work at the woodpile?" "No," he replied. "This is Sunday." (He never attended church).

In those days boys were usually clever at making their own toys. We made stilts, flippers, sling shots, darts, bow and arrows and willow whistles. I built a "railroad" with engine and boxcars from match boxes, complete with bridges and tunnels, at the edge of the neighbor's woods near our house. I ran a "mail route" for awhile, mail boxes strung along the well-worn path, for the edification and information of my cousins. For a time I ran a "restaurant" in a small outhouse where I sold sandwiches swiped from the table, bacon and pickles, to Joe and his ever-hungry older brother Harve, at one cent a sandwich. Joe, Harve and I cut one of Papa's small but tall, straight poplar trees and erected a flagpole where Old Glory waved for several months. I dearly wanted a tool chest and a miniature toy steam engine with which I naively believed I could really saw out little boards and build a playhouse. I wanted a red wagon and a bicycle. (I never owned a bicycle my entire life). Joe rode me on his handlebars. I wanted a real Culver small motorized vehicle advertised in the magazines. Of none of these were my wishes ever fulfilled. There was one very strange thing I wanted, for a boy as young as I was and that was pompadour hair, combed straight back. For a long time I would wet my hair and wear a skull cap. But even now my hair wants to part to the left.

Indoors, "playing house," a natural for girls, was a big thing with me in the winter months. I cut out many paper "dolls" from the Sears catalog. I lined up cardboard houses against the living room wall and did a lot of role playing. May it be that this was aiding me for later social contact and interaction? I had no thought then of how these boxes might be in the way of my grandparents. It was not only paper dolls I played with. I also collected some miniature clay dolls which, of course, had to be dressed with fragments from the loom rag bin, courtesy of Popo and Papa. From boxes of Tiger brand oatmeal, which contained little prizes much like Crackerjack popcorn, I got an especially beloved clay dog. I slept with it. It got damaged once and I stuck it back together, probably with sorghum molasses. Whatever happened to my dog? Memory fails me. Almost equally treasured was an all-white glass elephant, really a beauty.

"A fishing we will go"

In the succeeding lines I must act the self-critic. Under "Skinny" Joe's tutelage I smoked some cigarettes, he at age 13, already a confirmed smoker. His favorite brand was a small package called Favorite. We made all the community shivarees where we accepted and smoked the groom's cigars. Sometimes we smoked grapevine sections under the very eyes of Popo and mother, but a burning tongue kept the experiment to moderation. I learned to cuss and to tell white lies. Skinny and I would leave the house for all day, fishing, hunting and whatnot, without permission from our mothers. Sometimes we had an inclination to rowdyism. I was no cherub even though I had been born on All Saints Day and never as bad a Peck's Bad Boy. Nevertheless, it must be owned that Joe had a bad or mixed influence upon me and was abetted by cousins Bob and Lloyd.

Of all places some of these wayward tendencies were exhibited at the church night services attendance. We boys stayed mostly outside playing games and running all over the grounds, sometimes so noisy as to draw the attention of those inside the church. The truth was that I had too much freedom. It was partly due to the lack of my father who was at war and to my mother's lack of firmness. When it came to discipline Papa and Popo hardly counted. Again, it was the company I kept - my cousins. I suppose at that stage in my life I was both a sort of primitive animist, or better maybe to say, an animalist than anything else; a little animal with buoyant health and uninhibited vitality. A consciousness and appreciation of nature had hardly begun even though I was close to nature every day. Matthew Arnold says this love begins at about age 10. As to my childhood I will not go into the anal stage, the Oedipus stage, narcissism, or engage with an Freudian jargon. Enough to say that my moral consciousness developed imperceptibly - despite my boyhood friend's influence.

I spent the most of two winters at the Mt. Pleasant School located on the mail route and an eighth of a mile from the Laird farm. It was an old school district but at the new location and with a brand new building. My great-aunt Lizzie Brandon taught the 1917-18 term, followed by Mary Bremer 1918-19. I have told earlier how I came to reading skill. Before this Joe and Harve read portions of Alger, Henty and Castelmon to me. I have them to thank for my early introduction to the most popular of the boy's books of the era. When within a few month's living with Papa and Popo I read those book myself. The series of travel books (six books, one for each continent) *Carpenter's Geographical Readers* was a metaphor for travel and I have read them several times since I began them at age 8. I took *Hiawatha, Alice in Wonderland, Seven Little Sisters, Water Babies, The Little Lame Prince, Two Little Confederates* and other children's classics in succession.

On Oct. 5, 1918 the little war baby Glenn Woodrow May was born to our mother, a cause for celebration. Thirty-seven days later on November 11 came war's end. We boys, Joe, Bob, Lloyd, ran to the Macedonia Church on that clear, frosty morning as soon as the news came through via neighbor's telephone (about 9 a.m.). We rang the church bell quite awhile. I was happy because Dad would be coming back, not soon because it was six months more with the Army of Occupation in Germany and Luxembourg.

My Washington, my Lincoln, my Franklin, but as with most boys in those days Dad was my hero *par excellence*. He was honest, intelligent, confident, possessed of common sense and supportive. We lament here in 1997 that there are no heroes anymore. Maybe we're not looking in the right place.

As long as Papa and Popo were with us (until 1941 and 1949) I had a very close relationship with them; almost as close as with my parents. Count them my heroes also and this as a tribute to them. In his talk on grandparenting in *Modern Maturity* (January/February 1997 issue) Arthur Kornhaber said, "Kids raised by their grandparents are broader and deeper people. They have a sense of the past. They know other languages. They do better in school. They have a good sense of family and family values." I am deeply grateful for those years.

"Childhood memories are even more reliable than birth order as an indication of 'why you are the way you are'." Yes, Dr. Kevin Leman. The memories as imaged by the boy 80 years later bear you out.

"I love to think of my boyhood days
I cherish them more and more,
As clearly I see, at last for me
Life's voyage is almost o'er."

George Whitefield D'vys
–Vol. 15 No. 3, p. 42, June 1998

The Magnolia Tree

"They won't come up," declared my amateur, horticulturist orchardist friend. We were standing that autumn day in 1988 underneath the noble magnolia tree on the grounds of the Curtis House, headquarters of the Massac County Historical Society in Metropolis. Many cones lay under the tree. I picked up one and examined it closely. Embedded in the cone were many bright red seeds and I extracted one.

"I always felt that the magnolia was a beautiful tree," I said, "and I wonder if I planted this seed it would come up. Then I could have my own tree on my lawn." Which question led to the opening, vigorous denial. But before I relate my experiment I would like to make some remarks on this noble specimen of nature.

Named for Pierre Magnol (died 1715), a French botanist, there are at least 85 species, native mostly to the United States, Asia, Central America and Venezuela, some being evergreen and some deciduous. Many species are mere shrubs but trees can attain heights of 100 feet or more. The *magnoliaceae* are possibly the most primitive living family of flowering plants. In our country we commonly think of the magnolia as a Southern tree. In fact, the tree symbolizes the South, shared with the live oak and the cypress.

However, the magnolia, by one species or another, also grows in the North. We may condense by saying there are three major species. (1) the *magnolia grandeflora* or southern magnolia or bull bay. (2) the *magnolia acuminate* or cucumber tree (3) the *macrophylla* which is very different from its namesake *acuminate* (#2). The deciduous species (#3) can be grown as far north as New York but evergreens are not hardy in cold weather.

The bark of the southern magnolia is gray or light brown. The leaves are oblong or elliptical, five to eight inches long, sharp-pointed, edges smooth and leathery, shiny and bright green; rusty and hairy beneath. The fruit is cone-like, three to four inches long. But it is the flower which draws special attention. They are cup-shaped, six to eight inches across, creamy white and fragrant spring and summer.

The cucumber magnolia exceeds the other magnolia flowers in size. Whereas the sunflower, the water lotus (four to eight inches in diameter), the "Sacred Flower" lotus (the Giant Indian Lily, which grows in Illinois with a diameter of eight to 12 inches) are certainly large, the cucumber tree has the largest leaves (one to three feet long) and flowers (10 to 12 inches in diameter) of any hardy indigenous North American tree.

The smaller varieties of magnolia are ornamental. The saucer magnolia is one which "when its flowers come into bloom before the leaves, the whole neighborhood knows about it." The flowers are more than six inches wide and hundreds of them. The Youlan, the Star and the Kolus are similar ornamentals.

As I read encyclopedic texts on the magnolia I was amazed to learn that the cucumber tree and some other species had been grown and probably yet in New York and New England. Never would I have conceived such a range and that the tree could survive in the North. In most minds the magnolia is associated only with the South. But many plants as well as animals are quite adaptable. The mimosa tree is an example of a tree which has been taken from Arizona and other Southwestern states and California to thrive in extreme Southern Illinois. I will not venture to say that there are no magnolias north of the Illinois Ozark Ridge (Harrisburg, Marion, West Frankfort, Carbondale, etc.) for if I did some reader would be sure to call my hand. I will say, however, that if there are any, they are receiving some special attention and protection in winter, as many exotic ornamentals should. I was told that some years ago a West Frankfort family had a magnolia in the yard but, when still young, a hard winter killed it.

The prime value of the magnolia anywhere is as an ornamental, the "glorious magnolia," as William Bartram praised it in the 1790s: gracious shade, unparalleled blossoms. Other uses are

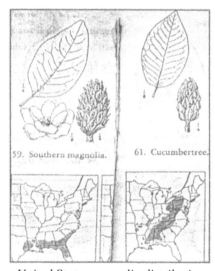

United States magnolia distribution

lumber for furniture, Venetian blinds and the soft wood for flooring and boxes. Although not edible, the tree possesses some medicinal qualities.

If propagated by seed one is instructed to first free the seeds of pulp (the outer layer). Then stratify four months or so mixed with damp sand or earth or peat moss at 40 degrees. In the warm south this period may be spent outdoors. In the cold northern winter, the seeds may be potted and kept indoors. The key words are keep moist and warm. Even so it may take months for germination. The tree may also be propagated by layers or graft. In any case it will be many, many years before the tree reaches heights of 50, 70 or 100 feet, depending on species and culture. Since there are comparatively few magnolias in Southern Illinois there is less chance of natural propagation-they like to grow in groves. Most or all the Illinois tress have been propagated by nurseries and set out as exotics.

As said earlier, the magnolia is an icon or symbol of the Southern states. Our images of the Southland include it. It is the state tree and flower of Mississippi and the state flower of Louisiana. The nickname of the former is the Magnolia State. I find towns and villages named Magnolia in Arkansas, Kentucky, Mississippi, New York, North Carolina, Ohio and Texas. Magnolia, IL was a station on the Underground Railroad in the 1840s, '50s and '60s. There is a Magnolia County, KY (pop. 13,000). The noted Magnolia Gardens are at Charleston, SC; Magnolia Bluff in Hickman, KY has been caving in for some years into the Mississippi River and the city is rebuilding Magnolia Street. There was once a Magnolia Oil Company which, I believe, operated in Southern Illinois. Metropolis has a Magnolia Manor nursing home. The elegant three-story Magnolia Manor house is owned and operated by the Cairo Historical Association, a mansion "capturing the charm of the Victorian era." I have no data on hotels, motels, business establishments, etc. that carry the magnolia name, but there must be several, especially in the South.

The magnolia seems to occupy a minor role in literature except incidentally. In the 1700s William Bartram wrote his *Travels in American* in which he writes quite a bit on "the grand magnolia." He saw Laurel magnolias 110 feet high and under date of December 1765 along Florida's St. Johns River saw "swamp magnolias 70 feet high, straight and a foot in diameter." Lovers of nature will find this book rewarding. It is reprinted by Anchor books, Doubleday and Company, 1957.

Magnolia (Hawks) Ravenal is the protagonist of Edna Ferber's *Show Boat* and purportedly she and Gaylord Ravenal were married in Metropolis, IL (Chapter 10). How many other girls have been or are named Magnolia? Perhaps legion.

I have searched almost in vain for any poems saluting the magnolia; some of the cypress, live oak and pine, yes. "Faint was the air with the odorous breath of magnolia blossoms," writes Longfellow in *Evangeline.* "and many a broad magnolia flower, within its shadowy woodland bower, is gleaming like a lovely star," writes George D. Prentice in *To an Absent Wife*, stanza two. Declares Maria Brooks in *Written on Seeing Pharamond*: "Fragrant o'er all the western grooves, the tall magnolia towers unshaded." More ambitious lines are spoken by C.P. Cranch in *Poem to the Magnolia Grandelfora*:

"Mystic flower! How purely beautiful
Thou art, as rising from the bower of green,
Those dark and glossy leaves so thick and full,
Thou standest like a high-born forest queen
Among the maidens clustering round so fair -
I love to watch thy sculptured form unfolding,
And look into thy depths, to image there
A fairy cavern and while thus beholding,
And while thy breeze floats o'er thee, matchless flower,
I breath the perfume, delicate and strong,
That comes like incense from thy petal-bower;
My fancy roams those southern woods along,
Beneath that glorious tree, where deep among
The unsunned leaves they large white flower cups hung!"

"Way down South in dear old Georgia, where the sweet magnolias bloom," sang Andrew B. Sterling in 1898 in the song by the same name; music by Harry Von Tilzer and popularized by Fannie Da Costa.

Lately, I made a cursory survey or tree count. Two small magnolias stand on the northside of Golconda. There are perhaps a dozen on the southside in the hill area, a few quite large and tall. Near Big Bay on the "4 Acres" farm along Route 145 is a small tree. The Gillespie farm (perhaps formerly the same) used to have a large cucumber magnolia with the extra large leaves. I saw only one tree in Vienna's northside but there may be others. The Vienna Nursery used to propagate seedlings, the seeds being taken from a large wide-leafed magnolia growing near the Church of Christ building, a mile southeast of Vienna. The tree is not there anymore. J. Bon Hartline owns an arboretum in Anna, IL which although specializing in hollies, also works with pine, cypress, cedar and magnolia. It is doubtful if there is a specimen of grandeflora in all Anna. (*Paducah Sun* Sept. 19, 1998). Karnak has a small tree at First and Main streets. Grand Chain has a tree on the shoulder of Route 37 near the Cantonment Wilkersonville histori-cal marker. Despite the hostile location, its di-ameter is 15 inches, but it is not very tall. Down-town, on the west hill are two other small trees. Mound City has two or three trees in the Court House area but at the US 51 junction at the Na-tional Cemetery are five or six trees in-line on the highway shoulder. Cairo, of course, has those grand trees on the

A row of magnolia, National Cemetery, Mound City

A hardy magnolia, New Grand Chain

lawn of the Magnolia Manor. There are many other trees in the city, especially on the west side, many of large size.

Turning to Massac County: Joppa has a nice, small tree near the Meth-odist Church and a very spindly sprout at the stop sign. At Ninth and Piland streets in Brookport stands a graceful tree and a very small tree a few doors away. I think my eye caught another, viewing from a distance.

Consistent with its size, Metropolis has perhaps a score of magno-lias located in the older part of the city, some of them fine specimens of middle age, but I will not locate them by street or house. On the old Gibbons lot (now the *Planet* newspaper) stand two trees whose image is traced on my mind from boyhood days. Tourists can hardly fail to note them near Metropolis's busiest corner at Fifth and Ferry.

I reserve the most noted southern magnolias until last. (1) The Curtis House tree at 405 Market Street (Massac County Historical Society) is a giant of its species. The height is perhaps 60 feet with a trunk circum-ference of 15 feet at 3-1/2 feet from the ground or a diameter of 57 inches. The age is unknown but early pictures of the lawn, surrounded by a paling fence, do not disclose such a planting. The house was built around 1870 by Maj. Elijah P. Curtis. It is safe to say that this grandeflora is 100 years or more old. What is distinctive is that three huge branches arise at the 3-1/2 feet level. Of late years the branches have been braced by metal bars to avoid splitting. (2) Until recently two large beautiful magnolias graced the lawn at 709 E. Second Street. One had to be removed in 1975 and the other subsequently, but a small tree grows there at present. Alfred Cutting built the house in 1867. It had a cupola from which he could view the Cutting Shipyards on the Ohio River. In the late 1860s he planted the original magnolia which was shipped by barge from Florida. The Trousdales were the next owners of the house (1904), with the Jacksons succeeding (1987). The house, minus the cupola, is now owned by the David Kruegers since 1990. One of the trees taken out was estimated to have been 150 years old (probably nearer 130). It was this tree that Roger Taylor (occupant, but not the owner) in the 1970s nominated it "the largest Illinois magnolia," citing figures of 10 feet, 5 inches for circumference at 4-1/2 feet above ground, height of 44 feet, a spread of 58 feet (*Illinois* magazine, April 1979, p. 23). Magnolia aficionados may wish to compare this with the Curtis tree or one or more in Cairo.

For the patient reader I will now return to my experiment. By Easter 1989 the seed I had potted in October had come up and on June 19 I set out a seedling. My daughter also came up with a seedling that year

Our Magnolia, 10 years old, ten feet tall

but unfortunately ruined it by accidentally breaking the pot and damaging it beyond hope of a growth and she did not replant. As of now (1998) my little tree, my "pet tree," is thriving at a 10 foot height but has not blossomed yet. Experiment closed. But I planted more seeds in November 1998.

–Written for *Springhouse* December 1998
but not published

The Avenging Serpent

Our expedition threatened to be a failure. Not because we lacked purpose nor because the Javanese wilderness stopped us-we had an able party, but a difficulty had arisen which threatened the very life of every member of our party. Thirty minutes before, as we were ascending the slopes of Mt. Bromo, Gronheim, a literary professor in The Hague, had died in excruciating pain. Our Javanese assistant, Nikyti, was even now in mortal pain and in spite of all the knowledge and skill of Dr. Zora, was expected to die any moment.

It was for no idle purpose that Von Schlegel, the chief, had begun the expedition. He had heard intelligent rumors that the famed "Thousand and One Nights" tales were originally told in Java. Their precise origin had long been a matter of debate. Mr. Itoska, of the Surabaya normal school, had studied the Kawi and Sanskrit languages. He had already shown that fables written in pure Kawi, a Javanese high-cast language, resembled the "Arabian Nights." It was the intention of Von Schlegel to study an ancient, untouched temple on Mt. Bromo. I was somewhat of an adventurer, but had been with Von Schlegel long enough to give him reason to believe I could be depended upon.

The three women of the party were Dr. Zora's half-breed daughter, Koja, by his deceased Javanese low-caste wife; Mrs. Itoska and Miss Ila Rongas. She was intimate with the latter. It had been rumored that she had spurned Dr. Zora's proposal of marriage. We also had five native carriers.

The slopes of Mt. Bromo are forest-clad almost to the summit. As we ascended, open spaces appeared and the tree-growth became scraggy. It made the going easier, but soon I was to view these open spaces as symbols of fear and death.

Gronheim had preceded us by a hundred paces. Suddenly we were aroused from our increasing physical lethargy by two sharp cries of pain and horror. "Oh, God," cried Gronheim, as he and Nikyti stumbled back toward us. Almost at the same time a kind of liquid was heard to patter on the leaves ahead of us. Gronheim was holding his hands to his face and Nikyti wringing his.

But that was not all. "Look!" I cried. A hundred paces from where the men first stood, stretched the most hideous looking serpent I ever saw in the tropics.

I had little time in which to observe the snake or its actions. Simultaneous with the loud report of one of our short-range guns, poor Gronheim reached us. The snake came down from its partly upright position and scurried away, a sinuous hateful thing.

"Bring them over to this clump of trees," directed the doctor. "Now, please retire if you will. This is terrible." He proceeded to examine the afflicted parts. A strong, but strangely familiar scent permeated the air.

"Retire I say," repeated the doctor.

We all began to obey except Von Schlegel, who remained close at his side.

"Is this pleasurable to you?" Remarked Zora to the chief, rather impatiently.

"No, it isn't, but the least I can do is to stand by and sympathize with his suffering."

"All right," said the doctor. I noted an inscrutable look come over his face, then I withdrew.

Within half an hour the two appeared and announced the death of Gronheim. Nikyti lingered on. "A terrible death, sirs," the doctor said. "A thing I have never seen before. Evidently, the poison permeated the tissues almost at once and took effect."

"And the needle?" suggested Von Schlegel.

"No good," returned Zora evasively.

"A true doctor," I thought to myself. "He does not wish to excite the women."

This was the reason why, I say, that our expedition threatened to end. Dr. Zora's knowledge of medicine seemingly had been surpassed; Mr. Itoska and I were unnerved; the women were horrified and the Javanese carriers huddled around us dumb with fear. Hishto hung sadly over his brother Nikyti. Only Von Schlegel concealed his agitation.

We now had two alternatives before us: to return with Gronheim's corpse to Patjitan and abandon the enterprise temporarily; or to send the Javanese with Gronheim and continue our climb.

"If we do the latter," Von Schlegel said, "there would be small hope of getting any more carriers from the village. The men are frightened and if they were to return, every man in the village and for miles around, would soon learn of our misfortune. No one could be found to accompany us again."

"It seems to me," I volunteered, "that the best thing we can do, if we do not wish our research to fail, is to send the Javanese down and proceed as usual in the morning."

"That is my desire exactly," rejoined the chief. "Deeply grieved as I am over the unfortunate and terrible death of our friend, we should not permit the incident to deter us in the least."

"If that is your purpose," said Dr. Zora, "I advise dispatching some-one to Surabaya along with the party bearing Gronheim down and I fear, the Javanese also. We may have more difficulty then we foresee. I can think of several things we shall need if we are to proceed with safety." Then turning to me he said, "Mr. Casper, you would be a good man for that job."

"Why me?" I asked. I had felt from the start that there was a slight dislike, an undefinable something about me which the doctor did not like. Perhaps it was my natural inquisitiveness and exuberance which jarred upon his unruffled disposition.

"No, I need Mr. Casper," Von Schlegel answered for me. "Have your list made out by morning, Doctor. We must make camp here for the night."

We made our camp with no intimation that the sinuous character of that day would deter us in the least from our purpose. That a mere snake could withstand and defy us was least in our minds. For awhile, we were silent as we sat around the fire. A lurid light seemed to glow over Mt. Bromo. We were even now sitting on a mountain of fire but which had not burst into great rebellion for a long time.

Then Dr. Zora spoke. "Many is the fair maid that has met her death in Bromo's fiery pit. Into its seething pit were hurled human sacrifices to appease the Fire God."

"Is that true?" I asked.

"Yes, but long since. Now chickens and corn are offered. That lurid light you see is caused by many fiery crevices, but sometimes boys go down and rescue the chickens."

"Then there is no danger to Koja and me?" laughed I.

"There might be," He jested, then musingly, "Could the serpent have anything to do with guarding the ancient temple you have come to see? What do you think, Mr. Itoska?"

"In my studies," returned the teacher, "I have not run into any such fancies."

We slept in four tents. We posted no watch but felt secure in the recesses of our tent. As yet, the tragedy had not reacted upon the simple Javanese carriers so much as to cause sleeplessness; certainly not upon the white people. But certainly the day had been no picnic, was my last thought.

I awoke in a sweat from a bad dream about a snake to hear light footsteps outside. I stuck my head out of the tent in time to see Dr. Zora about to enter the tent of the Javanese, with whom he had been bedded. He was fully dressed.

"What's up?" I inquired.

"Nothing," he returned grouchily. "Have just been out walking thinking over my medicine. Damned bad business," he added seriously.

Early in the morning the camp was astir and breakfast prepared over red-hot coals of teak-wood, dead for two years. Mr. Itoska was given instructions for the disposition of Gronheim's body. Nikyti had passed away in the night and he too was placed on an improvised stretcher. They were secured by sarongs of cotton. Mr. Itoska was given full directions for the purchase of two longer range guns; gas shells, if available in Surabaya and several new medicines upon the doctor's list. The wife accompanied him, but Miss Ronga would not go in spite of all our entreaties. Maybe, she loved the doctor after all.

Though cautioned against it, I wandered some distance from the camp as soon as the party had gotten under way. An insatiable curiosity now impelled me on to the point of the serpent's attack. But I did not follow the exact path which we took in coming from that scene. I had proceeded on the alert even as far as the snake had been seen. Here a huge rock jutted out from the strip of bushes. Should I round the base of the rock and see where we had not yet reached? I was impelled to do so.

I rounded the corner of the rock and looked around. There was nothing to be seen except more clumps of bushes and rocks. Then feeling that all was safe, I looked down to scrutinize the ground. It was made up of sand and volcanic ash, in places ankle-deep; in others just deep enough for permanent impression of footprints.

I had hardly noted the character of the footing, when a low exclamation of surprise escaped me. A footprint! A footprint where we had not been! I fell to my knees and examined it closely, unaware of any danger that might be near. Yes, there were footprints, many of them. All seemed alike, Javanese sandals, except one. Just one! It was made by a high-caste shoe. All the others of that kind were filled with running ash and sand.

I hurried towards camp intending to report the discovery. But an inner something, perhaps it was my recognition for once of my fault of exuberance, told me to withhold it. I sauntered around the camp, observing furtively the footprints. The closest resemblance I could find without exciting attention was the doctors. Had he wandered that far in the night? And for what purpose? Whose were the other footprints? I could not be certain that the single footprint was his. To question him would throw him on guard, if there was anyting shady about him.

I was aroused from my speculations by a shrill cry about 300 yards up the mountain. Screaming with pain and fright a Javanese came running from around a clump of bushes.

"The snake! The snake!" he cried wildly. I ran to meet him, at the same time unconsciously reaching for my pistol.

"Where? Where?" I yelled, starting to pass him.

"No! Don't go," he said as he fell clutching at my legs. Recalling that caution is sometimes the better part of valor, I stopped and helped the poor fellow into camp. He mumbled in the native dialect about being rushed upon by the murderous snake, scorching Death issuing from its wide, hideous mouth in a spray.

He fell in a heap, alternately wringing his hands and clawing crazily at his face. With an air of despair, Dr. Zora gave him a shot with a needle and left him to such care as we could give him.

"Doctor, isn't there anything in the books about this reptile and its poison," asked Von Schlegel.

"No," replied he. "It is another cobra. In all my studies I have never heard of this particular species of serpent. It is strange that in a country so densely populated as Java, no one has described or gave warning against such an evil enemy as ours is becoming. No, gentlemen, I am afraid we can do nothing. It seems like a case of an avenging serpent, which we mentioned last night."

"You mentioned it; we didn't," I burst out. I did not like his easy manner.

"Well, I mentioned it then," he corrected.

"Bosh, all bosh," cut in Von Schlegel abruptly.

"The Javanese have remained silent," I continued heedlessly. "It seems, living as closely as they do to this particular mountain, that they would have heard long ago something about the guardian reptile."

"The best we can do now, unless we wish to retreat, is to stay here and await Mr. Itoska's return," said the chief.

"But might not he be intercepted by the Thing before he reached us?" I asked.

"Not likely," answered the doctor. "Besides, armed as he no doubt will be, he will be able to take care of himself."

"I still do not propose to abandon my original search," said Von Schlegel decisively.

A groan emitted from the Javanese lessened and we turned to see the puffed-up countenance of our third corpse. The best we could learn from the brown men, he had no relatives and we buried his body soon afterwards.

The remainder of the day we erected a rough barricade around the camp. Von Schlegel gave us warning to stay in or near the enclosure. The Javanese needed no warning. They slunk together timidly. I noticed a more than usual conversation among them.

Each one now wore a charm around his neck. From time to time those objects would become the center of interest. I supposed they were warding off the evil spirits, or trying to invoke immunity from the serpent's attack.

"What is that?" I asked my chief, pointing toward the Javanese over in one corner of the enclosure. "Black magic, divination, or what?"

"I don't know exactly, Mr. Casper," he said. "I suppose some sort of nonsense, something that will excite them and will cause us to lose them to their village before we are through with them. Suppose you try, undesignedly, to see what it is all about."

"I don't know, sir, if I can make myself understood or not, but I will try." I had once docked at Batavia a good many years ago and having occasion to spend some time there, picked up some of the dialect. Coming up the other day, I had addressed the men. We had carried on a limited conversation. But to talk about occult things was a different matter.

I met Von Schlegel an hour later. I burst out with "Say, sir, there may be something in the way of spiritual adventure on this mountain. It seems that the Javanese have heard that in the dim past, the disembodied spirit of a man guarded the temple in Bromo's grim crater. They seem to believe that the snake is ruled by this spirit and is trying to drive us back."

"Bosh, is all I can say to that part. But, say," and he looked at me interestedly, "There may be something to some of this. I wish that Mr. Itoska were here now. Perhaps if he gained as much information, accordingly, as you did with your imperfect use of the dialect, we might have something of real worth. You never can tell how really important a thing is in research work until you have every possible particular before you."

As the ennui of close camp life came over us, I had a better opportunity to observe the character of the members. Von Schlegel chafed at the unavoidable delay. Dr. Zora irked me with his unruffled, serene matter. Koja said little, but seemed sad and depressed. I was everywhere trying to keep up the gayety of the group, perhaps overdoing the thing in so doing. For the first time I appreciated the presence of Miss Rongas. At first, I had inwardly objected to the women accompanying us. I did not see where they could help. After the attacks of the snake, I felt more strongly that they should have been left at home. I had urged Koja and Miss Rongas to go back with Mrs. Itoska. Now I saw that perhaps Miss Rongas was the saviour of the expedition. I do not doubt that some of us would have quarreled if it had not been for her presence.

I began to hate Dr. Zora more and more, why, I could not say. I must have knocked him down for his condescending manner of answering my questions. Orphaned though she was, Miss Rongas resided with responsible kinsmen and occupied a high place in high-caste Javanese quarters. She was beautiful, it was beauty unmarred by hard work and which destroys the natural beauty of the Javanese. Well, I could not blame Dr. Zora for falling in love with her. Nor, I had to admit, was he a bad-looking man though twice her senior. Why not a match? I remembered what Mr. Itoska had told me coming up on the train from Surabaya. How the doctor had a great hold on the natives throughout the district and no wonder, for he, a high-caste, had married a low-caste woman. How Koja now increased that influence, but how the doctor wished to marry her to a high-cast and so retain his standing in both circles.

Languor begets indiscretion at times. The third day, as we were lying around dozing from the effects of the tropical sun, Dr. Zora arose abruptly and announced that he was going for a walk.

"Better stay here" advised Von Schlegel. Of course, he had no powers over anyone if we so chose to walk off.

"I'll risk it," said the medico. Then he added as an after thought, "Want to go with me, Ila?"

"Certainly," she answered.

"Please don't go Miss Rongas," I begged. "You realize the danger?"

"I appreciate your effort to keep us diverted," she returned, "but quiet pastime and repartee doesn't take the place of action. I am ready doctor."

"I beg you again, Miss...!" I cried.

"Jealous?" asked the doctor in a manner I felt as a hiss of disapprobation.

"No," I said confusedly, turning away. It was not that I was beginning to love her, but that his manner stung me as nothing he had said before had done.

I abhor eavesdropping, but I felt justified for Miss Rongas' safety, in following the two as soon as they were out of sight. I walked five minutes, until I came to the large rock, on whose other side I had seen the footprints. The two were not to be seen. Two pairs of fresh prints indicated they had just passed on. "How foolish they are," I thought. "We are on the same ground where the attacks were made." I quickened my pace, determined to overtake the two and have it out with them.

I had hardly determined on this action when I heard a terrifying cry of fright ahead of me. It sounded and resounded as the rocks answered it back. It was Miss Rongas' scream. I ran my best, stumbling and falling a time or two in my haste. My hands were cut and bleeding but I gave them no mind. Involuntarily, I drew my revolver and fired two quick shorts. Would I arrive at the scene in time to help? That was my agonizing thought. Curse Zora! Why did he have to lead her off.

The cries continued and led me on. I could distinguish the doctor's cries for help. Though I was obsessed with the one purpose, I was feebly conscious that the cries seemed of fright and horror and not of pain. I had not heard a single scream of "Oh."

I rounded a clump of bushes and in an open space, got my first good view of the snake. There was another clump of bushes just back of the snake, from which probably it had emerged. The doctor was shouting and wringing his hands at the near side of the open space, which was a 100 yards across. Miss Rongas was being held by the torso with her limbs struggling in mid air and screaming in an agony of fear. Cold terror seized my heart and I could not move. I gazed at the monster enchanted.

"Do something man!" cried the doctor seizing my shoulders.

I awoke and seizing my field glasses still unbroken by my fall on the rocks, focused them on the horror. Its head and about a fourth of its body was held erect. The head was large and globular - the poison sacs puffed out - an evil cobra of Java. It seemed to be about 12 feet long but disproportionately large and powerful. That, I thought, must be the source, in part of its power in throwing out is poison such a remarkably long distance.

The Thing began to move! It began to crawl leisurely around the clump of bushes up the mountain. I was surprised at its unbelievable clumsy motion. It seemed to hump along like a grotesquely-painted mask. It was moving away, but I was afraid to shoot for fear of injuring Miss Rongas. I gazed fascinated as if charmed by its deviltry.

By now my shots had brought the other member of the party. My view was cut short by the loud report of a gun. Von Schlegel had risked a shot. Allowing only a glance to see that it was he, I hastily raised my field glasses again just in time to see the serpent disappear quickly around the bushes. Apparently, the revolver shot had missed its mark.

I looked at Dr. Zora, the cause of all this. His face was red and horror-stricken. I said red. I thought that a man's countenance, when horror-struck would be white. There was a peculiar glint in his eye which I took for a glint of sadness and remorse. But these speculations were shattered by his next action. I had misjudged him. His whole fiber had been concentrated on it.

Seizing and tearing a sarong from the waist of a Javanese, he enfolded his hands and almost his entire face in it. Then he seized the chief's gun and hurried after the snake.

The action was so quick that it stunned us. Of course, that was the thing to do! Protect the skin by clothing! It was so simple that we stood abashed. Why hadn't we thought of it by now? The doctor arose six feet in my estimation.

But even then, could we be sure that we would be sufficiently protected? From rash action and certain death in case the liquid touched our skin, we hesitated.

We crossed the open space to the bushy clump and found where the bullet had kicked up the earth. We were now at an altitude of 10,000 feet. The Javanese said that it was only a 10 minute climb to the rim of the crater.

"We can't follow," announced Von Schlegel. "Mr. Itoska is not here with the arms. Let us return."

"But, sir," I said. I had never directly opposed the chief, but for the first time I felt some repulsion for his seeming inhumanity. "Sir, can't we do something to rescue Miss Rongas? Isn't there some chance that she has not yet been killed? God! We can't leave her there with that writhing horror. We must do something!"

"Do as you like!" he answered shortly.

We returned to camp to find that Mr. Itoska had just come up. The two brown carriers had been procured in Jokjokkarta, that they would know nothing of the tragedies. We gave the teacher a hearty welcome. He and the chief went into conference for a hour.

They emerged from the tent and Von Schlegel came to me. Mr. Itoska mingled with the carriers.

"Mr. Casper," he began kindly, "I hope you will pardon my curt reply this afternoon. Truth is, I did not know what to do; I was agitated more than I have ever been before."

I was reconciled.

He continued, "Perhaps there is more seriousness concerning the enchantment of the temple above us. Remember you learned about a spirit which guarded it. Mr. Itoska says he remembers dimly a legend about Mt. Bromo. He is over there now interrogating them."

"Do you really believe it will concern our object?" I asked.

"Yes and no. You know I could not believe in such superstition. It may hinder our progress, it seems that it is doing so now, but if a legend appears which is connected in any way with Scheherazade and the 'Arabian Nights,' the object of our climb up this volcano, then certainly we shall investigate it, be it snake, man, or spirit."

Itoska was singularly pensive during the evening meal. We did not question him. He seemed to be reconstructing or calling to memory some past experience. "Could it be possible," I thought, "that Mr. Itoska, an educated man, a teacher with a mind above the intelligence of the lower-castes, was he succumbing to fear or to some sentiment engendered by his conversation with the carriers?"

Around the evening fire, Mr. Itoska spoke. "As you know, much of the ancient charm and seeming magic of the early centuries of Java are retained by the natives in their customs and beliefs. Stories, legends and petty superstitions have been handed down through the generations, each succeeding one, of course, adding exaggerations to those stories.

"Since talking with the men, especially in regard to our strange enemy, I have pieced together a legend I heard years ago, one which I had almost forgotten. The tradition (and I draw it mostly from my questioning awhile ago) is that centuries ago, there came to Java a man by the name of Scheherazade, of whom the Javanese became enamored. He told them stories of his homeland, Arabia and they in turn told him their stories. These, being highly imaginative and fantastical, made an instant and popular appeal to the Arabians. I make this last statement myself.

"Upon one of his trips to Java, he wandered far into the interior, even to this same Fire Mountain. Here he met his death by unknown means. The Javanese, having an ardent admiration for him, buried his body high on this volcano, far from prying eyes. An earthly memorial was erected over his body. It is that temple which perhaps now we will find in ruins, we wish to reach."

The teacher paused; then noting our intent attitude, continued. "Here begins the incorporeal side of the talk. Scheherazade's memory gradually dimmed in the eyes of the natives, until he became a myth. Few people had occasion to climb Mt. Bromo, it being frequently in action. Only the tradition remains to us and to that I have added some. I do not even know if this venerated character was Scheherazde. Only this remains to the carriers here tonight: The upper slopes of Mt. Bromo are guarded (the reason they know not) by some spirit or ghost and whosoever invades these regions are liable to destruction. Now they connect the serpent and the death of our men with that belief."

Some moments elapsed after this relation. Von Schlegel was the first to speak. "Is that all?"

"All but one thing. All are liable to destruction except the elect. Evidently, we are not the elect," concluded the teacher.

"Then who are the elect?" asked the chief.

"Those who bring up the sacrifices, the natives I suppose, or one who orders it done - one who is a leader or advisor in such matters - who has a great influence over them."

"And who is this leader?" His eyes narrowed.

"Why, Dr. Zora is the avowed patron of natives in Patijitan," said the teacher. then realizing that perhaps he was compromising his friend, he burst out, "No! No! It is impossible. Patijitan is 50 miles away."

"Why not the doctor," I cried impulsively.

"Enough of this, men," said the chief coldly.

More calmly I asked, "Do you think then that our efforts are likely to collide with these fancies, even though we, as intelligent men, know that they are not real?"

Von Schlegel said sarcastically, "I do not think the recital of this legend need deter us in the least from going ahead. This snake is only a Sinbad monster. I think we have here," pointed to the new guns and charges, "sufficient artillery to dispatch the creature. As for the ruins, if they be yet present, guarded by either animals or spirits, we shall reach them. I do not discredit Mr. Itoska's story as a story, but I do discredit the existence of anything so fanciful in reality."

"Then we break camp and start in the morning?" I said precipitately. I have always hated indecision and waiting.

"Most certainly," agreed Von Schlegel. I loved the blunt old Dutchman more than ever for saying that. "It would not be wise to proceed tonight, I think. Let us practice caution and keep under cover as much as possible. Remember, the snake has attacked three times in open spaces. It seems to be unable, at least disinclined, to recoil and force its liquid out in undergrowth."

I drew Von Schlegel to one side before retiring. "What do you suppose Koja knows?" I sympathized with her. Though she had not said much, she had been very quiet all along, I knew she must feel anxious for her father.

"Why Koja?" The chief asked.

"She's half-caste, you know. She might know half as much again as the carriers."

"Still wide-awake are you?" My employer laughed. "You quiz her," was his parting reply.

The long tropical nights were on. I could not sleep. Von Schlegel had only temporarily stopped my intense desire to follow Miss Rongas also, as the brave, rash Dr. Zora had done. Where were they now?

I awakened from a doze. Fighting down my feelings no longer, I jammed a revolver in my belt and crept stealthy out of the sleeping camp. I was guided by the lurid, grayish-orange flickerings of the crater. Led on, as I was by an intense passion of curiosity, I made somewhat better time than could be expected. I reached the rim. I glanced at the eastern sky and guessed it to be three o'clock, but the continual flashing of light from the fiery interior made it difficult to tell.

I looked over the rim and gazed entranced into the pit. It was not a solid caldron of fire, but here and there were fiery pits, baby volcanoes and seething crevices. Flashes of light shot up and displayed a boulder-strewn floor. Clouds of stinking smoke drifted about. Space intervened between them to allow of possible human passage. I could see no signs of life. Were Dr. Zora and Miss Rongas in that Hell? I hesitated to plunge into that eerie hole, where weird shadows played with fervent flashes of light.

Suddenly I grew tense. What was that? Was it something moving in the semi-gloom of that miniature cone? Yes! It was! I saw a struggling bulk of people, three of them! I heard a cry, Miss Rongas!

I clutched my throat to stop a smothered cry.

Two beings pulled her up to the rim of a fiery pit. There in the light, across the space of 100 yards, I could see them poise her body. She ceased to struggle but the two men retained their hold. I gazed transfixed, realizing numbly that she was a sacrifice to the Fire God.

I could tell insensibly that they had now relaxed their hold. She had fainted. The two infernals now tore her clothes and exposed her fair breasts. The beautiful, smooth body lying helpless in their hold had overcome them. They were now creatures of eroticism. Their maddened passions flew at each other. Their hold on her entirely relaxed.

Cursing myself for my inactivity, I tumbled incautiously over the rim, whipping out my revolver and firing two quick shots as I did so. But it was not so easy to navigate the floor of the crater. I fell into a deep crevice before I had gone 10 steps. Luckily, it was not a hot one. A bright light flamed up and blinded me. I saw I would have to pick my way with care. I fired two more shots. Then I shouted. Faintly I thought I heard an answering cry. Then silence again. I started to shoot again, then realized that foolishly, I had left with only one round of ammunition. I might need those two last shots.

I picked my way for 15 minutes. It was like treading a sea of needles. I decided not to shout again. I might be ambushed by the devils. Besides, in this hole, a shout might so reecho as actually to mislead Miss Rongas.

A shadow blacked my passage. I looked up and started to turn the cylinder. It was Miss Rongas!

"Come with me," I said. "But where is Dr. Zora?"

"Forget him for the present," she answered vehemently. "Let's get out of here."

We arrived at the camp just as it was stirring. "Your shots aroused me from my faint," related Miss Rongas. "I saw the two men fighting and seizing my chance, slipped away. They pursued and must have overtaken me, but I slipped into the shadow of a rock. They stopped very near me. One said 'Bring Zora'. The other one stayed. I crouched breathlessly. Soon the doctor and the messenger came running up. He said, 'Damn it, how did you let her escape? Let her go now.' Your near approach moved them on and I overheard no more.

"The snake carried me to a large cave or crevice," she said. "It was so dark I could see nothing. Evidently it went away, for two men tied me. It was not long until Dr. Zora was brought in, tied fast. I believe now that it was a trick to deceive me. The two men left us. Within an hour they returned and said that I must promise to marry the doctor or be a sacrifice to the Fire God. Dr. Zora remonstrated, but they were firm. The doctor showed me how that if I did promise I would have to keep it. Secret priests of the Fire God would seize me at the first chance. But he only insisted, he said, for my own life, to obey. I would not give up. 'Why the condition, marry you?' I asked. He said that I was granted this condition only because he was an avowed friend to the natives. Several hours passed but we were separated part of the time. Then I was seized and carried to the pit."

This diabolical plot registered internally with all of us. Of course, we could not be absolutely certain, but wasn't the overhead dialogue sufficient to prove the case?

We soon reached the scene of the last attack. Well armed though we were, we proceeded cautiously. We had climbed for perhaps 10 minutes when we were startled by a loud cry from M. Itoska. "There the snake is!" he cried.

Following the point of his finger, we saw at 100 yards the serpent. It was swaying its hideous head to and fro in a zigzag manner. We fired the long-range guns. It tuned into some bushes in a most grotesque and awkward way. Half through the thin clump, it stopped with a convulsive movement. We poured successive shots into it, body.

It did not move. Apparently it was dead. To make certain, we crept closer and poured more steel and gas into its hulk. Still it did not move.

We prodded its body. It resounded with a stupid-hollowness. It was a Javanese mask of paper-mache!

We tore open the mask with mounting fury. Inside were bottles of sulfuric acid and the extremely corrosive hydrogenfluoride. We found a very powerful handpump which had been used to force out this blistering mixture.

"A perfect piece of Javanese art," said Von Schlegel. "They are masters of the mask dances and shadow plays. But it came near undoing us."

"What is this?" I cried. "Blood!"

The snake men must have misjudged the range of our guns. One or more was injured. They had escaped around a rock without our seeing them. They had not taken the time to extricate the 'snake' and hide it, if that had been their plan.

The snake hoax unfolded, Miss Rongas said, "Now I feel sure that the doctor is in back of all this. I know he communicated with the snake men. He must have sent them out this morning."

We advanced to the rim of the crater. As we craned our necks for a first view of the beautiful but grim crater, we came face to face with Dr. Zora!

"Thank God!" he cried excitedly. "I have just loosened my bonds and escaped."

"Better pray to God," I lunged furiously and seized him in an iron grip.

"You are discovered, doctor," we shouted in chorus.

The doctor protesting, denying and cursing, we turned back down the mountain.

"To the camp!" thundered Von Schlegel, "and we will open his medicine chest and see what other infernal poisons he has."

We threw open the medicine chest. Vials, liquids and needles, all legitimate for a doctor.

"What's this?" Shouted the chief, taking up a small bottle.

"Curare."

"A most deadly poison," exclaimed Von Schlegel. "So you finished them by injecting this most horrible drug?"

"As you say," returned the doctor weakly.

Loathing hatred overcame us. Passion had made a murderous criminal of him.

Dr. Zora was speaking calmly. "I hoped to hold you off, by one way or another until I had captured the heart of...well, forget it. This morning I detailed the snake men to hold you off one more time..."

"Until you could kill us," I yelled.

"...but it seems they got too close, I had warned them of your higher powered guns. Surely, they must have depended too securely upon your fear of the snake."

Koja ran up and embraced her father. Pity for her began to soften us.

"Say it is not true, father," she cried.

He looked at her calmly but lovingly. "Too true, Koja, dear. I would do no good to deny it here, for back in the cities it would be proved true."

"Then I hate you!" She cried and before we had time to realize it, she had seized a long knife from a Javanese and plunged it deep into his breast.

"Why Koja...why...why?" he gasped.

"You killed Nikyti. I loved him."

We returned to Batavia, where Von Schlegel made known the great find in Mt. Bromo's crater and which will forever settle the "Arabian Night's" debate.

Only one possible flaw could have been found with Dr. Zora's diabolical plot. Might not the party have been frightened back and he lost the chance to rescue Miss Rongas? No. He guessed well the bull-dog character of Von Schlegel.

-1930s

Printed in the USA
CPSIA information can be obtained
at www.ICGtesting.com
JSHW022210140824
68134JS00018B/976

9 781681 622934